The Five Hurdles to Happiness

The Five Hurdles to Happiness

and the Mindful Path to Overcoming Them

MITCH ABBLETT, PHD

Foreword by

CHRISTOPHER K. GERMER, PHD

Shambhala Boulder 2018

Shambhala Publications, Inc.
4720 Walnut Street
Boulder, Colorado 80301
www.shambhala.com

9 8 7 6 5 4 3 2 1

First Edition
Printed in the United States of America

♾ This edition is printed on acid-free paper that meets
the American National Standards Institute Z39.48 Standard.
♻ This book is printed on 30% postconsumer recycled paper.
For more information please visit www.shambhala.com.

Distributed in the United States by Penguin Random House LLC
and in Canada by Random House of Canada Ltd

Designed by Greta D. Sibley

LIBRARY OF CONGRESS CATALOGING-IN-PUBLICATION DATA
Names: Abblett, Mitch, author.
Title: The five hurdles to happiness: and the mindful path to overcoming them /
Mitch Abblett, PhD; foreword by Christopher K. Germer, PhD.
Other titles: 5 hurdles to happiness
Description: Boulder: Shambhala, [2018] | Includes bibliographical references and index.
Identifiers: LCCN 2017049715 | ISBN 9781611804492 (hardcover: alk. paper)
Subjects: LCSH: Happiness. | Happiness—Religious aspects—Buddhism. |
Meditation—Buddhism.
Classification: LCC BF575.H27 A23 2018 | DDC 158.1—dc23
LC record available at https://lccn.loc.gov/2017049715

Contents

Foreword

This book could not arrive at a better time. Now that mindfulness has gone mainstream, practitioners often wonder, "What next?" This does not mean that mindfulness is limited in any way—it is as spacious as loving awareness itself—but mindfulness can be integrated into our lives in new and interesting ways to realize its full potential. One such way is by bringing mindfulness to the "hindrances," an ancient taxonomy of mostly unconscious habits that diminish our happiness and wellbeing.

In this book, Mitch Abblett unpacks each of the five hindrances in a unique, experience-near manner, especially showing how they manifest in our daily lives and what we can do about them. Dr. Abblett shares candid accounts of his own life, removing the distance between himself and the reader, and he brings to bear a wealth of experience as a psychologist working with individuals and families. He also shares ancient and modern tales of wisdom, historical insights from the Buddha, cutting-edge science, and practical exercises to illuminate the hindrances. It is clear that the author has been working with the hindrances for some time, and the fruit of his efforts, contained here, is an integrated, psychologically sophisticated reinterpretation of this important topic.

The maturity of Dr. Abblett's efforts can be seen in the threads of wisdom and compassion woven throughout this book. To begin, the hindrances are really patterns of *relating* to our experience, and these patterns emerge out of an unlimited field of interacting factors and forces, both personal and impersonal. That's wisdom—the insight of interdependence. And because the hindrances are multi-determined, they "are not our fault, but they are our responsibility."[1] We cannot change the past, but what we *do* with the hindrances during the 1440 minutes contained in a day can significantly impact our overall life experience.

Another thread of wisdom and compassion is that the hindrances— the five Ws: *wanting, wrestling, wilting, worrying, and wavering*—are hardwired into our psychological makeup through evolution and there is no way to eliminate them. This insight is an important tonic for zealous self-improvement practitioners. It does not imply, however, that our efforts are for naught. The issue is not *whether* we can be free ourselves from the crippling effects of the hindrances, but *how* we do it. In this book, the wisdom of changing our *relationship* to the hindrances is key, and the primary guidance given in this book is loving awareness of the hindrances themselves—mindfulness.

Recognizing our hindrances requires courage. For example, the process is not just saying, "Oh, I'm wrestling with anger!" That's a good start, but a fuller, more liberating approach is to recognize the impact of anger on our lives and those of others, to understand the origins of the anger, and to meet the pain of anger in a new way. In other words, working with the hindrances is a real engagement with real life. Fortunately, this is a process of *awakening* rather than elimination.

As this book beautifully describes, the process of loosening the grip of the hindrances is subtle and paradoxical. One example is the notion of "progress." Actually, to make progress, we need to abandon the idea of progress. Although this may sound disappointing, it can also be a relief. Progress is a refinement of intention, moving from striving to feel better—which might just strengthen the hindrance of restlessness—to holding ourselves and the hindrances in tender awareness. As Jack Kornfield noted, "The point of spiritual practice isn't to perfect yourself, but to perfect your love."[2]

Of course, the practice of working with hindrances wouldn't have existed for two and a half millennia if it didn't actually make us feel better. Practicing in the manner described in this book will definitely make you feel better. It is possible that when we begin to practice, more difficult emotions will emerge. Rest assured, however, that as the fire begins to burn the smoke will clear. This book throws new light on how to work safely and effectively with the hindrances. There is no time like the present, so let's begin!

Christopher K. Germer, PhD
Lecturer on Psychiatry, Harvard Medical School
Author of *The Mindful Path to Self-Compassion*

Introduction

Brutal Honesty Regarding the
Hindrances to Awareness

I RESTRAINED my out-of-control six-year-old this morning. Somehow, even as I gripped her shins to keep her from kicking me in the groin, I knew this could have been avoided. I knew my surge of anger—a frustrated sense that "I'm tired of this!" and "Why does she keep doing this to us?"—had boiled over, leading me to raise my voice and ultimately take hold of her to stem the flow of her flailing foot strikes.

In this current moment of open awareness, I know I could have more deftly managed my experience, and I know things might have played out differently as well. I know I reacted and that the reaction was indeed old—ingrained and well rehearsed. And now, in this moment of breeze and afternoon sunlight, I can give a pained smile to this pattern—this familiar, hated friend—and know I will meet it again soon, perhaps with a new reception, perhaps not.

My six-year-old struggles with significant, copiously diagnosed anxiety issues, and my higher, aware self—the one peering out during many moments of meditation and daily life presence—knows she is not choosing to become locked in the current fixation on counting spare change, of earning money so that she can compulsively buy a small, plastic piece of crap that loses all value as soon as she's bought it. I know this from my meditative practice, and I know this from my training and hundreds of patient experiences as a clinical psychologist (ironically, a child one at that). And yet, there is no training, no meditation that prepares you for your own anguish-lashed child. In many brief moments, I am all too aware of the suffering she experiences as these loops of thought and behavior trap her mind and bind up her precious heart.

And then there's my pain as her father. It's the familiar pain of fear for her future, uncertainty for mine and my family's, and agitation that "this" is what life has become, which quickly couples with angry pushing and pulling or outright avoidance by various means of my own compulsive grasping. Usher in alcohol, and say hello to fixation on fitness programs and fads, and even give a knowing nod to my raging addiction to Amazon book buying. My deeply empathic (arguably too deep) daughter anticipates my wife's reactions when we all arrive home to yet another stack of Amazon packages addressed to me by the front door.

"Mommy, don't be mad at Daddy. It's not *too* many books today."

So here I sit on a beautiful July afternoon on an idyllic porch overlooking a village common in upstate New York, a scene rivaling any for Americana tranquility, and the glare of the honesty is what burns me, not the sun. Instead of absolute ease dictated by the setting, I sense the settling in of an old cramped feeling in my chest, a restriction that says I'm staying a tad too open to the pain, and my well-tracked patterns pull at me to close things up. Go drink something; smoke something; buy something. Hell, go meditate even (but instead of it being a mere vehicle, I would do so with a "goal" in mind of being the "best" meditator).

Instead, I sit, listening to breeze in leaves, feeling feet in sandals, and hearing murmur of election-year blue-versus-red conversation around the corner. I'm staying open to the pain. It curdles and twists, eyes brim, and I allow it all to be. I penetrate it with the breath. I present myself to what's most important in this moment—the brutally honest rendering of what this book is about and why you might benefit from continued reading.

This book is about the patterns we've all inherited, less from parents or forbears (though there is indeed a biological and learned part), and more from our own mindless moments, our thousands of decisions to wear blinders instead of inquiring with honest awareness into both the beauty and the pain of our daily lives. As the book's title indicates, and as the Buddha said thousands of years ago as relayed in the Majjhima-nikaya, "Beings are owners of their actions, heirs of their actions; they originate from their actions, are bound to their actions, have their actions as their refuge."[1] And what he meant is that each moment's choice breeds the ingredients of the next moment's experience. What we intend and what we do set the stage for what comes. We largely unwittingly write our lives with what we've known or, more accurately, repeated.

Amid patterns "large" (addiction, abusiveness, hateful violence, self-injury, self-loathing, and abject despair) and patterns "small" (relationship struggles, reactive parenting, career burnout and dead ends, edginess and angst with loved ones), we all pass our days largely on autopilot, sheepishly enslaved to old scripts of thinking, feeling, and doing.

So why do I, a longtime meditator, therapist, and proponent of all things self-care, have any credibility to lecture on these patterns—these hindrances to awareness and flexible living? Considering my own on-going failings, would you not be better off reading a treatise from a truly awakened being? Perhaps not. My sense is that you'll need someone relatable to hear from as you learn about the hindrances of your own life. Perhaps I am the psychologist, meditator, father, son, brother, friend, colleague, husband, writer, and hypocrite perfectly suited to such teaching. I aim for this book to take stories of honesty and incongruity, science and contemplative practice, and drill them down into the open wellspring of our collective and yet individual cores. I therefore believe I have something to say as much to myself (and my children) as I do to you, and that makes the words all the more accessible and valuable.

So here are the questions that rise up to be addressed in this book:

- What are these hindering patterns of reaction that block us from lives of awareness, creativity, productivity, and connection?
- Can we, as heirs, have any say in the effects of our inheritances?
- What can we do about these patterns?

The answers lie at the crossroads of ancient Eastern contemplative tradition and modern psychological science. The solution derives from the daily practice of meditation, and it is not only supported by research; it *is* scientific in that we are each living laboratories, each day afforded precious lab time for collecting data amid the blips and ignitions of our moment-to-moment experience. The patterns of hindrance that I inherited in this (and every) moment can be observed, tested, and, when I make changes, observed again.

In Buddhism, these five hindrances (*nivarana* in Pali—the dominant language of the historical Buddha's time and region) are described in the Pali canon as impediments to the development and deepening of one's meditation practice. They "hinder and envelop the mind in many ways, obstructing its development."[2] They are obstacles on the path of concentrative absorption (the various *jhanas*) weaving toward enlightenment and arising for all who choose to walk the path of cultivation of awareness. In a wicked brew of reactivity, they rose up for me in that moment prior to placing my hands on my dysregulated daughter. They poke ever so slightly at me even now as I write this chapter, inciting thoughts of authorial insufficiency: "No one will buy this thing, so why even waste your time writing it."

Specifically, these hindrances are traditionally listed in the following order:

1. Desire (*kamacchanda*): This being the *wanting* of people, places, things, and experiences leaving us always hungry for more.
2. Anger / Ill Will (*byapada*): The *wrestling* we do out of frustration and resentment for the wrong we believe others (or life in general) have brought us.
3. Sloth/Torpor (*thina-middha*): The *wilting* we experience in body and mind when fatigue and sluggishness cloud our faculties and weigh us down.
4. Restlessness (*uddhacca-kukkucca*): The *worrying* we do when our minds and agitated bodies get lost in what might be based on a constricted view of what's been, our thinking anytime but now.
5. Doubt (*vicikiccha*): The *wavering* as we stiffen, hold back, second-guess, and, at least temporarily, lose our way.

These inner obstacles do not require you to be a Buddhist, or even a meditator, in order for them to take hold. They are not ancient mystical concepts, but rather, contemporary, mundane, and familiar emotional companions to us all. While the Buddha may have spoken of them as barriers to awareness in meditation, we each (in varying emotional fingerprints) know them as the *w* patterns entangling our daily lives, in or out of meditation.

The hindrances are not a mere list of feelings. They are pointers toward the conditioned patterns of reaction in each of us, clouding clear seeing and binding us from effective action. They are made of thought as well as our felt senses, and they are, in simplest terms, a self-protective "closing" from the pain we've learned to move away from over time.

When we close, we are indeed protecting ourselves—the limited, conditioned self—from the experience of pain. If I were about to step off a street corner in front of an oncoming bus, my mind's rapid self-preserving clenching would indeed serve me, and so closing is not all bad. As a short-term strategy, and in life-and-death scenarios for our bodies, closing up deserves our vote. It's in the long term of consciousness that the hindrances—modes of closing—get in the way. We can't see or go far if we're averting our eyes and hesitating to move. I can sit here and watch YouTube and be "entertained" (that is, numbed), or I can sit here and write and be engaged (that is, enlivened), though doing so may risk the pain each of the hindrances I've accumulated in my life has kept at bay.

Do we want our days to be small and safe or large with loving awareness? Do we prefer to sleepwalk or to truly awaken to the fullness of life we already are?

You picked up this book and opened it, and you open still by reading this far. But do you notice the pull of your mind toward a particular, and perhaps familiar, habit of closing? A tug toward restless worry that your time is best spent elsewhere, or perhaps a subtle internal tickle of want for chocolate cake or a three-finger-deep highball of bourbon? A wavering of doubt that you'll find any answers here of any merit?

Are you willing to listen to all this conditioned chatter, feel the bodily experiences of mild to major bodily discomfort linked to these thoughts, and to keep opening? If so, we'll take a tour of what the Buddha taught about the hindrances and the path through and away from them. And as we open, we'll hasten our footfalls with the findings of modern science. As the Dalai Lama stated in his book *The Universe in a Single Atom*, "if scientific analysis were conclusively to demonstrate certain claims in Buddhism to be false, then we must accept the findings of science and abandon those claims."[3] This book's journey will not get lost in the nether regions of mysticism or stop short with reference to dharma tradition; it will integrate the ancient truths borne out by the findings of modern science.

We'll learn how the brain evolved amazing capacities for processing billions of bits of information regarding our daily lives and how this mere three-pound universe weighs consciousness down with its evolutionary baggage. We fight a war of awareness on two fronts: there are psychological lessons of our families, work-life imbalances, and environmental traumas and deprivations that block our opening from without, and then there are the cognitive and perceptual biases that do so from within.

And we'll also peruse the recent findings of positive psychology that foster our practice of opening. The practices and overall approach of this book are informed by the work of psychologists such as Carol Dweck ("mind-sets"), Robert Emmons and others (relative to their key research on the liberating power of gratitude), Mihaly Csikszentmihalyi's findings on psychological "flow," and Angela Duckworth's research on "grit." And throughout, we'll examine the common ingredient of mindfulness.

Mindfulness will tie all the science and thousands of years of dharma tradition together as we open out and away from the five hindrances. To venture an inevitably incomplete definition, mindfulness can be considered intentional awareness of the present moment, on purpose and with kindness,[4] or "the summation of all energy . . . the energy of a state of mind in which all conflict has completely ceased."[5] Or you can simply look into the eyes of a loved one and notice the mutual impact of doing so—the loss of "time" and gentle, felt push-pull of loving interconnection—and you'll have a more accurate definition of mindfulness. Or consider an unselfconscious belly laugh. Notice a stop-short moment of awe at the rising up of a spectacle of nature or the dawning joy of the sight of one's newborn child. These are better definitions of the mind that is full of what *is* versus the mind hampered and clouded by the five hindrances.

In this book, you have the opportunity to begin (or continue) the process of gradually dislodging the crutches out from under your efforts to navigate your daily life. I say "process" and "gradual" because there is no self-help silver bullet for ending the hindrance patterns that block self-awareness and lead to unhelpful reactions in relationships (with yourself and others). And as you'll likely see, some strategies and approaches recommended in the following pages will resonate for you, and others will fly like leaden balloons. You will benefit from taking heed of the Venerable Ajahn Chah's admonition: "if it works, use it."[6]

Chapter 1 begins with a discussion of what emotional and psychological closing, versus opening, means and how we each approach any given moment with our personal inheritance of patterns for doing both. We'll reframe the ancient concept of karma (a kind of dharmic black sheep) in simple, nonmystical, and practical terms, and discuss how working with the hindrances is basically a working through of one's conditioned karmic patterns. No white-bearded Big Brother in the sky is determining your karmic plight. We are largely the makers of our own mindless beds. The chapter ends with a guide to assessing your areas of strength and challenge among the five hindrances and how you might strategically plan your journey forward to build on what's already open and whittle open what has grown closed in your mind and body.

Chapter 2 takes a more focused look on how the hindrances are most typically discussed—as impediments to meditation itself. We'll look at traditional and current ways of accounting for and addressing how these internal states and external patterns of action show up and block us up during formal meditative practice.

Chapters 3 through 7 take each of the hindrances in turn (and in the order in which they are traditionally taught: desire, anger / ill will, sloth/torpor, restlessness, and doubt) and examine their daily life implications. Understanding and resolving each hindrance is heightened when we marry the contemplative practices tested by thousands of seekers over the centuries with the scientific assessments of the comparative few who have begun to unearth the measurable variables of what creates and what binds the growth of open, compassionate awareness and action.

Chapter 8 brings the book to a close by helping us all consider how closing has its rightful place in our emotional lives. The endgame of working with the hindrance patterns is to learn to sidestep the achieving, striving mind-set so common to Western ways. As the artist and mindfulness teacher Rupert Spira suggests, awareness is the thread of the necklace of a lifetime of moments.[7] Our lives are less a crowning jewel to behold, and more a series of moments to mindfully engage and open to as much as we are able.

The best way to make use of this book is to indeed consider it a map for a journey—a journey into brutal honesty with the dark corners of your ways of being and moving in the world. The book is one map among many, and as you have often heard the saying profess, it is not the territory itself—rather, the true landscape is your aware nature, your mind a full nest of unhatched possibility.

So start with chapter 1, and then as it suggests, feel free to either move toward an area of hindrance you've already found yourself opening to (in order to build even more momentum) or address a domain of more pressing concern. Proceed with caution if you take the latter path, however, because these more overgrown, oft-repeated hindrances give way least readily, and the unforgiving travel might sap your resolve (and render the book a mere inch-wide reminder of yet another false start on your bookshelf).

Wherever your journey starts in this book, do not expect a fast unfolding and quick coming of gains as if ascending a seven-habit staircase or drilling down suddenly into some self-helpful inner giant. You must simply show up and let the awareness that comes from reading, contemplating, and truly applying the suggested practices seep into the fissures of your patterning; they will give way like warm water dripping atop a glacier—according to causal, inevitable, observable laws that will have absolutely nothing to do with your wishes or wants. You will find the living questions that spring up from this melting far more compelling than any hindrance-encrusted answers your mind had anticipated.

Make no mistake as you take your first steps with this book: you're really going nowhere, because the honesty is always available; your birthright is true, open knowing of when you're living from a hindrance and merely reacting to circumstances, or when you're listening with accepting awareness to what's occurring. You also know when you're willing to lean into the now, listen to what's happening in your senses, look toward the moment with curiosity and clarity as to what direction matters most, and commit to a leap into the unknown you're embracing.

I am the heir of my actions, as are you. But if that is not motivation enough, consider the heirs all around you—the loved ones, young and old, who are always watching (consciously or not) how you manage and hold your own experience. Your choices now as you hold this book and in next moments as you perhaps engage its offerings will do much to provide stimulus to their own inheritances. You are neither responsible for nor capable of truly opening others' lives, but you provide much indirect grist for their pattern-making (or breaking) mills.

When he was two years old, my son, Theo, loved a "sleeping" game. The game was simple: I fell over on the floor and proceeded to fake sleep, replete with snoring (which my sleep-deprived wife can well attest is far from inauthentic). Theo chuckled at the sight and sound of me dropping into a sudden Rip Van Winkle impression on the living room carpet and then ran up to me, falling with his full twenty-some pounds onto my back. "Wake up!" he called. And that was my cue to dart up, smile, and tickle him into giddy oblivion.

And there you have it—truly from the mouth of my (I must admit) adorable babe. That's the call of this book: are we willing to see (with compassionate, unflinching knowing) how we've been closed and asleep, and to wake up into open awareness?

When I began this introduction's writing, I told of my angry wrestling match with my anxiety-racked daughter. In the moments after her anger and mine had abated, I remember sitting on the edge of her bed as she slumped up by the headboard. She looked so much younger than her six years from the inward pull of her limbs into a fetal pose. The echo of my angry, worried, fatigued, and self-doubting patterning pressed tears to the edges of my eyes. It felt like more pain than my meager skills of awareness could hold.

Let's be clear: I've ventured this honesty to begin yet another round of my son's wake-up game with you. I'm hoping you'll play. I don't always open, but in loving contemplation of the inheritance I've received these past four and change decades, as well as all the possible heirs of my doing so, I'm increasingly willing to do so. May you be willing to do so over and over as well until there is no more life-clouding closing, no more hindrance, no more suffering—just the openness we all truly are.

1   The Karma of Closing

Our Emotional Inheritance

OPENING INQUIRY

Will you merely crack this book from time to time, or will you truly open it? Might you stay open awhile yourself?

For most of the three months of my training rotation at the clinic, I believed myself to be outmatched and ill equipped to be of help to the men. They were Vietnam War combat veterans, many of whom had been coming to this particular group meeting for over fifteen years. I was there for just a few months. I'm fairly certain I reminded them of the wet-behind-the-ears, overeducated platoon lieutenants who came over to the war straight out of officers' training: young men with no concept of what real war meant, let alone how to lead men, some of whom had already seen the darkest corners of it during their tours in-country. I sat across from them with the naive look of the officer who was going to screw up and get men killed. I held that sense of myself like a hot coal in my rumbling, anxious gut throughout most of the group sessions across my own tour of duty as a trainee. I was burying something I dared not let escape.

And in one particular session, the conversation strayed into the jungle, the places where the vegetation had long since died and renewed.

One particular man in his fifties, his appearance grooved and callused, talked of the "atrocity" he committed there among the tall grass, his rage swirling down and out through his clenched hands. His aging body had, of course, changed significantly since his days in uniform, but his aggrieved mind had known only glacial psychological change in all the years since he and his fellow GIs had exacted revenge on the Vietcong.

"I'm a monster," he said. "What sort of man does something like that?"

Round and round he'd gone in the gap of years, never stepping off his macabre merry-go-round. He aged. He worked. He stumbled across and through relationships, managed to do his best to raise his own children "who deserved better," and yet his mind was locked. The image of himself as a fanged demon clenched the pain in his heart and caged up his entire life.

I wanted to hold up a mirror to all that had changed, to all he'd done that was so unmonsterly in the years since the war: children, a wife, a job, support to his fellow group members. I wanted to show him all the obvious evidence of humanity and softness, and yet I found it difficult. I felt as though I was holding up a double-sided mirror, each of us only seeing ourselves—the same face we'd wrangled with in the bathroom mirror each morning for years. I had my own frozen image I was clinging to: the nice boy, the straight-A student, the applause junkie, the divorce-on-the-way, needy do-gooder. I lacked the looking glass for us to see each other clearly. My patient—I—needed a fresh perspective. In reaction to the pain we'd each experienced, we'd closed down our minds to new possibilities. Our respective reflections were laser etched into the solitary confinement of our bathroom mirrors.

At the time, I'd yet to become acquainted with the Buddha's teaching of how we are each the "heir" of each moment of our actions. By our attempts to avoid discomfort and garner pleasure, we condition ourselves into patterns of closure that carry forward like ripples on water in our lives.

Just This Life: A Contemporary Take on Karma

The meandering Charles River is across the street from my house in Newton, Massachusetts. There is as a small gorge there spanned by Echo Bridge, a footbridge built in the early twentieth century. My wife and I once took our then three-year-old daughter there for a walk on a Saturday. I'd lived in the area for fourteen years and had only recently discovered the bridge, let alone the small platform at its bottom, poking unseen from above out over the water's lazy flow. Though I adore my kids, my weekend tendency was to be lost in thought and anticipation of creative and professional tasks undone, the never-ending eddying of to-do items. I'm not usually focusing so much on fostering such family moments (to my wife's understandable frustration). But for some reason, I wanted to teach my daughter about echoes, knowing that she'd never experienced them before. We walked down the embankment, down a small flight of stairs, and out onto the small wooden balcony directly underneath the stone archway of the bridge.

As my daughter chattered excitedly about the water, the birds, and the sensory rush of it all, I smiled as I pressed my back against the bridge's cool stone and let loose a loud declaration of my daughter's name. "Celia!" echoed back to me, and her face lit up with the surprise of my voice bouncing down at her from the stone above. Her eyes brightened, and a smile broadened as she took in this example of lawful ordering of action and reaction. I didn't realize until later that this experience I'd allowed in myself and for my family was an example of what I'd call karma—a lesson about "then" and "this" and the echoing now. I've always resisted this lesson, and even though I'm a psychologist—a "change agent"—I'd struggled against the changes that karma teaches, a lesson I and all of us in the contemporary West have needed.

In that moment, karma—the Sanskrit word for "action," with "result" embedded within (*kamma* in Pali)—was in evidence all around me, and I was just beginning to see it. As we stood for a few minutes listening to the swirl of water and Celia's energetic experimenting with the bridge's acoustics, I perused the graffiti, the adolescent angst, written on the railings of the platform. There were declarations of love and pointed questions as to the truth of what the water had to say about teens sitting hunched together in the dark holding lighters and smiling at the glow of their illicit embers. There was a regularity, an echo of sorts, to the youthful searching there. This inner reaching and shoving were familiar to me, and I felt them still, if but faintly.

As water moved by, and as I read the pain gouged into wood, I noted my own well-worn grooves—from the minor ripples of diet soda, compulsive

Amazon shopping, and straight-A validation yearning over the years to major tidal waves of divorce and restless, grass-is-greener career flip-flopping. There was what I did compulsively and reactively to close down in hundreds of ways with body and mind that echoed out, buffeting me and those I've been connected with. And there at the base of the bridge was evidence of the antidote prancing about the platform—the marveling and mindfulness of a three-year-old's open holding of the moment that suggested a way into and out of the karma I'd inherited.

I've always either been skeptical of karma (due to my scientific training as a psychologist) or, more deeply and honestly, afraid of it. The fear was not just of the heretical branding I might receive for secretly checking out karma-related books from libraries, but rather the prospect of actually facing myself, my echoes, squarely. Like many, I viewed karma as a belief system that required full buy-in with reincarnation. There was also the distasteful sense of a universal, fatalistic accounting and justice-rendering system, and the accompanying mysticism that turned me off. Historically, and particularly in the West, karma has been passed around as a conceptual hot potato—few touting it for fear of being tagged New Agey or out-of-date. It has been mishandled out of anxiety born of misunderstanding—the conceptual reject, last to be picked for the dharma team out at spiritual recess. This is truly unfortunate because karma, at least for me, is becoming the fuel, the empowering nudge on the path. It's the patterning of conditioning there with us in every moment of experience of one of the five hindrances, daily obstacles of inner experience. It's there as a simple echo that can, if we're willing, become a mindfulness bell for opening our minds and hearts.

As I've acquainted myself with karma, I'm learning to let go of the sense of it being pessimistic. I'm moving away from a sense of fate and destiny. Karma is much more than "what goes around comes around" or "you reap what you sow." There is no karmic justice of the peace out there and no blame to be had in thinking of the cause and effect of one's actions. Through our actions we shape that which comes to us in the next moment. There's an anonymous saying on karma: "To see what you've done, look at what you experience now. To see what you will experience, look at what you're doing now."

Ken McLeod, a meditation teacher in the Tibetan tradition, writes:

The essence of karma is that actions determine experience: actions based on reactive patterns reinforce patterns and lead to suffering; actions based on attention in presence dismantle patterns and lead to opening. When we understand how behavior affects experience, we understand karma. Belief in past and future lifetimes isn't an issue. Appreciation of karma does not come from intellectual understanding or belief. It comes from seeing directly how patterns in conditioning operate, a seeing that comes about only through cultivating attention in uncovering awareness.[1]

Our past culminates in what comes to us as patterns in the present. Our future is created largely by what we do with the inheritance we've been given—by how much we open to our present-moment experience. We only have this moment. We've all heard many people touting this—a sort of urgent infomercial underlining the call for mindful living. It's the modern-day magazine cover message of well-being. To give it a moment's thought though renders the truth of experience: we can't live in our past, and the future is always out of reach.

If I'm open, I'm aware there is only this moment of fingers on my laptop's keyboard, only the next moment I'll have if my daughter walks down the stairs looking to engage me. The thought of the last sentence and its tapping out onto my computer's white space is gone, and so will the writing session altogether if Celia appears in the stairwell. The problem karma points out is that we tend to close up so easily into our patterns—our reactive, unaware conditioning. We quickly shake off realizations of nowness as hiccups of consciousness and fall back asleep with a sense of fixation on pathways past or eyes glued to the horizon. Or at least let me speak for myself—as a colleague, therapist, friend, family member, husband, and even as a father. I've been a Rip Van Winkle of wakefulness. I've been asleep to the role of karmic patterning and am only now standing up and stepping out of the trees and beginning to see the forest of things for myself. Only now is opening becoming the only viable option.

When the Buddha said that I am the heir of my own actions, he did not intend for me, for any of us, to beat ourselves up. He was likely aiming to wake us up to the hopefulness of the present moment for liberating ourselves from the momentum of our karmic conditioning.

We bequeath ourselves vicious cycles of action and reaction based on our years of struggle with the hindrances to awakening—to clear, compassionate consciousness. The Buddha pointed out that we all look to avoid suffering. Our karma is the collection of our understandable, good-faith best efforts in doing so. We are looking to shore up our store of good stuff and stave off the experience of pain, loss, and discomfort. There is no blame to be had here, because we don't willfully close and create the process of karmic return. It just *happens*. In fact, to deeply consider karma is to really experience a sense of possibility—there are patterns we've each inherited manifesting now, and then there's the next moment: either constriction, repulsion, reactivity, and pattern repetition *or* attention, awareness, openness, possibility. No matter what we've done that hems us in, there is the spacious capacity of the present moment. Close or open? That is the essential and only choice.

I once heard a recorded lecture of the philosopher Alan Watts using the metaphor of a sailboat in capturing the movement of karma in our lives, and it's perhaps my favorite.[2] Here, according to Watts, we create our past in the present moment through our actions. There is only now, so there is no past or future to fixate upon. Does a boat's wake move the boat? Does the horizon fill its sails? Only what the boat does with the wind it's given in the present moment determines the vessel's movement. And here's what I love most about this metaphor: it's pliable; it has creative possibility in it. Stand on the ship's deck and carefully and with engaged attention look about—and realize there is no boat. There's no vessel, no "you" separate from the ocean. It's only the open expanse, moving into and through itself.

As tempting as falling asleep (sloth and torpor, "wilting," as presented in chapter 5) is to the brain of a father of a young child, it also helps keep me awake to the truth of karma to consider an anecdote from Mahatma Gandhi's life. As the story goes, a woman once came to Gandhi with her young son.[3]

"Mahatma-ji," she said, "tell my little boy to stop eating sugar."

Gandhi looked at the boy and his mother. "Come back in three days," he said.

In three days the mother and son returned, and Gandhi addressed the boy. "Stop eating sugar," he said.

"Why was it necessary that we return after three days if that was all you would say to my son?" the mother asked.

Gandhi smiled. "Three days ago I had not stopped eating sugar myself."

If Gandhi can acknowledge and open amid his less-than-ideal karmic conditioning, so can I and so can you. Other than clear, mysticism-free explanations and nifty anecdotes, it has also helped me to consider karma from other perspectives—such as what can be rendered of it from philosophy, science, my clinical work, and even the rubber-meets-the-road aspects of my own life's history.

The Psychology and Science of Karmic Patterning

Long before I began work as a clinician, I was a teen growing up in a beach town in Florida. I can remember many Saturday afternoons when I had little to do but lie flat on the couch and stare up at the twirl of our living room ceiling fan. It was too hot and humid to spend much time outside, and often I felt too crimped by social anxiety to venture far from home anyway; therefore, I became more than expert at professional fan-gazing.

To stare at a ceiling fan is to know the perceptual parlor trick of how the individual fan blades blend and blur into a "solid" disk when the spinning reaches a certain velocity. Sometimes I would be sufficiently bored to play a game of "catch the fan blade." Flicking the switch on the wall by the front door to turn on the fan, I then bolted across the room, launched myself onto my back on the couch and looked up to see how many separate fan blades I could count before the whirling got the best of me, and the fan became a buzzing plate, spitting air down at me as if panting from the effort. Clearly, my family's move from Ohio to Florida had been hard on my social life for a ceiling fan to become my closest thing to a junior high summer fling.

Our eyes lie—whether in looking at ourselves as therapists, or as kids staring up through adolescent angst at ceiling fans. That is no disk or plate. We are not the monsters or the do-gooders we reflect upon. We know the blades are there, and yet, because of our narrow window of perception, our limited ability to track and accurately see "what is," vision gives way to illusion. The movement is beyond us, and therefore things solidify and seem as fixed as Rodin's *The Thinker* statue in Paris—not going anywhere, locked in frozen, eternal contemplation.

It's also easy to stare up at Rodin's statue and conclude this poor guy will never make up his mind. Similarly, my personality and everyone's personalities (the habits of action and inaction, emotion and thought, that reappear across our lifetimes) are made of a similar marble, are weighty and resistant to change; they're used to protecting and serving themselves by closing down as hard as any statue. Ask most people the one word that comes to mind to describe personality, and they come up with things like "fixed," "static" or "unchanging." I never liked large parties as a kid; I wanted to fade into the cracks in the gymnasium's cement-block walls during semiformal dances in junior high, and I still want to be similarly suctioned out of these situations as an adult. Yes, the fan blades shift from single blades into a pattern, change form before our eyes, but surely not *The Thinker*, not *this* thinker. There is no real change there to be had.

And yet, the patterning in all things—ceiling fans, statues, and ourselves—changes when you assume a large enough scale of observation. Put another way, you can see the spinning "solid" disk when the blades slow sufficiently for your narrow range of human visual perception to make them out. (Just consider how other beasts with better eyes might see the blades sooner.) If our perception of statuesque stubbornness did not rest on a time scale of our limited eighty-something years of existence, if we watched such objects across the span of dozens of decades, or if we zoomed into the subatomic vast openness in the individual molecules of marble, we'd see the motion. We'd see thought in flux. Similarly, with enough time, or with a scalpel sharp enough to split our cells open to a microscope's gaze, we'd see the same transience in ourselves.

Any rational mind must admit the changing nature of the body, and yet there's more if we're willing to look. Here is where karma comes in. Our personalities as well—they are patterns that form, continue with subtle and sometimes significant alterations over time, and eventually come apart. Yes, our parents pass us genetic raw material and provide the early breeding ground for our peccadilloes, but somewhere between diapers and dustups on the school playground, we begin choosing in present-moment consciousness how to manage our experiences—we begin adding to the growing pile of personality. The shifting motion is there, however, when we look deep and long enough.

"Me" has rigidity and immense momentum, and yet I'm inevitably shifting. Think Grand Canyon and the carving influence of the Colorado River over millennia. Consider the feel of an ice cube in the palm of your hand sitting across a span of minutes. Think time. Choose to open to whatever arises in your conditioning, whatever emotional obstacle crops up. Feel the melting.

As the late philosopher and self-proclaimed "spiritual entertainer" Alan Watts was apt to say, "everything is pattern." Look at anything outside and everything inside, and with sufficient scrutiny we'll find the woven fibers, the beat, rise, and fall of contour, the familiar texture of repetition and cyclic movement. Lunar and menstrual cycles, genetic and conditioned disorders of body and behavior, the stitching of my shirt as well as the front-to-back, top-to-bottom ordering of the structures of the brain—all are a regular, discernible cadence of consistency.

In the open now, five fingers left and five right tap out the consensus of squiggles representing specific vibrations of air molecules when human vocal cords twang in moments of meaning in a communicative context. In this act of writing, I am engaging patterning at multiple levels—physical, linguistic, interpersonal, and likely many others I'm only dimly, if at all, aware of. And in this same moment, there is the rhythmic pulse of my daughter's dancing footsteps on the living room floor above me, the dull cadence of the throb from a shin splint in the wake of yesterday's running, the relentless tide, the metronome, of my breathing. No reincarnation. No mysticism. It's there in the genetic and environmentally conditioned unfolding of moments. It's karma. I can open to it and watch as it disperses in awareness, or if emotional circumstances shove or pull at me, I can follow suit and close ranks with it, go to war with my inner life and lose every time.

I even take my shower along the outlines of a pattern: hair first, then body, and the soaping always proceeds toe to top, my behind-the-ears move saved for last. The fact of life's patterning seems certain, perhaps as comforting to us as an existential lullaby. It's there to be seen such that life becomes reliable, predictable.

We most often miss the subtle play of the patterns of the hindrances or at least fail to see there being enough at stake to take them to heart and motivate ourselves to relate to them with awareness. "Yeah, yeah, I see you," we might softly say under our breath when desire, anger, dullness, worry, or doubt emerge, and though we are momentarily aware of their inevitable destructive outcomes, we plunge forward into them anyway. Spouses push each other's well-worn buttons. We let things slide just one more time with a neglectful colleague. The addict tips the glass yet again to his lips. The unseen and neglected patterning of our emotional and behavioral inheritances unfurl.

Near and far, quantum quick and glacier slow, inside and out, up, down, and all around—patterns swirl. Everything moves, and our minds, due to the processing demands of it all, opted eons ago for a mental shortcut of separateness. It's just too much to sit around meditating on the nonduality and interpenetration of it all, particularly when hungry saber-toothed sorts are breathing down our necks. We couldn't afford the luxury of the cave time necessary to meditate upon the connectivity of "things" and "me." And just because our brains looked away for want of sufficient RAM (or, to use a psychologist's term, working memory), it doesn't negate the inevitability of universal patterning one bit.

Draw a circle around something, anything, that is not in some way the result (and cause) of a pattern. Touch stuff. Sense stuff. Think stuff. Cry a river and raft down it far enough to see the inescapable eddying about the shoreline. A dog's barking, a kid's whining, a car and a spouse's stalling—all are the flow of patterning. We'll never know all the reasons why we lifted that extra piece of fried chicken to our desirous mouths, though it won't be because of a willful CEO of the universe deciding to keep the recipe of our actions a secret—it will be because there are simply too many contributing factors to ever account for.

We need not stretch out toward complete intellectual understanding of why we inherit all that we do. The Buddha laid out his eightfold path as a way to put down that drumstick (much to Colonel Sander's chagrin) and to let go of the cycle of suffering that shows up in each new moment of our lives. But whether you're Buddhist or not, you can still choose to open, versus close, when the emotional clutching-and-shoving match begins within.

Again, there is nothing here that's fateful, New Agey, or pessimistic. There's no need to even pull the reincarnation tarot card. We can focus simply on the karma of just this lifetime. In fact, it all dovetails nicely with modern science.

The relationship research of the psychologist John Gottman and his laboratory have shown the effects of parents' "meta-emotional philosophies," or their overarching approach to managing emotions across generations.[4] Glimpsing the psychological mechanisms that I liken to karma, Gottman's work has shown that parents with a more balanced, equanimous, structuring style of approaching emotion raise children who are less physiologically reactive to stress and exhibit less negative socialized behavior.

Research on "intergenerational transmission" has supported the role that conditioning plays in patterns such as abuse, domestic violence, substance abuse, divorce, and health-related behaviors across the lifespan of families.[5] Research is beginning to codify the traps of patterning that clinicians like myself have seen in at-risk client populations. And there is a growing swell of studies outlining the epigenetic effects across generations—how human experiences can create physiological changes that impact how the next generation's genes are expressed. For each of us, it appears likely that karma is the behavioral and emotional patterning transmitted to us genetically and by the environmental contexts we're born into, as well as by our actions in the present that shape our inheritance in the next moment.

And karmic conditioning can go in positive directions as well. For example, the organizational psychologist Adam Grant's research has shown that if you provide cues for helping-related behavior in peoples' contexts, it can increase their chances of actually being helpful to others.[6] When simple changes were made to the wording of posted hygiene signs in hospitals studied by Grant, 45 percent more soap and hand sanitizer was used. Instead of sanitizer gel use preventing "you" from catching diseases, signs were altered to read that the protection would go toward "patients." That simple change in context increased peoples' patterning for the good of all.

More than metaphors or scientific findings, what's clinched the imperative of karmic understanding for me is what I've seen in clients and in myself. I've worked with parents whose tearful agony over their children's dangerous behavior sparked old patterns of closure—parental

rejection and avoidance—further solidifying this patterning in themselves and their kids. I've sat with addicts and inpatients whose knee-jerk
repetition of reactivity had momentum like a lava flow, with me trying
to arrest it with frantic spitting. I've listened to promises made and
witnessed their repeated undoing. I've heard avowals of collaboration
for the good of children and watched as divorced parents did the emotional equivalent of a medieval racking of their sons and daughters. I've
had clients in tears over the changes their very survival required, and I've
heard later of their near-death reenactments of the parts they've been
playing since childhood. I've seen far too few closings in my office.

And I've sat the silent hypocrite in sessions as they've wrung themselves out over their karma—the "shouldn't be this way" of their lives—
and I've flicked the scabs of my own patterning. With two divorces,
the Oscar-worthy role of family "magician" / disappearing actor I've
rendered, and the things compulsively going into my body and the deeds
and words obsessively coming out over the years, I've filled out an entire
how *not* to self-help book. I've stood on the deck and shaken my fists
at the wake I'm undeniably made of. I'm the therapist whose flow has
been such that my own therapist spitting on me would seem insufficient
to wake me up. The mantle to carry is that karma is inescapable. It is
around and within us all. To live is to inherit what is: mantle, yes, and
more if we look closely without closing to the obstacles our patterning
presents.

Our Lives as an Open(ing) Question

Why worry about being lost in a ceiling-fan illusion of solidity and me-
ever-more-ness? Very simply it's because failing to create a flexible,
accurate view of karma—of shifting, changing patterns of thought,
feeling, and action in our lives—leads us to perpetuate and bestow
unnecessary suffering. We'll keep filing for divorce when we might
learn to let go, open, and live for each other. We'll continue looking at
a bent world through the bottom of raised and drained glasses of booze.
We'll work too much to accumulate piles of stuff to bury our well-being
beneath. We'll turn away from moments of beauty because we're following the bread crumbs of unmet expectation or gut-on-fire fear. We'll
clench and collapse when a fully lived life would have us lean in to the

open expanse. In big ways and small, in moments of addictive craving and parental caving, we'll suffer. And it will largely be due to the failure of the predictive lenses we've purchased and worn for years without question. Standing at the lip of the Grand Canyon, our eyes see only the blur of patterning that we perpetuate mindlessly. "When's lunch?" we ask, blinking our eyes closed, completely missing a moment of timeless grandeur.

If we choose to open, if we rest in mindful awareness, we can hold patterns as if handed them by a mute, faceless mailman, deciding each wakeful moment to (again for the thousandth time) live it in repetition as patterning or hold it up and drink in the ferocious perfume of presence. Henry David Thoreau lingered by the doorway of his mindful pond-side shack-o'-presence-and-life-pondering and talked of our "lives of quiet desperation."[7] We can choose to either sleepwalk through life or wake up in awareness. For me, for those I work with and those I love, it's become increasingly important to come home to the good, bad, and otherwise of karma.

Only when we hold the dead carcass of our patterning without breathing new life into it can we embrace freedom. As Ken McLeod writes, "You have to die to the pattern's world. You have to die to the belief that your ability to survive rests on those patterned behaviors."[8]

Be it a habit of blowing off intimacy, chasing away pain with sex, booze, or pills, souring a marriage with lack of attention, dousing fear with work or family ambitions, or "small" patterns like refusing to tip more than 10 percent because our own efforts have been insufficiently noticed—or any of an infinity of other patterns that we've inherited— there's a bank account you walk around with, and it's crucial to ask what it means to gently, compassionately hold it, perhaps even to the point of feeling our arms breaking. And as McLeod's statement suggests, we resist the death of our patterns because it feels like suicide, a killing of that which is inextricably linked with "us."

A final metaphor: In any moment, we can choose to reach out with our attention to lift a shiny, mirrored wide-open bowl. Mindfulness is our attention to whatever appears inside, patterned or not. Our practice of doing so consistently, not reactively closing our eyes and looking away and chasing our patterns' demands, but gently holding the bowl, prompts the bowl to expand in all directions. The bowl includes, contains, and reflects more and more in open, flexible, spacious awareness.

When we're willing to gently hold (not grip) our bowl, we're willing to open to understanding how patterns bind and block us from doing what we know in our deepest corners of heart-body-mind to be healthy, ideal, and life-at-stake worthwhile. We learn to see the obstacles that land in the bowl as opportunities to turn it into a crucible of awareness, where we can press the bowl out wider, holding more and more of what life has to offer. We'll deeply experience what it means to inherit patterning. We'll begin seeing how patterning manifests in our daily behavior. "Oh, I know you," we'll declare as we wake up, Van Winkle style, and see the forest for the trees we've been sleeping under for years. Such holding is what I've seen in moments of compassion as a clinician, when a father took hold of his family's pain of a baby's sudden death and spoke and led from his heart, moments when other clients held tongues instead of lashing out, when colleagues leaned in toward angry parents and distasteful situations calling for avoidance.

I'm reminded of a very angry mother of a client I sat with recently. Her rage covered a vast vat of fear. I had filed a legally mandated (though these mandates seem to offer little solace of certainty to treatment providers) abuse report with the state after this very loving and treatment-availing parent had struck her special-needs child during an intense behavioral outburst by the girl at home. Contrary to my lavalike patterning of avoidance of conflict and angry barbs sent in my direction, I opened and allowed that not-so-pleasant failure feeling to sit inside me as the mother pointed dagger fingers in my direction and talked of how I'd "f——d" her and her family. Though I have much bowl crafting left to do, I *consciously* opened in that moment to this woman's fear and pain, and more accurately, I opened to the pain and chaos in myself. I decided to stay quiet and let the tears hover unhindered about my eyes, and I rode out my urge to debate and counter the charges this mom filed in the air between us.

Later, after time had allowed the weather to clear for her, and after this mother returned to meet with me again, I asked her if she'd noticed my tears, my upset during that tough conversation.

"Yes," she said.

"And did it help in some way. Did it help to see how I was reacting?"

She softened, much unlike that day of daggers. "Yes. I knew I could trust you."

I had luckily learned a bit about minding the present and doing the opposite of what patterning nudged forward in me. Luckily, I'd started opening and thereby slowly letting some of the karmic echoes in.

For me, for clients of mine, and with what science suggests, it comes down to willingness to lean in to the pattern, the emotional hindrance, and open to what happens in us when we do. There's the validation and freedom of the inevitability of patterning. We all dance, and we wish it different (even if only in passing glances of each other as we whirl about the floor).

My self-tortured Vietnam veteran client thought himself a "monster." I thought myself the young lieutenant who had to do something to prove himself. A former supervisor once suggested I say in such moments: "We're both right, and we both get prizes. So now what?" This man's life had swirled about in a dank eddy of muck along the shore for years. Until recently, I've spent my life craning my neck to catch glimpses of adoration, avoid angst, and detour from difficulty. As much as any client, I've been locked into patterning as sure as the solid-disk spin of a ceiling fan, as certain as the mentally constipated *Thinker* in a Parisian garden.

So our ever-present task is to shock our systems to the core and stand up together, stretch our marbled legs, and take a new, pattern-breaking step forward. Our choice is open if we're willing.

Pointing Out Your Patterns

To help as you move forward in this book, take a moment to do some self-assessment as to the current patterns of the hindrances in your life. By estimating your areas of strength and challenge among the five hindrances, you can strategically plan your journey to build on what's already open and whittle open what has grown closed in your mind and body. Here again is a list of the hindrances:

1. Desire (kamacchanda): This being the wanting of people, places, things, and experiences leaving us always hungry for more.

2. Anger / Ill Will (byapada): The wrestling we do out of frustration and resentment for the wrong we believe others (or life in general) have brought us.

3. Sloth/Torpor (thina-middha): The wilting we experience in body and mind when fatigue and sluggishness cloud our faculties and weigh us down.

4. Restlessness (uddhacca-kukkucca): The worrying we do when our minds and agitated bodies get lost in what might be based on a constricted thinking from anytime but now.

5. Doubt (vicikiccha): The wavering as we stiffen, hold back, second-guess, and, at least temporarily, lose our way.

Which do you find yourself reflexively drawn to? Which have the quality of familiarity? A sense of "Yes, that's one I struggle with a lot"? Perhaps one or more are no longer as thick and salient for you as in the past; maybe there's an area where you are confident you've not stumbled to any significant degree—in fact, you've rarely ventured in that direction. Regardless, notice (and trust) that you already have a fair degree of intimacy with your own patterns. You've ridden these waves of unrest for much of your life. If you're at all in a self-reflective mood, you know quite a bit about yourself already, warts and all.

Review the figure here with an eye toward discovering your areas of strength and challenge. Consider the figure a "pattern pointer" of sorts—an aid to noting the patterns of mental (thoughts/images) or sensory (bodily perception) activity in our moment-to-moment experience. The figure draws your attention to a given situation and asks the core self-inquiry of this book: in this moment, am I opening or closing to my experience? This pointer is a compass of sorts—a karmic compass of the patterns you stand heir to in any given moment.

While we all experience all the hindrances at various times and to varying degrees, consider the following situations to narrow in on the ones most prominent for you. Take your time, and approach each statement as a meditation in and of itself—go behind and beyond analyzing or merely thinking *about* these. Notice what arises in both your bodily sensations and in word-based thoughts and images. If a memory shows up, pay attention to what you remember sensing and thinking, as well as what shows up *while* you're remembering. There's no way to "fail"

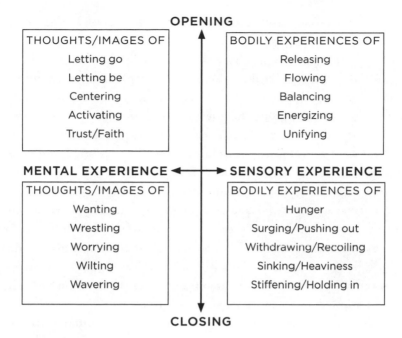

at doing a self-assessment of your patterns. If you're willing, you're opening and patterns will inevitably reveal themselves. The unseen is only so because we're not looking.

- Pain or the threat of it has visited you as a result of your own or another's actions.
- Pleasure or the promise of it has arrived as a result of your own or another's actions.
- Pain or the threat of it has arisen out of the context or circumstances you find yourself in.
- Pleasure or the promise of it has arrived as a result of the context or circumstances you find yourself in.
- Pain or the threat of it has remained over a significant period of time.
- Pleasure or the promise of it has remained over a significant period of time.
- Pain or the threat of it varies in intensity and is unpredictable as to when it will show up.
- Pleasure or the promise of it varies in intensity and is unpredictable as to when it will show up.

I would also recommend selecting a day for self-observation, for pattern detection. As you go about your daily business, try to keep your eyes open for aspects of the hindrances. Consult the questions and/or the figure above. Use a journal if it helps, and simply note your tendencies of body and mind when pain and pleasure arrive or depart. Don't let them visit without signing the guest book. The point is to get curious about the hindrances and let this become a contagious habit all its own.

What were your tendencies of bodily reaction/sensation and thought in response to all this self-inquiry? How much did you notice patterns of energy suggesting your body and mind's habits of flight from pain or fight against its perceived sources? There are no judgments to be had and no diagnoses to be rendered. These are merely the habits of closing you've inherited to which you can learn to increasingly give compassionate glances. And the looking will be enough. Do your eyes have to go in search of light for vision to happen? Or does the opening let the light do it's natural "thing" on your waiting retinas?

Self-assessment is a process, not a simple cosmopolitan quizzing for mere entertainment. Don't be fooled by the list of five and fall prey to the belief that this is more of the same stepwise "self-help." Centuries of Buddhist teaching have relied on numbered lists to get the point across that mindfulness (or mindlessness) is the predictable result of specific conditions. Put certain ingredients together, and things happen in a cause-and-effect sequence. The five hindrances are not an arbitrary list that merely looks great as a book's title (though it does, right?). They are the mental habits that together knock a meditator's mind off the cushion (perhaps literally in the case of sloth and torpor). The next chapter examines meditation as the laboratory of the mind and how the hindrances traditionally and scientifically muck up the experiment.

CLOSING INQUIRY

What is the cost of your hindrance patterning? To the repetitions of wanting, wrestling, wilting, worrying, and wavering?

2   Meditation and How the Hindrances Have Us over the Barrel of Our Monkey Minds

OPENING INQUIRY

Are you willing to step onto the path of meditation and its hindrance–laden twists and turns and do so with the right intentions and with the necessary knowledge to guide your steps?

Act now! Limited time offer! Can your health and well–being afford for you to flip that channel?

"Of course I can't!" my mind screamed. "I need this. I deserve this." I only required the slightest nudge in the direction of the "Buy with One Click" button. It's impossible to tickle yourself, so why can't we be equally unable to push our own impulsive buttons?

I was carried away by the impulse at the close of the holiday season several years ago and ordered a collection of "power yoga" DVDs for use in home practice. It was P90X meets yoga, wherein you were challenged with a daily regimen of intense hour-long practices performed on the video by studio sets filled with svelte, unfairly flexible twenty-something yoga instructors. It was daily, it had a progress-tracking chart, and by God, I, in my early midlife-crisis drive to get lean and prove something of my power, was going to bang this out.

I made it a month or so into the program, but only by sheer, wrenching force. It hurt, and I had no idea what I was doing and how I was the source of a lot of the pain. There were some guided *pranayama* breathing and meditation sections, but these seemed on another planet from the sessions in which I was straining, agitated, falling over, and literally aching as something unnaturally popped in my anatomy. I ended up with a ferocious case of tendonitis in both elbows, with an inflamed irritability to match my tendon discomfort. I underwent surgery and began a slow, painful process of physical therapy to rebuild a modicum of strength in my arms.

I missed a crucial lesson on my first blitzkrieg pass at yoga. I somehow missed the DVD teaching that the essence of good practice of yoga is an abiding presence at the seamless juncture of mind and body. In the healthy practice of yoga postures (*asanas*), you don't shove your body into pretzeldom just to prove you can or to wring your midlife angst out of your joints. Instead you patiently rest in the middle of physical tension at the edges of your capacity. You rest there without forcing or straining, patiently and mindfully breathing into the mild aversion—the discomfort—waiting for the body to respond, to open, and for the tension to leave of its own accord. You'd think I would have learned this already from my experience as a meditator. Alas, I was approaching yoga as a means to a fantasized end. I've done the same with my meditation practice over the years:

> An aching half (or maybe only quarter) lotus sitting position . . . guided practices on CDs . . . eyes closed . . . Zen, *zazen*, breath counting . . . expectations of sudden enlightenment or perhaps a mystical experience or two . . . *vipassana* anchoring on the breath and noting of distraction/thought (because all the "going back to one" with zazen was just too boring) . . . eyes open . . . guided practices on CD in my car (ergo eyes open) . . . kneeling on a bench (I "caved" in service of comfort) . . . *metta*/loving-kindness practice (short-lived due to my penchant for vengeance fantasy life) . . . me, ten or so middle-aged women in a yoga studio on a Sunday morning, and face-to-face "insight dialogue" relational meditation (prompting my abrupt, insecure return to eyes closed practice) . . . *tonglen* (Tibetan for "sending and taking") com-

passion breath work . . . nondual open monitoring, "choiceless awareness" . . . stacks of unread and compulsively purchased meditation books . . . two Tibetan singing bowls (because one was insufficiently resonant) . . . mindful self-compassion practice (because at this point, I was feeling quite the meditative failure) . . . a *zafu* cushion that is now being used as a crash mat for my kids in their play area in the basement . . .

Throughout the years, I've gone more horizontal than vertical (i.e., toward depth) in my own practice. It's not only failing to see the forest for the trees—it's hacking away at one trunk only to abandon it and turn my ax on another. I end up with nothing to build upon. What I needed and what we all need if we're to have any chance at chipping away at the obstruction the five hindrances cause is what the psychologist and meditation teacher Jack Kornfield has called taking the "one seat." What this means is that we need to understand that meditation is not a "technique" to be dabbled with. It's not a quick fix or means to a desirable end. We need to show up to practicing in a consistent manner that reflects the dignity, beauty, and ultimately the immense demands of meditation. I—we—need to stop hacking at tree trunks if we're to build a house of awareness that only meditation, rightly and consistently practiced, can bring.

Beware the Guillotine during the Mindfulness Revolution

Over 11,000 search engine hits for products on Amazon, a seemingly endless array of articles, books, mala bracelets, incense sticks, and cushions of all shapes and sizes: indeed mindfulness has made the cover of *Time* magazine as a "revolution" in 2014 and with a special edition in 2016 as "the new science of health and happiness."[1] A 2016 article in the *New York Times* referenced the research of IBISWorld, which estimated that meditation-related ventures and products scooped up $984 million in revenue in 2015.[2] Books promise mindfulness in a mere minute, and courses suggest you will master meditation. Slap the word "mindful" on a book, product, or service, and you'll benefit from the automatic branding the word delivers. Mindfulness has done for self-development what Kleenex did for flu season.

While there is much to celebrate about the popularity and interest in meditation in recent years, there's cause for concern as well. This chapter aims to put meditation in its rightful place as a purifying path of liberation—specifically, from the patterns of hindrance that cloud our clear seeing—but as we'll see, we need to be aware (which is a word at once bigger and perhaps better than "mindful"). Mindfulness as a term may be somewhat new (first coined by the Buddhist scholar T. W. Rhys Davids in 1881[3] and popularized by the author and researcher Jon Kabat-Zinn starting in the 1970s[4]), but meditation is anything but new. And, as we'll also discuss, the West is prone to grabbing onto the clarion calls of "health" and "happiness" (Hint: check this book's cover!). In doing the hard work of true liberation from suffering, it's important not to clutch at promises fit for magazine covers and Times Square neon. To move into and through the hindrances, we need more secure footing for the path of meditation.

The psychotherapist and longtime meditation teacher Bill Morgan writes in his 2016 book *The Meditator's Dilemma* that the Western mind, with its predilection to fast results, thought-driven self-management, and independence and self-development, is at odds with the primarily Eastern mind-set in which traditional meditation practices first arose.[5] In those cultures, an internal, contemplative (versus thought and action) focus was emphasized. Interdependence versus independence was the norm, as was an acceptance of gradual versus immediate change. Morgan argues that "for mindfulness practices to become more deeply rooted in Western society, the differences in inclination and disposition must be addressed early on in mindfulness teaching and in the instructions themselves."[6]

Dr. Miles Neale, in his article "McMindfulness and Frozen Yoga," takes things a step further regarding a proper frame for the practice of meditation in the West.[7] He argues that the outcome-driven, quick-fix frenzy in our society (which he deems "McMindfulness" relative to many current meditation invocations) leads Americans to be "notorious for extrapolating what they idealize, plucking the desirable from foreign cultures and simply disregarding the rest . . . seeking quick fixes and inciting temporary trends, lacking the patience and long-term commitment needed for lasting change."[8] We may focus (and I certainly have) on culling out the meditation techniques and severing them from the ethical foundations and pillars of wisdom on which the techniques rested thousands of years ago. Neale worries that we're at risk for "diluting" meditation, and this is crucial if we're to embark on the difficult journey of engaging meditation as a tool in overcoming the obstacles posed by the hindrances in our lives.

Neale cites a personal example of the need for embedding meditation practice in an ethical and wisdom-tradition framework. He bought and diligently (and with mindfulness) attended to the care of his plants. He lacked, however, the "wisdom" that comes from knowledge of "right actions" to foster their health and development. "Because of my inaccurate knowledge," Neale writes, "I and my plants suffered."[9] Neale had good intentions (ethics) and was focused and attentive (mindful), but he lacked knowledge.

It is for this reason that working with the hindrances requires a full toolbox—meditation technique to foster concentration and open awareness of the patterns of mind, emotion, and behavior, along with ethical intention and wisdom. But an ISIS terrorist can muster (and "benefit" from) meditation techniques in isolation from ethics and wisdom. He or she can, with calm and deep concentration, press a suicide bomb belt's trigger button. Working with undesirable, hindering patterns (karma) requires a team effort—from meditation, healthy/compassionate intentions (ethics), and knowledge (wisdom) from both those who have walked farther down the contemplative path than we, as well as what contemporary science has to say about best practices for well-being and compassionate connectivity in society.

In his wonderful short book *Zen in the Art of Archery*, Eugen Herrigel tells of his quest to learn the ancient art of Japanese archery.[10] What he learned was far more than how to penetrate a target's bull's-eye. In holding and aiming the bow, Herrigel's master taught him that "by letting go of yourself, leaving yourself and everything yours behind you so decisively act that nothing more is left of you but a purposeless tension."[11] He would hit the target less because of a desire to do so, but because he'd actually given up the desire and lost himself in the tension of the act. "Now, at last," the master broke in, "the bowstring has cut right through you."[12]

Before we delve into each hindrance in the coming chapters, it's important that we set the frame of our expectations. As Bill Morgan and other teachers have suggested, it's crucial for us to let go of the quick fixes and drive-through-window aspirations for a happy meal to be made of our meditation practices. For us in the West, this is indeed a challenge, as we love the promise of possessions obtained and goal lines breached. The actor Michael Douglas (as *Wall Street*'s socially sanctioned 1980s psychopathic investor robber baron, Gordon Gekko) announced that "greed works."[13] Though most of us (some presidential candidates excluded) might hesitate from being so brazenly direct, the truth of our straining for tangible, Amazon-boxed evidence of success is no less for us in the West.

Meditation is the mirror that accurately reflects how each of the five hindrances is warping our view of life. These hindrance patterns are not obstacles "out there" in the world, nor are they defects "in" us—they are the inevitable imprint of our body-minds trying to make their way forward on their own. As soon as we emerge as individuals, we're looking to set ourselves apart from the world we're intimately and inextricably connected to. Meditation is the vehicle that reminds us of ourselves—that we've been asleep at the wheel dreaming a life of "me," "yours," "mine," and "evermore." Meditation is the movement of the mind out of the hindrances—the karmic "genetic conditioning"—meant to keep us safely and separately asleep, and to keep us self-protecting and greedily possessing. The real deal meditation—the authentic reflecting pool of practice—is the movement of the mind away from its temporary, swarthy, elusive, herky-jerky, persistently shortsighted and distorted smallness to the open, clear, even-tempered, long-viewing inalienable and untainted smiling awareness.

In essence, meditation *is* awareness. The noted twentieth-century philosopher Jiddu Krishnamurti referred to meditation as:

- "the total comprehension of the whole of life"
- "not sitting cross-legged, or standing on your head, or doing whatever one does, but having the feeling of the complete wholeness and unity of life"
- "perceiving the truth each second—not the truth ultimately—to perceive the truth and the false each second"[14]

What he meant is that there is actually no true separation between meditation as formal "technique" and our daily life. We are intelligent (a word Krishnamurti uses with precision) not when we're analytical and smart in the standard sense; we're intelligent when we're seeing reality clearly and without the obscuring influence of our thinking. For Krishnamurti and many teachers of such nonduality perspectives, things like meditation, you, me, the stuff around us—it's all the same. On the surface, this may appear to be meditative, philosophical gobbledygook and have little relevance to living life with greater awareness, but that would itself be a limiting result of your own thinking! In meditation— more correctly, *as* meditation—we realize that awareness contains every- thing. All thoughts, bodily sensations, and mental images (which is what the "world" ultimately breaks down into) are contained *in* awareness. The hindrances are simply the conditioned patterns of thought, images, and bodily sensations/emotions that show up "inside" our body-minds. They arise close and quick, and meditation helps us to see them and learn to rest in the gap of awareness—our true identity.

I've listened to recordings of Krishnamurti's talks. (He died in 1986, at the age of ninety, after having traveled and taught for more than sixty years.) I've heard the story of how he disavowed his appointment as a spiritual leader (the "World Teacher"), his only official action being to disband the entire Order of the Star in the East. There's a credibility earned in such selflessness—a lack of hypocrisy that has eluded me as I've pursued my own path into the hindrances. Without being Buddhist (he dismissed any organized tradition as inherently of the mind rather than truth), Krishnamurti spoke of the meditative mind in a way suggestive of the journey into the hindrances. "Therefore you must die to every- thing you know psychologically, so that your mind is clear, not tortured, so that it sees things as they are, both outwardly and inwardly."[15] An unhindered way of being indeed.

In talks I've given, I've asked the audience to give me their own def- inition of mindfulness. Usually they happen upon the components of the definition originally offered by the author Jon Kabat-Zinn—"paying attention, in a particular way, on purpose, in the present moment, and non-judgmentally."[16] Most in the audience are busily writing the defini- tion in their notes once we arrive at it. I wait until the writing stops, and then I ask them to take their pens and vigorously cross out the defini- tion. No offense to Kabat-Zinn, but it's seemed important to me that we get closer to true mindfulness—true meditation. Words (i.e., thoughts) will always fall short. Meditation/mindfulness is an experience of pure awareness. I play a short video clip of a young boy who'd recently received one of the first successful cochlear implants. He'd been born deaf, and this was the moment he'd be hearing his father's voice for the first time. The surge of awareness on his face is quickly reflected in the emotionally moved glistening of awareness about the face and eyes of the audience. We've all just meditated in a true, most wonderful way, with most folks likely experiencing at least the briefest hiatus from their unique imprint of the hindrances.

The Leaning Tower of Meditation in Our Lopsided Lives

As I've abashedly listed above, my own meditation journey has included many detours and dead ends—a lot of grass-is-greener, restless practice hopping. Three things were lacking—a depth of meditation practice (i.e., planting my flag in specific practices and cultivating the benefits of insight into my patterning), careful forethought as to the ethics of my practice (my early intentions were much more akin to producing a 007-degree of proficiency and smooth daily operation), and wisdom (which was in short supply). As I've read and talked with teachers, and as I've explored what science has to say about building awareness (and sidestepping its obstacles), I believe I've grown in that regard. Without any of these three to offer, this book would be flaccid in its helpfulness, better as a paperweight on your desk than a guide to opening your life out from under the repetitive, compulsive karma choke hold you're likely experiencing.

The practice of meditation can be considered a microcosm—a proving ground for our relationship to our daily experience. It helps us learn about the workings of our conditioned (and hindered) minds and builds our capacity for resting in the awareness we truly are. To take the transportation metaphor out for a spin a bit, I'll go further and say meditation practices are best as vehicles we're meant to merely lease, not own. To the degree we try to possess our favorite make and model of meditative technique, we're letting the car drive us instead. We're taken for a ride that can last our lifetime if we're not careful.

Again, we need meditation technique, ethics / good intentions, and knowledge to really make a go of getting away from the hindrances. We need to heed Bill Morgan's and Miles Neale's words as to the binding aspects of the Western mind-set from getting the most out of meditation.[17] Yes, we can be more focused, effective, and less stressed in our daily lives—there's nothing wrong with such goals. We simply need to hold them lightly, without all the gripping and grasping. We'll find, as Eugen Herrigel did with his archery lessons, that we actually hit targets quite well, and we'll do so despite the "selves" that had previously suffered with all the striving and straining.

The hindrances can't be "beaten" or "obliterated." They can become the fertile ground for our true growth. Their uncomfortable "garbage" can, as the Zen teacher Thich Nhat Hanh wrote, be seen as transforming into the brightest of flowers, if we maintain awareness. According to Hanh, "roses and garbage inter-are."[18] These hindering obstacles are actually karma's offerings to us for growth beyond ourselves.

Traditionally, the Pali canon addressed Buddhist monastics and provided instruction on clearing away the hindrances as part of their work in laying the foundation for the ripening of the conditions for a liberated mind. In the Anguttara-nikaya, the Buddha states:

> If a monk has overcome these five impediments and hindrances, these overgrowths of the mind that stultify insight, then it is possible that, with his strong insight, he can know his own true good, the good of others, and the good of both; and he will be capable of realizing that superhuman state of distinctive achievement, the knowledge and vision enabling the attainment of sanctity.[19]

And these conditions required for a monastic to reach absolute enlightenment appear virtually impossible. There's a certain fanaticism in Buddhism around the lists of factors required for advancement of the mind and the endless rungs of the ladder as one climbs higher toward liberation: *four noble truths, eightfold path . . . three characteristics of existence . . . five aggregates . . . twelve links of dependent origination . . . five precepts . . . ten perfections . . . five hindrances.* My son likes to stack blocks on our living room carpet, but even at two years old he seems to know his limits—he knows when to call it quits and just smash them all to the ground. In Buddhist psychology, it can seem there's a perfectionistic striving that itself verges on hindrance.

And yet, consider an analogy from nature—the extraordinarily rare conditions required at a planetary level for life to have a chance. Just last week, there was international news about a possible "artificial," strong radio signal from a star ninety-four light-years from earth. Could it have been emitted by an advanced intelligent species? Alas, it appears the signal was of our own terrestrial making (a bouncing back of man-made emissions). We've yet to find conclusive evidence of life (past or present) on Mars despite probes, scans, and laborious analysis. Life emerges amid a very narrow sliver of conditions—millions of variables have to converge for the life fire to spark.

This is where karma comes back in—again, nothing mystical or faith-related. No voodoo and not even our wishes, fantasies, ideals, or politics have any say in whether the conditions required for the development of consciousness have developed. It's simple empiricism. It's the bouncing about of causes and effects, a gathering of patterns like clouds predictably swelling into a front, which brings downpour and the crashing of lightning. There's no consideration to be had and no forethought required. The causal conditions of body, brain, and social context emerge, and awareness follows as a consequence.

The tower of conditions may have to rise quite high, but any concern about the "impossibility" of what awareness requires is a label and judgment arising from the limitations of mind itself. Meditation, awareness, reality are independent of such sentiments of difficulty. For centuries, monks have stripped away conditions of daily life that might nudge the tower off its footing. I'm not arguing in this book for a retreat into robe-donning cloistering, but I am suggesting that we all consider creating not just a time and place for formal meditation practice, but the conditions on and off the cushion that make the path in and through the hindrances more likely.

Awareness and How Our Biological Deck Is Stacked against It

The Pulitzer Prize–winning naturalist Edward O. Wilson wrote, "Human nature is the inherited regularities of mental development common to our species . . . These rules are the genetic biases in the way our senses perceive the world, the symbolic coding by which we represent the world, the options we automatically open to ourselves, and the responses we find easiest and most rewarding to make."[20] What Wilson points to is how we inherit our brain's biological raw material, which shapes how we take in and respond to the world. We do not, however, inherit predestined *experiences*. We get to apply the greatest tool evolution has afforded—awareness—to the task of how we relate to the world in the forms of our thoughts and sensory experiences.

One example of the biological blinders that evolved within our brains is the adaptations we've developed over the eons in how we perceive one another. One well-researched brain-based bias is what social psychologists have termed the "fundamental attribution error": "the tendency to assume that an actor's behavior and mental state correspond to a degree that is logically unwarranted by the situation."[21] It's me assuming the guy who cut me off last week in Boston traffic is a "selfish jerk" to the exclusion of any sense of his personal context of lateness and/or family crisis. It's people assuming the emotionally and behaviorally challenged kids I've worked with are "bad" or "manipulative" and failing to see the biocontextual forces in a given situation that may have sparked their swearing or oppositional behavior, rendering them empathy hard to the onlooker.

So why would evolution deliver such a biological straitjacket to our mental wardrobe? As argued by evolutionary biologists, "cognitive biases are often not flaws, but design features that improve responses under uncertainty."[22] Overevaluating threat and deceptive intent or underemphasizing the seeds of forgiveness in another could (for our cave-dwelling forbears) have prompted avoidance of those who might be aggressive and take off with our food or mates, and may have prompted us to forge stronger bonds with our kin (and thereby promote genetic advantage). "Social cognitive biases should be viewed in terms of their ultimate adaptive effects, and not whether they represent logical or 'accurate' ways of thinking."[23]

As an example of the modern implications of this, Federal Rule of Evidence 403(b) prohibits the prosecution from introducing evidence of a criminal defendant's past "propensity" for criminal behavior.[24] Judges and juries are not to be trusted (due to social cognitive biases) to not overly weight past behaviors in assessing a defendant's guilt in commission of the crime being adjudicated. The law would have participants rely solely on a logical and unselfish weighing of facts, and yet we can't readily sidestep the ancient emotional architecture of the brain's hardware. It's for this reason that research suggests that people who are experiencing a temporary surge of fear are much more likely to erroneously perceive anger in another's face and miss cues of fear or other emotions, particularly if that other person is part of an "out group."[25]

So here's a question I've struggled with in recent years: if, as Buddhist psychology argues, the pure light of unhindered awareness is our birthright, why were we born with such constrictive neural hardware? It's like being told you are really the Deep Thought supercomputer, and after you've matured enough to open the box and peer inside, you find that you've really be given a mere Commodore 64. (Yes, I'm dating myself here.) So did the Buddha have the same mental RAM as we do? He decried any godlike status and referenced himself as mere mortal. Was his motherboard somehow better wired than ours?

The biological deck may be stacked against our ready access to the Buddha's attainment of awareness, but it doesn't mean we can't play our hand, learn about the karma of hindrance patterns clouding the mind, and take strides toward greater clarity. Evolution gave us our brains, but we can stand astride its fissured surface and reach higher. It's here that the array of lists of factors and conditions for the rise of awareness within Buddhist psychology reemerges. We must do the hard work of consistent, unrelenting practice—we must unpack the hindrances and climb higher in concentration (the various jhanic levels) and approach the example set by the Buddha.

The Buddha would not likely have unfurled into awareness and the subsequent teaching of his four noble truths and eightfold path if he'd found himself sitting not under the relative safety of the Bodhi tree at Bodhgaya in northern India in those centuries before the birth of Christ, but instead outside the mouth of a Paleolithic cave. The more physically treacherous environment of the cave's opening would not long have supported his peaceable lotus pose.

We are far more than the brains we are born with. Behavioral psychology (i.e., learning or conditioning), with its principles of how our habits are shaped by rewarding and aversive experiences, provides the steel girding of our mind-bodies. The early psychologist John Watson demonstrated the power-of-learning theory by conditioning a baby ("Little Albert") to fear a cute, white bunny rabbit (by clanging a metal bar loudly and in the boy's vicinity); Pavlov taught his dogs to salivate to the sounds of bells; and B. F. Skinner got rats and pigeons to perform circus-like stunts for the chance of a pellet of food in their glass cages. We are not immune to these principles and must learn to think outside of the Skinner boxes of human arrogance whereby we believe ourselves above such conditioning. The karma we're working with in addressing the hindrances is simultaneously a rising above the constrictions of our highly evolved brains, as well as the entrenched patterns of thought and action molded by our interactions over years with family, friends, coworkers, and the environments we find our-selves in. And this learning leaves its imprints in the neural networks of the brain.

Not only nearly impossible, this evolutionary brain and the behavioral conditioning creating our hindering karma can feel mute and uncaring. How does compassion and love figure into this perspective? How do we begin working with our karma, our hindrance patterning, in such a cold vacuum?

I'm reminded of a conversation a colleague and I had recently about our respective meditation practices and who we knew who seemed to have really "gotten it" regarding awakened awareness: who did we both know who seemed farther down the path than us? My friend and I have both mediated for years, and both of us are highly educated, trained, and experienced as clinicians and have read widely about the makings of awakening. And almost in synchrony, we each conjured the name "Jose." We were each struck with the simultaneous recognition of the true guru in our workplace. Jose is one of the maintenance workers at the agency where we both worked, with no graduate education or meditation train-ing. Jose is someone quite special. To me, he was always smiling and commenting to me about the look and feel of the day's weather. To my friend, he'd often say things like, "It's not easy," as my friend rushed about the building addressing some clinical crisis of the moment. We were both struck by the insight that Jose had not simply been chatting about weather and work stress; he was holding up a mirror of aware-ness to each of us. "Wake up!" his smile and gentle, engaged presence announced—and had been doing so for years. We, the "meditators," had simply failed to see it, clouded by the workday hindrance blinders we'd been wearing.

Jose, true meditation, love, awareness (synonyms to me)—these are not cold, uncaring vacuums. They are the agendaless openness to all conditions as necessary and sufficient in the now, the present moment. The arms of awareness are infinitely wide to hold every thought, sensation, and image that rise. They are compassionate because they accept what arises in the moment without hesitation. To Jose and in meditation, there is no mistake, no good or evil. These are the agenda of the limited, thinking, conditioned mind. Jose has always seemed open to every turn of the weather, to any of the demands his job, or we as his coworkers, sent his way. Perhaps I'm merely projecting guru status onto Jose, and I'm betting Jose, in the awareness he embodies, would agree.

The Buddha's Truths and Working with the Hindrances

In the coming chapters, we'll drill down into each of the hindrances, understanding their influence in our lives from both dharmic and scientific perspectives. We'll also rely on both realms for learning how to skillfully work with the hindrance at hand, how to turn it from "garbage" to "flower." Again, karma unfolds in this moment because it's been conditioned to do so when the context calls for it. If you follow your reactive conditioning, karma solidifies and repeats, thus solidifying a hindrance pattern. If you open, the karma shifts, loosens, unwinds, and there is change in brain, behavior, and mind. A new, more flexible pattern is born that enhances well-being.

To organize our efforts, each hindrance will be addressed according to the Buddhist principle of the three characteristics of existence.[26]

In the Samyutta-nikaya, the Buddha taught that "feeling is impermanent . . . Perception is impermanent . . . Volitional formations are impermanent . . . Consciousness is impermanent. What is impermanent is suffering."[27] "What is suffering is nonself. What is nonself should be seen as it really is with correct wisdom . . . When one sees this as it really is with correct wisdom, the mind becomes dispassionate and is liberated from the taints by non-clinging."[28] The Buddha suggested that we open ourselves to these essential truths of reality—that the emotions, behaviors, physical objects, people, and relationships of our lives are inevitably transient. Clinging to the mind's want for permanence is what the hindrances are about—they are the patterns meant to keep our minds to the smallish task of holding on, claiming, and keeping the ego going. The Buddha is recommending we learn to see clearly, with unflinching recognition of the truth of the inevitable dissolving of what the mind would have fixed.

From the Buddhist perspective, one's opening develops from practices that take into account each of the three characteristics of reality:

1. The universality of the unsatisfactory nature of human suffering (what the Buddha called *dukkha*)
2. The temporary, or impermanent, nature of all things (*anicca*)
3. The truth of interconnectedness and interdependence of all things, and therefore the lack of any "self" of ours being separate from others and the environment (*anatta*)

Don't take the Buddha's word for it—test it out for yourself. Take any thing, any noun of your life—person, place, or thing (or even an idea, emotion, or relationship)—and ask if any of these could exist absent the three characteristics. Try it out. Does anything exist fully intact and unchanging forever and ever? Is there any person who has not suffered? Is there anything that has not been influenced, shaped, affected by other stuff? The meditation teacher and author Sylvia Boorstein, in her book *It's Easier Than You Think*, suggests that we are more verb than noun. "Since everything is change happening," Boorstein writes, "there is no one who owns the changes and no one to whom the changes are happening."[29] We are truly be*ings*—do*ing*, feel*ing*, liv*ing*— rather than individuals who stay put.

These three characteristics will lead us to consider practices and the arrangement of one's life conditions for opening amid the experience of a particular hindrance:

1. Addressing inevitable suffering by practicing acceptance—abiding of the bodily discomfort arising in your sense experience
2. Getting clear on the truth of time and the passing nature of difficult experiences and situations sparking unrest and unclear mind states
3. Getting clear on how no one (to quote John Donne's famous poem) "is an island." We all are reciprocally influenced and

affected. Even the very fact of our breathing is a constant reminder of our dependence on the world around us at all times. We are in no true way separate, and this selfless clarity is crucial to the development of opening amid the hindrances.

A Universal Practice for Addressing the Hindrances, Humbly Offered

Again, there's a potential high cost to Western society's pursuit of meditation-as-corporate-profit-facilitating or even as a seemingly benign white knight for riding in to rid us of modern stresses and psychological ailments. Instead of emphasizing the benefits of "one-minute" mindfulness or how an online course will bring meditative "mastery," we're much more likely to unhinder ourselves to the degree we're willing to work beyond the hype and promises of meditation as a panacea and learn to relate to meditation directly. Instead of looking for a helpful meditation technique that will boost our career or improve our relationship, how about connecting meditation to the ethics of karma and your interdependence (and accountability) as a human being in society with access to scientific findings? Unveiling and unraveling awareness from the hindrances will require that degree of practice, intentionality, and know-how. Are you merely meditating for effect, or is meditation *you*?

In addition to discussing particulars and practices for each hindrance, I want to offer a practice we'll return to again and again. While acronym "McStrategies" might verge on the type of self-help ploy that Miles Neale and others have warned of, I offer it with the aspiration that it open you in moments of both formal and informal practice. Though it's a bit of alphabet soup, my intention is that its ready accessibility aids you in pouring warm awareness into a moment's hindrance reactivity. With consistent use, it perhaps fosters a gap (perhaps very small at the start) in which awareness, meditation, Jose (!) have a chance to wake you up to the possibility of choosing your true self, instead of the conditioned one you've inherited. Farmers and gardeners know that small gaps in the earth are required for the placement of seeds. Tossing them loosely atop the ground is unwise effort, and crops are much less likely to grow. Try snapping awake into gaps of awareness in which fresh, creative, compassionate, and, yes, effective seeds can take root.

Try "SNAPPing awake" in moments of patterned reaction by doing the following:

1. **Stop** what you're doing for just a moment when you can tell you're getting triggered, when a hindering pattern is on its way.

2. **Notice** with curiosity what is happening in your bodily senses and your thoughts. Witness and watch the energetic play in the body and the flow of thought and mental images as they are born, live, and die on their own.

3. **Allow** these experiences to be just as they are, without judgment or attempts to control them. This allowance is a choosing: you're not signing up for pain; you're choosing to recognize the reality that hindering, clouding intensity does indeed exist.

4. **Penetrate** these sensations in the body with full, deep belly breaths (slow, deep breathing that expands your belly on the inhale), and continue to breathe in this way until you notice your experience shifting, until the solid "thingness" of the pattern has begun to dissolve.

5. **Prompt** yourself to move/act in the direction that feels most important and in line with what takes everyone's perspective compassionately into account. Pause to send an intention of kindness toward yourself for your efforts in working with your patterns.

CLOSING INQUIRY

Are you looking for a mindful prize inside a hastily consumed drive-through meal of technique or self-help? Are you pushing or pulling toward a goal in meditation, or are you willing to be *meditation?*

3   Sidestepping Cookie Monster

Learning to Dance with Desire

OPENING INQUIRY

When in your own life has desire not ultimately disappointed—fallen short of its promise?

I still have some of my comic books from the late 1970s and early '80s. Spider-Man was my favorite, but it wasn't just the art and stories that drew me to my comics, and it wasn't even the supernatural personal upsizing I could do within those pages. Without a doubt, one of the biggest factors leading me to clutch comic in hand and—before I realized it—plop my spare change on the cashier's counter was the opportunity to find a new advertisement for a random piece of plastic crap I could order. For only two bucks, I would find myself dutifully popping open the mailbox at the end of our driveway in rural Ohio each afternoon after school. Where's my "footlocker" of two hundred army men? I'd ask myself, "Why isn't it here yet?"

Never mind the fact that the "footlocker" in the full-page color ad in the comic turned out to be a small five-inch-wide cardboard box stuffed with flat, cheap, plastic army men. And it's not all that important that I played with my new toy no more than thirty minutes before it ended up with the other rejects down in the basement. What's relevant here is that my nose very soon opened up in yet another comic book, with me circling other items I "desperately" wanted. And so the conditioning of my desirous, compulsive karma began. And so it continues to this day, as evidenced by the never-ending, steady flow of Amazon boxes to my front door.

This is why my mom branded me the "Cookie Monster" when I was a kid. My hand could frequently be found "randomly" grabbing about inside the yellow, ceramic smiley-face cookie jar in our kitchen. The blue fur was the only difference between my ferocious cookie flailing and the gobbling chaos of my Sesame Street namesake. If I had to pick one of the hindrances that has been my own personal weak spot, desire would be it.

What used to be plastic comic-book doodads morphed over time into compulsive clutching at grades in school, leapfrogging relationships, self-help schemes, and substances of various kinds. Desire and its nastier cousin craving pull hard at me, and I've gone off the grid of awareness many times as a result. Of the writing I've done for this book, this chapter has posed the greatest challenge—it's the mirror onto karma I've been least willing to look at.

Last week I had a rare opportunity to be at home alone for a chunk of the day. I'd been away for most of the week on the lecture circuit, talking, ironically (because hypocrisy has been one of my best teachers), about mindfulness and how to work with one's own karma/patterning and to address how it blocks effective action as a clinician. And here I was at home looking at the formidable pile of packages that had arrived for me while I was away.

Instead of following my impulsive childhood mailbox-and-cookie-jar grabbing, I decided to run an experiment in awareness with my packages. I cranked up some Christmas music on my iPhone, carefully placed my Amazon boxes under the branches of our twinkling tree, and proceeded to sit down facing my desire. I closed my eyes and meditated on what was showing up in me for fifteen minutes there in the rare quiet of my young family's living room.

Yes, I am a very busy professional, and yes, I had many things I could have been productively doing that morning. And yet, there were the results of my little holiday-desire laboratory. The Buddhist psychotherapist and author Mark Epstein wrote in his book *Open to Desire*,

"Desire always disappoints. But if we can make this disappointment the object of our awareness, then desire can become enlightening."[1] That's what I found by paying close attention: the wanting curdled into craving as I sat in meditation. Desire, when delayed, swelled and bloated until it became downright uncomfortable.

And yet, unlike years ago at the mailbox and cookie jar and in the many years since at the bar or my home's mudroom (where packages are delivered), I sat through the craving. I related to it with something other than grabbing.

And yes, when I finally opened the packages—more slowly than is typical for me—I found myself actually enjoying my solo early Christmas. I was able to bring a bit of awareness to the objects my impulsive, wanting fingers had fetched with a click of the "buy now" button on the Amazon cart. Usually, my Amazon package ripping quickly cascades into a dull thud internally, quickly followed in subsequent hours with the crescendo of another purchase and its promise of absolute satisfaction. This time, I stayed with the "presents" with an ounce of presence. I found myself jonesing less than usual for another Amazon fix later that day. There was a valuable lesson in this slowing down, in the relating to the experience of desire with flexibility and mindfulness. And yes, as Epstein wrote, desire indeed disappointed—it still fell short of the promise of all the swirling energy of craving.

Desire in Contemporary Society: Times Squared

According to "the official site of Times Square,"[2] an estimated 300,000 pedestrians enter the heart of New York City's Times Square each day. The estimate comes from an automated counting system that tracks foot traffic into what is arguably the beating heart of desire and craving in the Western world. To stand in Times Square (if one is at all mindful of the sensory experience and not simply on autopilot toward the next store, show, or fast-food dissatisfaction) is to have your senses assaulted by light, shape, motion, size, and sound—all manufactured for the purpose of tugging at the human tethers of craving. With our Amazon carts calling to each of us, desire in all its various forms is more pervasive than ever.

Consider the following sobering statistics:

- The United States spent over 180 billion dollars on advertising in 2015 (by far, the most of any country).[3]
- Americans were forecast to eat approximately $18.27 billion dollars of chocolate in 2015.[4]
- In 2013, an estimated 24.6 million Americans aged twelve or older (9.4 percent of the population) had used an illicit drug in the past month.[5]
- On average, American adults watch TV for five hours and four minutes per day.[6]

And then there are the alarming trends around the use of digital technology, such as our (not so) smartphones:

- The soreness in our fingers and wrists from texting too much is so prevalent that the term "text claw" has entered our lexicon.[7]
- Problematic Internet Use (PIU) is now considered a behavioral addiction, with almost half (48 percent) of participants in one study considered "Internet addicts."[8]
- A quarter of teens in the United States are connected to a device within five minutes of waking up each morning, and most teens send at least one hundred text messages per day.[9]

I just set my phone down to write this, but, thankfully and notably, it's well within arm's reach. Our desire-prone brains appear easily bound up by the craving digital technology affords. I'm not saying we should all throw our phones in the trash or that we should forgo Facebook or terminate our Twitter accounts. The technology may not be "evil" in and of itself. These devices and capabilities do bring incredible benefits and possibilities for sharing information and creating more global interaction than ever before. We simply (and yet with great difficulty) need to learn to hold our technology—and all the various objects of our desire—more lightly. We need to cultivate more awareness of the risk of unfettered craving and possibly even life-draining addiction.

It should be no surprise that we've become so enamored with TV, fast food, drugs, and our increasing ability to drive ourselves into a phone-checking frenzy. Desire is nothing new, and as we'll see in the next section, it directly links to our brains and evolutionary heritage.

The issue is that with today's immediate-gratification cultural gambit, the ways in which we can saddle ourselves with compulsive and addictive responses to desire are now infinite and at the ready at all times.

The goal is not to follow Thoreau out into the woods by Walden Pond and divorce ourselves of all desire, but to instead learn to relate more flexibly to the uncomfortable space desire creates in our bodies and minds. It's not the geography of an isolated grove of trees and a pond glistening with summer light that makes desire manageable and life meaningful. Instead, we can learn to stand in the middle of Times Square and see it all as a neon show—a temporary digitized fireworks display we might allow ourselves to enjoy but not fixate upon.

According to the psychotherapist and author Mark Epstein, "desire must confront the gap that our clinging wishes to eradicate. How we handle this gap makes all the difference in our own unfolding lives"[10] We grab and cling in response to desire to stave off pain and clutch at pleasure. As a result, we condition ourselves (i.e., create karma) into ever-swirling whirlpools of craving. Choice and peace are lost as we slip unwittingly into these currents of consumption.

Are we willing to come to at least a brief rest in that "gap" between desire and fulfillment—between anticipation and satisfaction—and hang out there a bit? Are we willing to relate with this ill-at-ease state and thereby claim a more fluid and flexible approach to our daily lives?

The pull of desire may be inevitable and even assistive in our enjoyment of life. The suffering and slavery of craving can become optional if we learn to insert mindfulness into the mix. Let's pause in this gap for a bit of practice.

AN OPEN INVITATION—TRY THIS

Mindfulness of Our Phone Addiction

1. Sit comfortably in an upright posture with your phone in the palm of your hand, which you can rest gently on your lap. Keep your eyes open for this meditation.
2. Turn your phone on, but do not open any particular app. Just let your thumb hover over the screen.
3. Take a full, deep breath into the belly. Let yourself feel the nuances

of how the breath enters and leaves the body. For at least a couple of minutes or more, practice mindfulness of the sensations of your breathing. Simply place your attention (even though you're looking at your phone) on the feeling of your breath coming in and out (without breathing in any particular controlled way). If your mind drifts away, just gently bring awareness back to the breath.

4. Notice any of the following, and if they arise, just gently label them as a "want" and come back to being aware of how your breath feels. See if you can keep your awareness lightly connected to the sensation of the breath, and simultaneously see if you can notice the bodily sensations and thoughts associated with desire that happen to show up.

5. Is there any impulse drawing your thumb or finger to open an app, check e-mail, or some other aspect of your phone? Is there a want showing up in you—a sense of being pulled toward something? Get curious as to what this want, this desire, actually *is* in this moment. What are its components in your mind and bodily sensations? Notice the pull and see if you are willing to just ride the impulse without following it. Is this want actually the driving need it seems to be?

6. Rest your awareness in the sensations of the breath for a couple more minutes. Just notice what it's like to allow your mind to settle there in this small, yet ever-available space coming after digital desire has shown itself.

The practice above is about opening up to how desire manifests through this small yet powerful piece of technology. Instead of closing down our awareness and letting this device's screen become a "rabbit hole" we fall mindlessly into, are we willing to make a habit of seeing the negative state of craving it can draw out of us? Again, smartphones (and the Internet, social media, and other digital technologies) aren't inherently "bad." (Some, such as Jennifer Jolly of the *New York Times*[11] cite apps and the capacities of this technology for speeding our access to health information and even 911 calls.) This technology is, however, dangerously addictive. Sure, guns don't pull their own triggers, and lines of cocaine don't march up peoples' noses unbidden, yet somehow we typically know it's not wise to place either in a young child's unsupervised and unaware hands. Somehow we're not so careful when it comes to our digital devices. (And feel free to ask my wife what she thinks of all this—particularly when she's trying to get me to engage a conversation about household logistics while my phone is open and casting its pale, zombified glow onto my face.)

So let's put our smartphones to the side and mindlessly stroll through the kitchen—passing the cake deposited like a dark brown fudgy black hole with immense gravitational pull there on the counter. Desire comes in all shapes, sizes, and decadent textures for us to struggle against and perhaps learn to practice with.

AN OPEN INVITATION—TRY THIS

Chocolate Cake Meditation

Perhaps you've meditated for years. I'm betting you've never tried a thick slice of my chocolate cake meditation though! (And if you're not a chocolate lover, think apple pie or whatever promotes cavities in your sweet tooth.)

1. With eyes closed and posture upright yet relaxed, prepare yourself for the onslaught of thousands of delicious calories. Take a deep breath into the belly, exhale, and repeat. Now set a timer for just sixty seconds. Your only task for this minute is to continue breathing and do whatever you can to force thoughts or images of chocolate cake from your mind. Don't allow cake to linger on your imaginary lips for one second!

2. After the timer sounds, keep your eyes closed and notice the quality of your experience. What's happening to your mind and body?

3. Now take in two more slow, deep belly breaths. Feel the sensation of your breath wherever it is most noticeable in your body—nostrils, throat, or belly. Let go of breathing deeply and just allow the breath to rise and fall naturally. Gently rest your awareness on these breath sensations. If your mind wanders in any way (to another sensation, image, or thought—even chocolate cake), simply and gently return your attention to the feeling of breathing. Set your timer for sixty seconds and continue resting in the breath, gently returning from any thought, even of cake.

4. Again, after the timer alerts you, notice your experience, and consider the following questions: Which manner of managing thoughts and images of cake required more effort? In which method did you notice

more thoughts of cake? What manages your relationship to cake craving better: force (method 1) or mindfulness (method 2)?

Of the hundreds of attendees I've done this exercise with at talks I've given, the vast majority find a mindful approach (method 2) more effective in managing the internal experience of chocolate desire. Control and force seem less useful, yet what is our dominant approach for regarding the gripping fist of desire?

Your Brain on Desire

There is not something wrong with you (at least in terms of the focus of this chapter!). Just because you fall prey to various desires, even if they hem you into the uncomfortable snares of craving, that is not something "broken" with who you are. As recent psychological and brain science has made clear, and as Buddhist psychology has suggested for thousands of years, our basic human makeup is to desire pleasure and the end of pain and to crave objects, people, and experiences we feel will lead to those ends.

The Wright State University philosopher William Irvine refers to us all as possessing a "Behavioral Incentive System" (or BIS): our brains are genetically wired to find certain experiences pleasurable and others aversive in order to set us up for survival.[12] According to Irvine, "We gained this system through a process of natural selection: our evolutionary ancestors who had certain built-in incentives for action were more likely to survive and reproduce than those who didn't."[13]

Irvine's BIS is given a nod by the Buddha's second noble truth—that the inescapable cause of all human suffering is dukka, or "craving." In the ancient language of Pali, this was *tanha*, or "thirst." As the Buddhist scholar Joseph Goldstein indicates, this thirst is a sort of "fever of unsatisfied longing."[14] So our BIS from the many millennia of a biological and evolutionary standpoint is equivalent with what the past two and a half thousand years of contemplative tradition have known and practiced—desire is part of our makeup. Irvine argues, "We have an unprecedented ability to alter our environment so adaptation is not required. But although our way of wanting has enabled us to thrive as a species, it has not, in many cases, allowed us to flourish as individuals."[15]

Humans climbed the evolutionary ladder toward ecological dominance on the wings of desire, yet once we made it to the top, we ended up gorging ourselves on our well-earned capacity to clutch at our every longing. This capacity to desire and grab at attempts to satisfy desire is what sparks human suffering. Goldstein references the Buddhist teaching on dependent origination: "Based on contact and feeling, whether pleasant or unpleasant, craving arises. Because of craving, clinging: because of clinging, becoming. And so the whole cycle—old results (feelings) causing new actions, which in turn bring new results—goes on."[16]

In more everyday terms, it goes something like this: my old job gave me an iPhone to keep me in the loop with work goings-on, which soon led to the intense pleasure of flicking through the app store and downloading my first version of the game Angry Birds, which led to craving of more apps. And so my phone and I became fast friends, though I was a jealous, needy friend and kept my (now version 6) iPhone clamped tight to my hip in a pouch, not unlike an Old West gunslinger and his Colt revolver. Ask my wife about my compulsive phone-checking at the dinner table, and you'll know a bit about what became my addictive cycle of non-work-related phone fun (and suffering). What have I missed on my children's faces there at the table in the many moments of my face lost in the flutterings there on my phone's screen?

Researchers like the University of Massachusetts's Jud Brewer have placed the Buddhist concept of dependent origination and the karmic cycle of desire in the discerning view of scientific study.[17] Brewer and his colleagues have documented how addictions operate through a conditioned process in which our bodily senses pick up on cues from our environments (e.g., TV, food, iPhones, sex, etc.), and our brains link these into feedback loops (based on experience of these sensory experiences as pleasant or unpleasant) in our brains leading to the experience of craving. This not-so-pleasant experience of craving leads us to actions to satisfy the desire, and thus an addictive pattern is born.

As Brewer points out, we are never in direct contact with the objects of our desires—only with our mental representations of them in our brains. And it's this fact that holds the promise of freedom from the destructive cycle of craving (particularly at the level of life-bleeding addiction). We can't change the objects that trigger our desire—those cues will continue unabated and unbidden. We can, however, change how we relate to our mental experiences of them—the word thoughts, mental images, and bodily sensations of desire. "Craving is the link that is targeted here in cutting through the cycle of dependent origination," writes Brewer and his colleagues.[18]

Brewer's research suggests that mindfulness is key to severing the link between conditioned cues of desired objects and the craving that leads to addictive behavior. "Mindfulness functions to decouple pleasant and unpleasant experiences from habitual reactions of craving and aversion, by removing the affective bias that fuels such emotional reactivity."[19] Whereas more traditional approaches to treating addiction focus more on shifting the environment, problem solving, avoiding addiction cues, and boosting positive feelings, mindfulness offers the possibility of severing the cycle at its source in the brain, and treatment outcome studies in areas such as smoking cessation are increasingly bearing out the promise of this approach.

Scientists are increasingly teasing out the brain circuits involved in our desire loops, as well as how mindfulness meditation may play a role in physically changing these structures in ways that might allow for a decrease in compulsive and reactive behavior. Neuroscientists like Kent Berridge of the University of Michigan have pioneered the study of brain mechanisms of pleasure and desire[20] and have, through brain scans, shown that desire/wanting might derive from a larger and more pervasive system in the brain, whereas pleasure itself might come from a much smaller and distinct area (the ventral pallidum being a key candidate) and is therefore much harder to spark into action.[21] This may account for Mark Epstein's "gap" between desire and satisfaction—a gap that mindfulness may be uniquely situated to help us navigate. I may spend an entire interminable meeting at work craving a slice of chocolate cake and, when finally indulging in it after dinner, find it falling a tad short of all the mental marketing leading up to an actual forkful. Sure, it tastes good, but I keep aiming for that small target of ultimate satisfaction and ultimately miss the pleasure bull's-eye. It's like my (and your) brain tugs the target at the last second, making a direct hit elusive and, ultimately, short-lived.

Regarding mindfulness brain effects, researchers such as Sara Lazar and Britta Hölzel at Massachusetts General Hospital have documented the changes in the "default mode network" in the brain (comprised of structures like the medial prefrontal cortex and posterior cingulate cortex) in terms of deactivation of these areas with meditation practice.[22] What this translates into is less mind wandering and less self-directed thinking, both of which are arguably ingredients of the craving mind. When our brains are trained (and biologically changed) to pull free of the mental surging and meandering of images, sensations, and thoughts of that next drive-through window or alleyway fix, then we have a chance to sidestep the karmic clamp of unrestrained craving.

We simply need lots of practice learning to let go into the gap of desire. Let's get in some practice right now.

AN OPEN INVITATION—TRY THIS

Taking Desire by the (Open) Hand

Conjure the thoughts, mental pictures, and bodily felt sense of some object, goal, or result you are desiring. Close your eyes and rest your attention on this desire until you notice it growing, as if the energy of your attention were its fuel, and it strengthens as you feed it with your interest. With the desire having developed in your mind and body, do the following:

1. Silently tighten one of your hands into a fist. Draw your attention to the sensations there in your hand—the pulsing and tension. Imagine all the tension clenching or surging in your body gravitating to the sensations of your fist. Imagine that this tension—this clenching of your hand—*is* what happens for you as you continue to fixate on obtaining the object of your desire.

2. This entire practice may only last a minute or two, but notice how rapidly and readily you can direct your attention to this one area of your body. Breathe into the tension in your hand. You get to choose how you relate to this tension. Notice the discomfort there in this tension—the pulsing, vibrating, nail digging, and ache of the gripping of this desire. In your fist are all those compulsive thoughts, the seductive mental pictures, the delicious sensations of the desire being fulfilled. But notice whether this

gripping of delectable thoughts, images, and sensations is pleasurable. Is this becoming more or less comfortable the more you fuel the desire?

3. Now let go of the tension and open your hand, facing the palm up. Notice the sensations there and the differences and changes as they occur. Watch how you can let go of the thoughts, images, and sensations and just witness the truth of what both your body and thoughts are saying. No need to grab onto or grip anything—if you're willing, you can just let it all be as it is: bodily sensations, thoughts, and images passing through your mind.

4. And now with a final, deep breath, ask yourself: What matters most to me in this moment? What serves my life more, the gripping tension of craving or the openhanded acceptance of the pleasure and pain once they've arrived?

5. Are you willing to hold your desires lightly, as if with an open palm?

Opening via Acceptance: There's No Divorcing Desire

In a tale of Mulla Nasrudin, while sleeping, he sees himself counting gold coins being handed to him one at a time. When he counts out nine in his hand, the unseen benefactor ceases doling out any more.

"But I must have ten!" calls Nasrudin in his dream, waking himself. As many of us have tried after awakening from a desire-laden dream, Nasrudin closed his eyes in hopes of descending back into the same dream to claim his gold. He found the gold had disappeared altogether. "OK then," said Nasrudin. "Give me just those nine!"

As the previous section emphasized, desire is a fact of our evolutionary heritage—of our brain anatomy. The pain of craving (and ultimate dissatisfaction, if not devastation, when our various feeding frenzies are done) can lead us to want to get rid of desire (a desire in itself—the mind is relentless!). In a sense, we want to divorce desire, and yet it's the spouse who refuses to leave. Desire is a squatter in our mental and emotional home, and no matter how we cajole, ignore, plead, and cater, we can't end the relationship.

Nor should we. That's the state of confusion we're in when it comes to desire. It's a misunderstanding to say that the Buddha's teachings were trending in the direction of some "desireless" state as our existential end goal. As Mark Epstein has suggested, that is the fundamental confusion about Buddhism and desire in the West—that meditation is leading toward a flat-line life free of desire. No, desire will remain (because it's wired into us). It's the karma of craving that mindfulness can help us slip free of.

Meditation, if correctly wielded, is not about shoving desire to the side. It's about learning to live with and learn from desire. Again, as the brain science is increasingly clarifying, desire is part of our evolutionary emotional inheritance. Our karmic patterns rest not in the fact of desire in our brains, but instead in how we *relate* to desire when it arises. The Buddha would have us aim "higher" than what craving can deliver.

Speaking to the wanderer Māgandiya, the Buddha offered the following perspective on a new way for us to relate to desire:

> On a later occasion, having understood as they actually are the origin, the disappearance, the gratification, the danger, and the escape in the case of sensual pleasures, I abandoned craving for sensual pleasures, I removed fever for sensual pleasures, and I abide without thirst, with a mind inwardly at peace. I see other beings who are not free from lust for sensual pleasures being devoured by craving for sensual pleasures, burning with fever for sensual pleasures, indulging in sensual pleasures, and I do not envy them, nor do I delight therein. Why is that? Because there is, Māgandiya, a delight apart from sensual pleasures, apart from unwholesome states, which surpasses even divine bliss. Since I take delight in that, I do not envy what is inferior, nor do I delight therein.[23]

I think what the Buddha meant is that consistent mindfulness practice can lead us toward new mental "grooves" of desire—that we become de-identified from the objects of craving. We basically learn to not take our thoughts and sensations personally and instead aim for the peace of interpenetration—of all things connected; therefore, since the manifestations of desire are part of "us," we have no need to push them away, no need to grab at the objects of our desire. We need only not get lost in the mental fireworks and believe the show was on our behalf. By all means enjoy the show, and yet mindfully remain with the awareness that it is indeed just a show—one where the curtain eventually falls.

In New England where I live, there are multiple chain organic grocery stores to ease the consciences of the health conscious (particularly those in the more affluent suburbs of Boston who will not be daunted by the prices). The argument to be chewed on here is whether we're willing to live "raw"—not necessarily in a vegan manner (as great as that may be for others), but instead in the sense that we're willing to live with the raw experience of pain and pleasure. Are we willing to be aware of desire and aversion (which we'll delve into more in the next chapter) without getting ourselves attached? Detachment is therefore something wholesome, as opposed to disconnection, which is often confused with Buddhist conceptions of the end game of desire.

The writer Solala Towler tells the story of an ancient Chinese teacher traveling with a student. Villagers hosting the duo served the meat of a pig, a forbidden food.[24] The student was horrified to turn and see his teacher eating and, daresay, savoring the meat.

Upon noticing the reaction of his student, the teacher replied, "This was a gift from our hosts," he said. "It comes to us at great cost and hardship to them. Alas, who am I to reject their generosity?" He leveled his gaze at his student. "It's not what goes into your mouth that defiles, but what comes out."

Again, we don't directly make any contact with the objects of our desire. It's more how we relate to them that leads to the cycle of suffering. Research shows increasingly more clearly that learning to "surf the urges" of craving can be a very effective route for managing addictive behaviors. Alan Marlatt and Sarah Bowen randomly assigned 123 undergraduate smokers with an interest in stopping smoking to either an experimental group in which mindfulness skills were taught or to a no-instruction control group. There were no differences between groups in terms of experience of urges to smoke, yet those who were briefly trained in mindfulness were much less likely to subsequently smoke (even at a follow-up assessment a week later).[25] Similar data were found for college-age consumers of alcohol.[26]

Other experimental data suggest that mindful "acceptance" (versus control or suppression) of negative emotions led to less upset and lessened the heart rate for a group of study participants diagnosed with anxiety and mood disorders.[27] Pushing away emotions (such as those rising up with desire) may be a less helpful response than mindful opening to these experiences. Opening (mindful acceptance) in this sense is not condoning smoking, drinking, or any other craving-focused behavior. It's an allowing of mental experience to move through once it's here. The mind pushes back when we try to push its contents away.

The willingness to fully engage the moment at hand and to sidestep the pull of the mind toward what was or what might be (which is certainly what happens to us all in the midst of strong craving) is highlighted by the following classic Zen teaching story:[28]

While out for a walk one day, a Zen master is met by a ferocious tiger. He slowly backs away from the animal, only to find that he is trapped at the edge of a cliff. The tiger snarls with hunger and pursues the master. His only hope of escape is to dangle himself over the abyss by holding on to a vine that grows at its edge. As the master hangs from the cliff, two mice—one white and one black—begin to gnaw on the vine he is tethered to. If he climbs back up, the tiger will surely devour him; if he stays, then there is the certain death of a long fall onto the jagged rocks. The slender vine begins to give way, and death is imminent. Just then the precariously suspended master notices a lovely ripe wild strawberry growing along the cliff's edge. He plucks the succulent berry and pops it into his mouth. He is heard to say: "This lovely strawberry—how sweet it tastes."

This fable seems especially relevant in that it's an indication of desire in its most "pure" form—a flexible experiencing of "what is" without allowing the karma of craving to contort and bind us up. Surely, this was the last moment in the master's life, yet instead of thrashing against his fear, he allowed the fruit of the moment to ripen in him. Mind would have us miss, keep moving, and not stop to smell roses, let alone savor a strawberry. Open awareness will. So ask yourself, which approach to any given moment is preferable?

AN OPEN INVITATION—TRY THIS

SNAPPing Awake amid Wanting

Are you willing to sit and breathe through a wave of wanting without grabbing that next self-medicating object, experience, or action? Are you willing to "surf" the waves of wanting by SNAPPing awake?

1. **S**top as soon as you can after the pull of desire has set in.

2. **N**otice how desire is showing up in your body and mind. Take your attention and lightly touch each sensation and thought as if with a feather—no need to shove at them, just a gentle touch of awareness.

3. **A**llow the bodily sensations and thoughts to flow in and through you just as they are. You may not like them, but are you willing to just surf them? Not liking a wave doesn't change whether the water will move. It will move.

4. **P**enetrate down through the sensations and thoughts with one or more deep belly breaths. You're not forcing the feelings of desire away with the breath, but instead you're breathing space in and around them.

5. **P**rompt your awareness toward a recognition of self-kindness for the effort you've placed into riding the current of this desire.

Repeat these steps as much as you're willing until you experience changes in the manifestation of desire. Even if you end up reaching for satisfaction of the urge, are you able to feel the space, if only small and temporary, your willingness to snap awake created?

The argument I'm making here is for a reframing of desire. To put opening in its rightful, elevated place in terms of a life stance leading to well-being, it's important to be clear about what opening to desire is: not a caving into craving, nor is it a deadened disavowal of all pleasure in life. A very bright teen therapy patient of mine said it far better than I could: "The opposite of desire is not satisfaction like you might assume," she said, after a moment's reflection about her own experience with how the newness of things desired always tarnishes. "The opposite of desire is an appreciation of what you have." This is proof positive that wisdom is not necessarily correlated with age; it correlates much better with awareness at the point of open contact with felt experience.

What we're talking about is adopting a more nuanced understanding of what it means to "renounce" our craving for experiences and "stuff." Mark Epstein refers to it as "a turning away from an entire approach to life—one that could be called completion by consumption."[29] We can't find ourselves by jamming down food, injecting drugs, having sex, or even meditating for "enlightenment." Renunciation is really about freeing ourselves by freeing up everything else to be just as it is. Enjoy the strawberry when it's ripe, and set down your fork when the load it carries is weighted by a craving to have more than a mouthful.

Studies by the researchers Emily Balcetis and David Dunning[30] have provided an empirical glimpse of the distorting impact of desire on our perception. In a series of experiments, the desirability of objects (such as glasses of water and $100 bills) varied, and then research participants were asked to rate how physically close or distant the objects were. As you might expect, the more desirable the object, the closer in proximity it appears. People's beanbag tosses even came up consistently shorter when the target was linked to something of greater value! Horseshoe players and hand grenade throwers take note.

According to the Taoist fable as told by Lieh Tzu,[31] there was once a man who was absolutely obsessed with gold. One day, while walking through a crowded market, he spotted a bar of pure gold sitting on a businessman's wagon. The man grabbed up the gold in front of many eyewitnesses and ran off. The man was promptly caught and carted off to jail. When asked why he would be so foolish as to steal gold in plain sight of so many, the man (not insane or otherwise lacking in faculties) answered without hesitation. "I did not see other people. I only saw the gold."

The desiring eye deceives. Particularly when desire morphs into compulsive craving, the mind digs grooves for the want instead of accurate appraisal of (and satisfaction for) what is. If the moment at hand carries the pull of craving, having a practice at the ready for keeping you on the track of renunciation can be very helpful.

AN OPEN INVITATION—TRY THIS

Use a "Mangia" Mantra

Perhaps you have dined at an Italian restaurant and been taunted by obsessive thoughts to simply "mangia, mangia" (Eat! Eat!) another cannoli or to thrust your psyche toward the ever-elusive satisfaction of any sort of craving. Next time (or perhaps now, just for practice), try using a personalized "mantra" to remind yourself of a decision to simply move on from the flash fiction of craving when it arises in the mind and body. Again, you get to choose where you invest the energy of your awareness.

1. Anticipate a situation where desire is likely to flood you—one where you'd like to increase your capacity to avoid indulging.
2. Decide in advance what you want to do in this situation. State your decision in precise, simple, unambiguous, and positive terms: say what you'd do, not what you won't do. For example, if you don't want to drink when you walk into the office holiday party, declare this to your mind with the statement "I'm only drinking soda tonight."
3. Personalize the mantra to anchor your attention on the decision to move on. Choose one or just a few (briefer is better) words that resonate for you—ones that echo the clarity of your most deeply valued intentions. Perhaps it is to say to yourself that you are "bigger than this" or "let go and move forward." It can be as Nancy Reagan simple as just saying "no!" But don't let it be anything that feels flaccid and false—let it be the words you're willing to invest in with conviction.
4. Give yourself a script for responding if others are involved: "No thanks, I'll have a club soda with two limes" or "No dessert for me—I'm good" or "I'm flattered but I'm not looking for anything physical right now."

This is not about getting rigid with yourself and your desires though. It's about sidestepping the suffering of craving. Again, desire is not something you can (or should) "break up" with.

Most of us have used the word *willpower* and immediately felt a tinge of letdown—that it's not our strong suit. We have the best of intentions for hanging in with delaying some gratification of desire, yet time and time again, we find ourselves falling short of the grit and resolve of most former US Navy SEALs and infomercial fitness gurus (some of whom are both!). Here's where a heaping helping of self-compassion can be useful. The research is clear that willpower is a limited resource for all of us, and it's something that can be cultivated with wise attention.

In his book *Willpower*,[32] the social psychologist Roy Baumeister, of Florida State University, summarizes the body of studies indicating the physical and psychological aspects of our capacity to hang in against craving and delay or avoid gratification. Physically, willpower appears to be mediated by levels of glucose in our systems: as glucose levels drop, so does willpower, and it's restored by raising blood sugar. As Baumeister summarizes, any mental effort during a given day for controlling ourselves against impulses depletes our reserves. Research suggests that when we're depleted of willpower (and glucose), our negative emotions and cravings escalate.[33]

So, according to these studies, at any point you have a finite amount of willpower. When you look to "control yourself," you expend willpower fuel, and when the tank gets low, your resolve weakens. This is perhaps why it's wise that you only tackle one self-improvement project at a time (and therefore not try to address all five hindrance patterns for yourself simultaneously). It's also why (as I suggested in the previous "Open Invitation" exercise) it can be helpful to make a commitment (via a proactive renunciation "mantra") *before* entering a situation full of temptation.

So if Navy SEALs seem to have more willpower, perhaps it's less because they're "better" than you, and perhaps it's more that they have developed habits that maximize glucose levels, which structure their responses to craving. Data indicate that what we eat, how well we sleep, and even living in a clean, organized environment can help augment willpower.[34]

As we demonstrated with the chocolate cake meditation exercise above, meditation takes a different route with desire than do aggressive attempts at self-control. Alan Marlatt and others'[35] research cited above also underscores that mindfulness makes for a less bumpy road for managing craving. Though the data are yet to be collected ("hint, hint" to researchers), experiments looking at whether those attempting to sidestep a craving via mindfulness fare better than those trying to "will" or "grit" their way through will be telling. Perhaps meditation dips less into our glucose reserves due to the lessened mental and emotional effort required.

And just for your information, mindfulness is part of many military personnel's training these days as well. Military bases across the country have included the meditation training program "Warrior Mind" into their training regimens.[36] So yes, the answer for our struggles with desire is to join the Navy SEALs!

Opening to Desire via Clarity Regarding Time and Impermanence

The Shambhala Buddhist *acharya* (or senior teacher) Judy Lief wrote in *Tricycle* magazine,

> Change is continuous in spite of our efforts to resist it. We begin to realize that we do not have any way to stop it or to slow it down. The more we try, the more we suffer. But there is a way to let go, to break this cycle of suffering. We can slow down and have a closer look at our experience of it. When we have a look, we begin to realize what we have been doing, and the whole enterprise begins to feel more and more dubious. It becomes more difficult to hide from what in our hearts we know to be true—the fact of impermanence.[37]

Some years ago, I lived in an apartment complex bordering a large cemetery. I was in the habit of jogging at the time, and I would occasionally go for my runs there on the cemetery grounds. While some might find this morbid, I viewed it as a good, practical decision. The roads near my apartment were congested, noisy, and presented frequent hazards to the runner in terms of various wheeled or two- and four-legged forms. It was just a quieter, more peaceful run there in the cemetery. When you're running with the dead, there's no one to interrupt you.

As I spent more time in the cemetery, I noticed a curious shift in my thoughts. I started runs with the familiar habits of my desiring mind wherein I conjured new professional schemes, fantasized a victorious resolution to upcoming difficult conversations, and obsessed about my personal and professional endeavors. Over the course of the runs though, my mind got quieter, and I found thoughts wafting into the sights around me. In particular, thought centered on the headstones of these hundreds of beings whose bodies were interred there around me, degrading further as I attempted to extend my own time through cardiovascular exertion. Their collective silence seemed to speak far louder than my one-man show of panting death denial.

Desire wanted an answer right then and there as I pounded the pavement and snaked my way across the cemetery. There was an urgency to the asking. Yes, they're all dead, I thought—but surely they were somehow quite different from me. Surely things were "solid" in my life. I wasn't going anywhere—ever.

As I looked about the cemetery during those existential jaunts, it resonated there on the headstones that "I"—"Mitch"—was not "it." I was not the answer to that question. The headstones were like most of those I'd ever seen: stone, usually marble of some shape and color, etched with the dead person's surname largest, first name and dates of birth and death smaller and beneath. Occasionally—rarely, actually—something specific indicated the person's life doings, usually a quick reference to "devoted fathers," military service to our country, or "loving mothers."

The older stones were doing what all stones eventually do—weathering, fading, and losing the boldness of their etched declaration of the snuffed-out life they represented. The stones inevitably changed. The life stories of all these hundreds of souls had all experienced crescendo in life with pull of desire and the crush of craving, and each crumbled in death into these one or two words in stone, which again wore down and away.

As my heart pounded out the next of its beats—uncertain in final number and yet certainly numbered—wishes abounded that headstones of the future, perhaps even mine, would tell a more authentic tale. Perhaps they could do more than spout name, rank, and one's timeline death digits? Maybe there would be a longer resonance, daresay immortality, for stones heralding that "this one lived for love and courage in the face of family's betrayal" or that "here lies a life emboldened by fortune and yet humbled by the suffering of a child's tragic death." My mind could barely imagine a stone crying out "for the fear here crippling this among many of the family's generations."

Even now, there's a quiet voice inside knowing that these deeper, more authentic words will not echo forever. The voice has a gut sense that these words, though resonant and true like the rush of water over a falls or compression of snow gathering at a high peak, will not long attach to any one person, any life situation.

Here, now, late-afternoon New England fall light is draping down and around the edges of clouds, also slowly withering. I know because I've walked there many times, but I can't see now that the Charles River's waters flow through the gorge a short distance away where that light has fallen from the clouds. I know the water glistens as it passes up toward the edge and cascades down over the small falls. I know the water's *whoosh* trumpets the transformation of water molecules passing over the lip into the mist that inevitably rises up from the crashing there.

And yet right here, now, these are mere thoughts pressed atop the sensation of light, air, and keyboard key pressure on my fingertips by my brain's neural networks of electrical exchange. The light out the window has already died, and the water at the falls has already passed away downstream by the time I can mark it here at the blink of the cursor.

There's no answer to be found on headstone, name, or any attempt at written or verbal rendering. Aside from my experience that everything does change, there's not much more this writer or the runner with the dead or the dead themselves can say. The silence after the asking seems important, however. It is in the awareness of desire, the willingness to rest in its tugging, that we cleave through illusion. That alone is worthwhile.

Impermanence is a cornerstone of open living. Once we come to rest in the timelessness of reality, we let go of all the by-products of mind, such as craving, because we feel our way into the texture of moments as essentially and eternally dying (or living, if you'd prefer). Only in the mind of time do things or moments begin, stay, or end. In reality there's just this rolling now, and the open mind knows this is so—no need to grasp and clutch at the objects of our desire because opening is in accord with untying all that leaves the thought-ensnarled mind fit to be tied.

AN OPEN INVITATION—TRY THIS

Dying with Desire

Either in memory or, better yet, in the red-hot (or at least pinkish) moment of a desire manifesting, pause to try this practice. Here, we're practicing toward the felt experience of impermanence—the more rapid access to the wise resolve that comes from awareness amid change on the playing field of desire.

1. Sit comfortably and look around the space you're currently in. What is there around you that is "alive"? What life is there? Was it always so, and will it be? What is there with you that was alive at some point?

2. Begin gently noticing your breathing. Watch the subtle changes in the pace and depth of it as you continue to sit and witness it. Is "it"—are "you"—as solid as you've typically imagined?

3. What is changing in you physically, mentally, and emotionally? Continue tracking the flow of the breath, and consider the desire, perhaps the craving, you're currently facing.

4. Continue noticing the breath and ask yourself: Has this desire always been? Where is it exactly right now other than in your thoughts and bodily sensations? Will it and your thoughts and felt energies around it change? If you do nothing, will they still change? How solid are not only this current desire, but all your precious things—your objects and relationships?

5. Continue breathing and see if you're willing to gently notice the quiet shifting of all things. What is it that's able to witness all these changes? Is even this "witness" solid or shifting?

6. Breathe. Watch. Ask. Notice.

7. How does this exercise inform your relationship with desire?

Opening to Desire: Clarity Regarding Our "Nonselfness"

One of the best-loved stories in mythology is the Greek fable of Daedalus and his son Icarus. Daedalus was a famous architect, inventor, and master craftsman. He worked for King Minos of Crete and built the labyrinth in which the half-man, half-bull Minotaur was imprisoned. Incurring the king's ire, Daedalus and his son Icarus were jailed in the labyrinth. As Minos controlled the sea around Crete, Daedalus realized that the only way to escape was by air; therefore, he built wings for himself and Icarus, fashioned with feathers held together with wax. They successfully flew from Crete and appeared to be in the clear. Unfortunately (as these fables tend to go) Icarus grew exhilarated by the thrill of flying and, desiring more of this excitement and newfound power, soared too close to the sun god Helios; the wax holding together his wings melted from the heat, and he fell to his death in the sea below.

Daedalus's flight has stood as a symbol of safety, temperance, ingenuity, and resourcefulness. But flying was also for the gods; Icarus, a mere mortal, should not have veered heavenward with a sense of his new god-like power. He was therefore punished for his arrogance.

I wanted to be my college class valedictorian in order to prove how smart I was. I went to law school in order to get the keys to "the good life." I then went to graduate school to become a therapist so that I could out-shrink Sigmund Freud and cure everyone in three sessions or fewer. It took me years and considerable suffering (and eventual personal meditation practice) to learn in my own experience what Mark Epstein rendered so succinctly: "Being close to ourselves is frightening when we are always trying to be something more than we are."[38]

When entangled in craving, we string together the fiction of our self-stories; we weave a blanket that, though it might keep us warm at times, covers up the truth—we don't see things (including ourselves) as we really are. Learning to open around desire (or any of the hindrances) is learning to relate to self and the hot-fudge melting of desirous thought, images, and bodily sensations with compassion and flexibility. It's scary to see ourselves, warts and all. We want to see ourselves as glittering and coiffed as we see people on the covers of *Esquire* or *Mademoiselle* magazines or as the plaques of Nobel Prize or Oscar statues, instead of the desirous and short-of-the-mark realities we are. We need to learn to give up trying to arrange circumstances and control the world in order to claim our true selves in the objects we crave.

In yet another parable,[39] Mulla Nasrudin stumbled upon a valuable ring with no apparent evidence of its owner. According to the law in his region at the time, Nasrudin could not claim the ring as his own until he went to the village marketplace and declared the find three times in a loud voice. And so, at three in the morning, Nasrudin went to the center of the market and yelled that he'd found the ring. After the third call, bleary-eyed villagers finally ran into the market to see what the ruckus was about.

"What did you find, Nasrudin?"

"Oh, what a beautiful ring! It must have fallen lost from the finger of royalty."

"Who is the owner, Nasrudin?"

Nasrudin smiled as he looked at the ring. He knew the law and knew well the answer. "Well, of course, I'm the owner."

Do you see the fallacy on Nasrudin's part? How often have you (and I) fallen prey to the conditioning of "I/me/mine"—of "ownership" as a path to wholeness and peace? Will the ring bring lasting well-being to Nasrudin? Your experience already knows the answer.

The core conundrum here is *thinking* itself. You would not be inaccurate to view thinking (particularly the self-related I/me/mine thoughts) as the core addiction in our lives. Sure, heroin overdoses kill thousands every year, yet how much suffering and death (particularly suicide) comes from a compulsive fixation on the self as the separate center of the universe? Pain and desire are inevitable. Suffering and craving are optional. When we focus less on the objects of desire and instead go "upstream" to the source—our addiction to the conditioned (and erroneous) thinking of separation, isolation, there and then, always will and never was—we have a chance at freedom. We have a chance at breaking the chain of craving.

Consider this: your "self" is the greatest compulsive ritual of all. Let's learn to relate to this aspect of craving in a new way.

AN OPEN INVITATION—TRY THIS

Desire and How to Use Your Internal "GPS"

Though I've never owned one, I've had occasion to drive a BMW sedan. It's an experience that sucks you in; you can lose yourself in the desire to possess such a car. Instead of BMWs, I've owned many craving-conducive thoughts over the course of my life. That is, I've regarded thoughts about the "nouns" of my life (the people, places, things, experiences, and stuff I've desired) as being *part of me*.

But I've learned that I feel better and am much more effective when I simply "drive" a thought instead of being driven by it. When I see a desire-related thought for what it really is—my behavioral incentive system (to use William Irvine's term) nudging me toward something pleasurable, rather than *who I am*—I don't get sucked in. I *relate* to the desire; the thought doesn't bind me.

I call this going BMW: going **b**ehind the **m**ind and **w**atching. During, after, or even while anticipating an episode of craving, try the following to get behind your thinking and more flexibly manage your desire.

Recognize to yourself, "I'm *having* the thought that [insert rigid thought]." This will help you step back and watch the thought. Imagine that it's the voice coming from your GPS—it's telling you about a possible pleasurable experience up ahead. You don't have to go that direction though. You can simply note what the GPS of your car is saying and sit back and "watch" (the GPS and the road!). This is very different than arguing with a thought or trying to force an impulse away.

1. Think to yourself, "Thanks, mind, for coming up with [insert desiring thought]."
2. Take a breath and mentally place the thought on the screen (if it's a mental picture), or imagine it as the voice of your GPS. Vividly imagine the shape, color, size, movement, and sounds that describe the thought. For a single, full deep breath, just watch it there in the corner. No need to debate it. It's just there. It's information coming from your GPS—information, not your full reality.
3. And now ask yourself: What will happen if I keep staring at the screen of my GPS as I'm driving? How will my driving pan out? You'll, of course, wreck the (very nice) car! Are you willing to merely consult the GPS— the desire-filled thoughts and images? (As we've discussed, they may actually be useful.) Maybe there's a wake-up call there as to something that would not just bring your pleasure, but might enliven your life, allow you to enjoy the ride?
4. Yet, are you willing to not just listen to and watch your GPS and also take in the full truth of what's happening both inside your body and mind and also outside the car—in the world around you? Are you willing to take it all in and then keep driving in a direction that really matters to you? Maybe you'd go in the direction the GPS commands, and maybe not. You—the fully aware driver—get to decide.

The goal with all of these techniques is to shift from a rigid, absolute frame of thinking to foster instead a more flexible relationship with your desires. This requires a lot of practice. To be of real benefit, this practice must become a habit. Such a habit will give you a measure of psychological freedom, whether it be a mild chocolate impulse or an intense self-destructive urge.

Part of the path of opening to desire is to let go of the little, craving "I" inside and to focus more on being satisfied with what is and what we already have, perhaps even making compassionate, open philanthropy our default mode of networking. Such a selfless stance of giving can become increasingly an option (and a satisfying one at that), rather than one of taking and craving.

In a traditional Japanese fable,[40] a man dies and finds himself in a heavenly realm, seated at a huge banquet table. All his favorite dishes are sumptuously prepared and within reach. As he goes to dig in, he realizes someone has strapped his arms to stiff boards, and he can't bend the fork to his own mouth. He looks around the table and sees that everyone else is caught up in the same awful plight.

"Surely, this is not heaven!" he cries. "I lived a good life, and this is what I get?"

As if heard by a divine ear, the man suddenly finds himself in an even more glorious hall, with even more wonderful food and drink prepared for him. Once again, he goes to bring fork to plate, and once again, he finds his arms strapped to a board, completely disabling his ability to eat.

"So, I guess I've ended up in hell!" he calls. At that he happens to look about him at the others at his table. He is struck by seeing all the others taking advantage of their straight-strapped arms for raising forks to one another's mouths, everyone being fed by their neighbor.

Opening to desire is learning to mindfully delight in the sustenance and joy that life gives us in a given situation. It is the mindful lightness of being with desire that connects us to life, versus the hard, self-laden taking of craving.

As I sit attempting to conjure a specific memory of an absolutely "me-less" episode of giving, I'm here sitting up tall and alert on the couch and coming up short. My two-year-old son sleeps beside me after falling asleep on our way home from the grocery store. My mind reaches back—recent, distant, close, and far away—for a clear example of selfless giving. I sit with fingers hovering, nothing coming for some time.

And there it comes—a quick pulse of remembrance of a moment with him this morning. The fact that it's Sunday played a role in the gift exchange in that I was not pressed for time—I had no agenda at hand. I sat with him in the rocker in his bedroom and paused for a few moments longer than my mind had told me was the plan. Thinking was poking at me to move things along—things to write, agendas to fulfill. And yet I lingered and turned him around to face me on my lap. I ended up tossing him into the air a bit in hopes of sparking the peals of laughter that light me up, sparking paternal things eons deep in my brain.

But he didn't laugh, instead just smiling a bit. Perhaps it was lingering fatigue from a choppy night's sleep. Maybe his breakfast was jostling distractingly in his gut. Who knows, and as I write, it seems I may never know exactly when gifts given are not fully received in the way I'd like. I can barely control the awareness leading to giving, let alone what happens when the gift departs for the other person's shore. None of us can really give an experience to someone.

I'm remembering a clinical supervisor of mine from many years ago: a wise, gentle older man with tufts of hair sprouting from ears that were always intent on compassionate listening. He waited one day in a supervision meeting as I ranted about my work with my clients, how things were falling short of the mark of my lofty, straight-A conditioned expectations. I was simply not knocking every ball out of the park, and I was finding the work less than exhilarating. I was not the good Dr. Freud I'd envisioned.

My supervisor listened and waited for me to take a requisite breath during my monologue, and then he leaned forward into the space between us—a space that, by the way, my mind then would have considered to be separating us, but now, in this moment as my now awake son watches from his car seat as his dad taps away at the keyboard, I realize was joining us. He leaned in and held a fist out, clenching it. "Mitch," he said quietly, "you seem so much like this as you talk." He clenched his fist such that it shook slightly. He then let it go slack. "I'm wondering if it could ever be more like this for you."

What my supervisor may have known—what my awareness seems to know just now—is that the best way of managing ourselves (particularly with regard to desire, be it for chocolate or clinical glory) is lightly and with openness. There's a giving over to others, the situation, and our true, felt selves without a return address, without any "taking" involved. My supervisor could not control whether I resonated to his simple gesture with his hand in the air joining us in his office that day. He had no way of controlling my response, particularly my internal flickering of thought and emotion. He just offered what was authentic and true from his engagement with what I was expressing.

I've sat with my own supervisees, often channeling my old supervisor, nudging them with my own version of an open palm in the face of the vast uncontrollable landscape of their desire for clients' "progress." Therapists are trained to view ourselves as "change agents," and it seems I've spent years unlearning this. I don't control change in others—I'm no change agent. I create a context in which clients, and my supervisees, must take from it what they will. The same is true for us as meditators, parents, friends, and workers: we do our best, and we live the most when we let go of any expectations of controlling the outcomes and marshalling satisfaction for ourselves.

In that moment in supervision, my answer sat there on the edge of my supervisor's palm. The message took hold in me long after he would have any access to knowing whether it would. It was here this morning when I paused to offer a moment of playing with my son. His giggle would have been nice, but as I tap out these words, I'm aware the gift is always there. I didn't need his laughter to confirm it. In fact, I might have been more likely to miss it if he had. I would have again convinced myself of my gift-giver status. I would have puffed myself up so large I would have missed what was there to see in Theo, in the space joining us. I can't give what's there already. None of us can.

And therein lies a key to managing desire—forsaking "self"-control over outcomes, appreciating the pleasure that comes, abiding the pain that does as well. The mind likes to make current experience into currency for future exchanges as in the Chinese parable[41] of the wise carpenter and his apprentice who came upon a large oak tree along the road. It was sprawling with many limbs and a large amount of potential lumber.

"Let's cut it down," said the apprentice. "Surely there is great value in this tree."

Silently, the carpenter moved forward down the road.

"Why are you leaving this tree behind, master?" asked the apprentice.

"This tree is useless," he said. "Its branches are hard. They are heavy. They are gnarled and twisted. The effort required is beyond any value."

They moved away, and the tree stood as it had for hundreds of years.

The value of the tree was in its beauty by the road, which the carpenter saw—not in the future-leaning mind's eye of the apprentice. We have to be willing to consult our mental "GPS" of thinking and self-reference and yet not allow these to get in the way of opening to the truth of a resonant response to the present moment. Craving leads to miscalculation. Desire (lightly held) can lead to wise, vibrant action.

Compass Check: Loving (Lightly) and Leaving

In this chapter, we've taken a deep dive into how desire emerges for each of us and tugs us away from open awareness. For folks like me (and perhaps you), desire quickly devolves from a natural brain-based nudge in the direction of pleasurable experience (which again helped us eat, make love, and nudge our genes deeper in the pool) into the compulsive craving that binds us into karmic patterns of suffering. We close down into the endless loop craving creates in our lives.

We've explored how desire is a natural component of our evolutionary heritage and the wiring of our brains. Mindfulness and positive-psychology practices offer supports to bring us into, and perhaps over, the gaps desire creates within us.

Mark Epstein writes[42] that we make headway by learning to shift from "object" to "subject" regarding desire. Whether it be a chicken parmesan sandwich (my favorite) or a long-anticipated night out with my wife, it's important to relate to these less as "things" with inherent properties and capacities to satisfy and more as ongoing, changing processes. We crave (and suffer) when we expect objects to "do" certain things for us. Instead, when we allow them to be the flowing flux that they are, we can relate to them and see the novelty and aliveness that's there in the nuances. As Epstein writes, it's why traditional Japanese gardens are designed so that some objects are hidden from view at particular vantage points: a dynamism is created, a flow and a mystery that allows for the healthy energy of desire, versus that full-on, Times Square assault of craving.

Though I've known my wife for many years and at times can convince myself I know her from every angle, this is of course false and a GPS-like illusion of mind. The truth (and the source of sparking desire in our relationship) is allowing her to be a changing, evolving wave of potential, versus the "Lisa" I believe I have sized up. What might happen to society's divorce rate if we married "waves," versus the "wives" we believe we know inside and out? Epstein writes: "The flavor of separation is what keeps relationships vital . . . a taste that came from both within and without . . . [the] possibility of working creatively, rather than addictively, with desire."[43] When we shift from object to subject, we allow the other's freedom and thereby have a chance at claiming our own.

This chapter has explored the possibilities emerging from learning to play within the gap between desire and satisfaction. We, particularly in the West, tend to rush through this gap as if it were an abyss to be avoided at all costs. In fact, it is a portal, an opening, that we would all be fortunate to learn to fall into.

Open Invitation: Additional Contemplations for Personal Practice

Below are further inquiries for learning from and working with desire. Consider each, and don't think your way to answers. Instead, notice and feel what arises in your experience, and then just wait. It's in the waiting and watching that learning happens.

ACCEPTANCE OF THE EXPERIENCES OF DESIRE

- Instead of beating yourself up for a binge, try breathing in the knowledge that we all have felt the pull of craving, and breathe out a kind wish that we all feel some peace from its pangs.
- Consider a recent experience of craving. Did you notice a gap between your anticipatory wanting and the satisfaction you actually received? Between the desire and the pleasure? What does your experience say as to any difference between desire and the felt pleasures of your life? Where do you end up investing more energy: the buildup of desire or the actual present-moment pleasures?

WORKING WITH TIME/IMPERMANENCE

- The American poet Robert Frost reminded us: "leaf subsides to leaf . . . So Eden sank to grief . . . So dawn goes down to day . . .

Nothing gold can stay." What aspects of your life are you hoping will hang around forever? Though it's natural to want to hold on to our loved ones, hard-won attainments, and the fruits of our labors, what happens in our body-minds when we regard them all as so much gold? Ultimately, what happens to even purest gold? Does resting in the reality of impermanence diminish or enhance our relationship with the things we cherish?

- When you meditate, do you expect to attain something "better" by having done so? That "you" at some point will receive a reward of some sort? Is there value in meditating even if you give up meditating beyond just this moment? What if meditating right now never amounted to anything?

CLARIFYING THE TRUE NATURE OF SELF

- Consider all the events of the current day thus far. What have you given? Notice the mind's reaction: "Not much," it might say. Perhaps "not enough." Maybe "too much, and what do I have to show for it?" Notice and allow whatever the mind tosses at you regarding your philanthropy (or perceived lack thereof) to others and the world. Notice how much these thoughts rely on "I/me/mine" and a sense of "you" being separate from the "stuff" you're giving (or not).

- Consider the breath at this moment—the give and take of oxygen and carbon dioxide, continuing the circulation of the world's ingredients, its nutrients. Consider the gift of awareness in this moment. How might that ripple out and "give" to many beings the rest of today? Now that we've established your inevitable "benefactor" status, what *else* have you given? Is the giving and receiving more or less apparent when the "I" is not doing the looking?

- And if you're feeling exceedingly (and excessively) proud of your giving today—if you're feeling spent as though you've "given at the office" (and perhaps at home as well), pause and ask: Has all your giving been without expectation of gain for yourself? Were there any strings attached? Exhale your breath fully. And then pause. Can you give out the breath without again taking? Notice how you inevitably receive when you give. Are you willing to give with awareness, with felt knowledge that what you need will come, and

that this moment—all that you ever actually have—is enough for
your happiness?

A few weeks ago, I stood in a high school auditorium and spoke to a
senior class about the importance of learning to relate honestly to one's
cravings, especially when it comes to the pull of high-stakes addiction.
I asked them to practice the chocolate cake meditation from earlier
in this book in order to experience the power of a mindful, versus a
controlling, stance toward the impulses of intense desire—to learn to
more flexibly relate to desire with compassion and gentle watchfulness
instead of trying to wrench the wanting out of their minds with
substances or behavior.

I looked out at the sea of young faces and knew some were currently
fighting the inner contortions of craving even as I spoke. I knew many
would likely use alcohol, drugs, sex, and even the glow of their cell
phones to sidestep the discomfort that is so rampant in today's teen
lives.

And then I came into my hotel room tonight after a long day of
looking out at another sea of faces, this time a room full of licensed
clinicians, looking to learn about methods of mindful communication and intervention with their patients. Alone in my room, and completely "off the grid" from observing eyes, I felt the old, familiar pull
of wanting. "Head on down to the hotel bar," it said. "You deserve a
glass (or more) of wine." Even though I was well aware of a very early
start and another long day of speaking to come, I could taste the delicate
pinch of a pinot noir as it first hit my palate. The familiar friend of
wanting would soon surge toward it its truculent cousin craving. I had
hard-earned wisdom enough to stop, to notice the swirling mental wine
tasting and the desirous thoughts, to allow them to move and flail about
unaided by any emotional investment on my part. I penetrated them
with the depth of my slow breathing and watched as the wanting flopped
like a fish out of water, violent at first and then more still across the
seconds.

I prompted my hand into my pocket and retrieved a small brass
Buddha statue I often carry—particularly when I'm off giving a talk.
Running my fingers over it, I knew I'd connected with the wisdom that

knows the difference between desire and outright craving. For once, I practiced what I preach.

Having opened our heart-minds to the lessons of desire, we now turn toward the heat of our hostility: the anger and aversion that fires us up and burns down our mental homes if we're not—you guessed it—mindful.

CLOSING INQUIRY

Instead of trying to force cravings away, are you willing to increasingly apply awareness of them? Are you willing to gently breathe into the energy of desire and remember that it's part of being human?

4   The Boiling Point

Opening Up to Turn Down the Dial on Hostility

OPENING INQUIRY

Fifty thousand years ago, the human species relied on reactive hostility to eke out survival in a harsh landscape. Though this is our inheritance, does the current state of human affairs require such easily sparked angry flames to light our way?

Before leaving to fight as an infantry soldier in France during World War I, my great-uncle fell in love with a woman named Sarah. The details are scant, and I'm sure the frequent retellings over the decades have obscured things, but what I've gleaned is the stuff of a page-turning novel.

I've many times stared at the image of my uncle standing next to Sarah, in the only surviving picture, faded and browned by time. He's clearly angled toward her, but in no way touching—maintaining a respectful distance. There's anticipation in his slight smile as he looks at her. She's wearing a white dress, appropriate to the modesty of the time. Sarah was a schoolteacher, and her posture suggested propriety; the soft beauty of her face indicated the warmth she likely brought to her students, and likely to my uncle as well.

Off Earl went to the war with reported promises of marriage upon his return. My uncle was not in France long before entering combat and sustaining a debilitating wound: shrapnel struck him in the face, blinding him almost completely. After arriving home from Europe and recuperating in an army hospital, he returned to the small town in Ohio where he, my family, and Sarah lived.

The short version of the story is that Earl and Sarah never reunited, never married. What I learned was how much my great-grandfather, Earl's father, dominated him and the entire family with his anger and consuming self-interest. According to my grandmother, after my great-grandfather realized his son would receive a full disability pension from the government for life, he set about a crusade of psychological warfare with Earl, convincing him over time that "no woman would want a cripple." He said, "Sarah can do much better than a worthless waste of man like you." Earl—by all reports a sensitive, quiet, caring wordsmith of a man—succumbed over time and never followed up on the prospect of marriage with Sarah. In fact, he really never followed up with Sarah much at all.

My great-grandfather secured his own finances by way of my uncle's disability pension. My uncle secured a life of lonely self-denial out of father-stoked fear and shame. Though Earl and Sarah evidently exchanged a few letters and many glances across the years following the war, both remained single the rest of their lives.

Across the articles, blogs, and books I've written thus far, I've held this story until the right time. For me, this story is a personal example of ill will and its opposite—an abiding, open, patient presence with difficult circumstances, both outside and in.

Despite her clear love and longing for my uncle, and despite the hardship and pain she surely suffered, she apparently never ceased her wait for him. When love is held in limbo, time's passing can leave most of us begging for release. Most of us cave in to some sort of shoving away or grabbing in an attempt to fend off the pain of unrequited love. It doesn't seem as though Sarah did so.

Though it's now a story as faded as that solitary photograph, the echo of Sarah's mindful example comes through clearly. She abided the pain of unrealized love and the undoubted anger she experienced at my uncle and my great-grandfather and continued about her life as a schoolteacher, friend, and family member. My grandmother, who knew her well, heard nothing of bitterness, resignation, or debilitation in Sarah's life, only a gentle hanging in—riding out the difficulty of a small town's microscope as she held on calmly to a love that would never materialize.

How is it that people cultivate such openness to experience without sinking into ever-increasing cycles of resentment and anger? Is this abiding something a lucky few are born with, or is it a skill to be honed? What is the juncture of what modern science and centuries of contemplative tradition have to say about the role and value of managing ill will and anger in our lives?

Wearing Thin: The Weakened State of Western Abiding

I grew up similar to many kids in the modern Western world. There were many admonitions from parents, grandparents, teachers, and so forth to not be "negative" toward others, to not be nasty, and to never lash out in anger. I'm personally not keen on definitions that fail the "dead man's test"[1]—"not becoming angry or annoyed" is *not* a behavior you can do. A dead man could "not be annoyed," but we can't—you can't see someone doing "not annoyed." Exactly what is this aspect of mindful opening? Even in modern psychology, our conceptions of opening around anger, ill will, and resentment can leave us needing footnotes in order to have a chance to walk in that direction.

When it comes to this hindrance, it helps to create some specificity. Anger, ill will, and resentment cover a lot of ground. For the sake of convenience and clarity, I'll refer to them all as "hostility." The Buddha's language for this hindrance was *vyapada*, which translates as "a desire to strike out at something."[2] That's the essence of this obstacle we all experience. Something or someone is blocking our way forward or causing us pain, and we want to lash out. And in this shoving, it's less that we're wanting the circumstances to change (though we might say we are), and it's really that we don't want to feel the sting of aversion, of pain. That's where the importance of opening comes in—learning to step into the experience of pain or discomfort, regardless of whether we take action to impact the circumstances we find ourselves in.

In my clinical work with children and teens with emotional and behavioral challenges, I frequently refer to how these kids need more "frustration tolerance," and I've many times used interventions aimed at developing their "anger control skills" and their capacities for "delaying gratification." It's important to pause and simply note how our Western minds have (to some degree) devalued opening and patient abiding around the experience of hostility. There's this sense of "grit" (also a term used in psychology these days)—of gritting one's teeth and bearing the burdens of unfavorable situations. Dead guys are apparently aces at it. But how does one "do" grit? How do you do opening around hostility?

In order to really understand opening to this obstacle, not to speak of practicing it, we need more nuance, more specifics. Though there might be other approaches of equal merit, we Westerners can benefit greatly from what Buddhist traditions offer in terms of the specific nature of mindfulness and acceptance, as well as concrete practices for cultivating and elevating opening around hostility as a core virtue of the heart with the capacity for creating a wellspring of well-being.

A Very Old, New Frame for Relating to Hostility

The story of the young, then midthirties Siddhartha Gautama's enlightenment under the sacred fig (or Bodhi) tree at Bodhgaya in what is today India is familiar to millions.[3] Beyond a tale of spiritual coming of age, the Buddha's awakening is itself a parable of opening in the face of provocation to hostility.

After having renounced the ease and pleasures of his princely birth, and after years of seeking to penetrate the core of human suffering by heaping it upon himself as a wandering ascetic, Buddha is said to have accepted some food from a young girl and taken up his seat under the Bodhi tree. The traditional accounts vary widely as to how long the Buddha sat in unwavering meditation under these branches (from one to forty-five nights), but all indicate that Mara, the mythic demon, sent all manner of temptation and attacks at him. Mara was intent on disrupting the Buddha's awakening into the greatest truth of reality, wanting to horde truth for himself. According to the tale, when the demons all vouched for Mara's rightful place on the throne of enlightenment, Mara taunted the still-meditating Gautama.

"They all speak for me," cried Mara. "Who will speak for you?"

And despite the long hours of enduring temptation and taunting, the former prince who'd lived a life of leisure did not flinch. He did more than "remain calm" or "not become annoyed." He truly opened to what most would find highly aversive. Instead of reacting or withdrawing, he slowly reached down with a finger and gently touched the earth, claiming it as his witness. And according to Buddhist scriptures, it was that moment when he became the Buddha.

This tale of forbearance despite provocation is not unique to Buddhism. Jesus was beset by Satan for forty days and nights in a desert wilderness. Adam caved to temptation and took a bite from the apple of the Tree of Knowledge. Religious traditions clearly underscore the crucial role of abiding. What contemplative tradition offers in particular is a series of concrete principles of what opening to the experience of hostility is and how one actually practices it. The Buddha did not consider such opening a "weakness." In fact, he considered it central and taught of its value often.

In one of the classic Jataka tales, stories of the Buddha's past lives (in which he, across life spans, "perfected" virtues), the Buddha tells of a stubborn, impatient monk in his group.[4] In this former life, the monk was a powerful spiritual figure (a Brahmin) and had the ability to perform a magical incantation that, when the planets were properly aligned, would cause a rain of precious gems from the sky.

As he and a student were traveling through a forest, bandits encircled them and took the Brahmin hostage, telling the student to go fetch a ransom from the village. Before leaving his master, the student told him that the planets were aligning that very night, but not to use his incantation—that ill would befall him and others if he did so. With his student gone and still held hostage, the Brahmin was not willing to endure his imprisonment any longer. In essence, he got annoyed. He performed his magic incantation, and the sky rained with gems. The bandits were amazed and offered to have the Brahmin leave the forest with them of his own free will.

As the Brahmin and the bandits left the forest the next day, they were suddenly surrounded by an even larger group of thieves who demanded payment. "I'm happy to perform my incantation for you and bring you precious gems from the sky," the Brahmin offered. "But we will need to wait an entire year until the planets are aligned, and then I will happily do so." Enraged, the thieves killed the Brahmin on the spot. They then began fighting among each other for the jewels, attacking one another until all were dead. The Brahmin's student returned with the original ransom amount to find the misery his master had brought upon so many with his impulsivity.

The Buddha's former lives (and that of this impatient monk) can be viewed with a modern lens as colorful pointers in the direction of truth, of opening to painful experience, in *this* lifetime. Here, the story underscores that, despite incredible wealth-inducing talents, lack of skill in opening to hostile inner experience can be costly. Such opening is central, even under today's non-gem-raining skies.

So the argument I'm making here is for a reframing of opening to the irritants and agitators the bring us to the boiling point—that prompt us to close up and strike out—holding it in a higher regard than everything our instant society calls for. To put opening in its rightful, elevated place in terms of a life stance leading to well-being, we must consider what it's *not*.

To summarize, opening to hostility is not

- Becoming passive and making one a pushover who will fail to act
- Suppressing and shoving down reactions and merely "grinning and bearing it"
- Something only people like the Dalai Lama are born (or reborn according to your beliefs) to exhibit
- Resignation in the sense of throwing up one's hands and sighing, "Oh well, I guess I'm going to have to deal with this"

This first misconception regarding passivity is perhaps a large part of our society's undervaluing of opening. In a time of trumping rivals and compulsively jonesing to keep up with our neighbors, to open and abide and not shove or lash out suggests coming in second or perhaps dead last. Opening is not flashy or overt—it does not put a person on display. There's little in terms of a Tony Robbins–styled inner "power" to it. In a word, opening amid anger and angst can seem weak.

In our society, patient abiding is a "nice" quality of teachers and talk therapists like your humble author. It's not the hard-driving, bull's-eye hitting, get-'er-done aspect we so admire in the West. It's more what leads people to say that it "takes a special person" to do the clinical work I do (which always seems a backhanded, defensive, hard-to-know-what-to-make-of-it sort of compliment). We give peacefulness and patience to saints, but the gold and the glory only goes to those scoring touchdowns.

Even in our own Western mythology, we somehow, however, know differently. Consider the classic Aesop's fable of the turtle and the hare wherein the patient, slow-moving tortoise wins the long footrace with the rabbit. My favorite Western version, by the way, is the Bugs Bunny cartoon rendition where, despite his wit and speed, Bugs's frenzied pace does not win out against the slower, persistent movement of the turtle. The turtle's fluidity and tolerance win. We know this and yet do not trumpet it. We know openness is crucial, yet it's not the flashiest of personal qualities. We see its potential, but we let others have it in our grasping for prosperity. We fear opening may close the door on winning.

And this leads to the second misconception. Perhaps another piece of our neglect of opening to hostility is that it feels at odds with our grasping at the good life. It's easy to misconstrue it as entailing a denial of our every desire and a lack of gumption for chasing American (or insert your nation here) dreams. Opening equals biting our sugar-seeking tongues during dinner and suppressing our true passion for the dessert to come. It's no wonder people devalue opening in the face of hostile experiences when it seems to suggest you have to crush your desires into oblivion and let others have their way. What sort of success is there in that? A Nike ad tells us that "yesterday you said tomorrow." We live in a world bombarding us with "do it" messages, and, though there's clearly value to initiative, there's risk in our prevailing attitude absent of waiting and wanting more than the highest platform to stand on.

Related to the sense of suppressive tongue biting is thinking of opening around hostility as imbued with a sense of self-defeat. It's the inner quality of "Oh well, I might as well put up with this." What sort of virtue would that have been for the scientists and astronauts struggling to get the Saturn V rockets from the earth to the moon in the 1960s when the task seemed impossible? Or for Martin Luther King Jr. to have stood on the steps of the Lincoln Memorial and instead of telling the world about his bold dream, to have instead said, "Hey, let's just make do with how society treats the black person." Of course we're going to demote opening to our not-nice thoughts and feelings when it's viewed as such a down-and-outer.

And now let's consider a final misconception of opening to hostility. When talking of paragons of open abiding, we think of people like Mother Teresa or the Dalai Lama. Many people jump to the conclusion that these saintly examples were born with a bottomless reservoir of acceptance. But before you assume folks like the Dalai Lama inherited a birthright of abiding, let's consider some specifics of the life of His Holiness. Yes, many Tibetans and Tibetan Buddhists regard the Dalai Lama, Tenzin Gyatso, as the latest incarnation of a being who has returned over thirteen life spans to lead the country and religion of the Tibetan people.

The Dalai Lama's life experience has been a long series of *practices* in cultivating tolerance, beginning in his early childhood. With tools deriving from his intensive daily meditation practice, this young boy learned to abide the pain of separation from his family. He was faced with periods of loneliness during his childhood and monastic training at the palace in Dharamsala. In his autobiography, *Freedom in Exile*, His Holiness writes,

> The evenings during my retreats were even worse than the days, as it was at this time that young boys of my own age would drive their cows back home to the village of Shol at the base of the Potala. I well remember sitting quietly saying mantras during the stillness of the fading light and hearing their songs as they returned from the pastures nearby. On a few occasions, I wished that I could change place with them.[5]

And he undoubtedly experienced pain and hostility following the Chinese invasion and decades of occupation of his Tibetan homeland—

the displacement and attempts at cultural decimation of his people. The Dalai Lama is typically very measured in his comments about the Chinese occupation of Tibet. During an interview, His Holiness was asked: "Do you ever become angry?" This was his reply:

> Sometimes, but generally as times goes by, the irritable side of my nature has subsided and changed. These days it is difficult to arouse my anger. If the anger were constantly there, then my anger towards the Chinese would also be there. But now that the anger has lessened in me, there is less anger to show to the Chinese. The main cause of one's suffering is based on one's karma, so we cannot blame everything on the Chinese. That would not be right.[6]

You can feel free to disregard any notion of this man having been born anger-free. His life experience—*this* life's experience—has been a nonstop series of episodes for him to practice the opening he preaches.

Considering all of these misconceptions, is it any surprise that we water down the value of opening, of acceptance and presence with hostile feelings? This is why we can benefit from some reframing, from inserting these obstacles in a place of prominence. This is why the cultivation of a daily habit of opening is crucial.

With practice, our lives shift from the mindless repetition of habit to the mindful opportunity for creative impact—that's what opening entails. The five hindrances become daily compass points for getting ourselves on track toward freshness and possibility, versus the stale odor of very old patterns.

Opening by Exploring the Pain of Hostility

To address inevitable and unavoidable feelings of hostility, key skills help build a person's capacity for acceptance of the turmoil of angry experience. This is a core aspect of opening and is reflected by how willing and able we are to hold these experiences without shoving them away (and creating more suffering). This is not a perspective of giving up or passive resignation to negativity in others or the situations you find yourself in; instead it has a sense of "of course" to it. A person skillfully regarding adverse experience with acceptance sees them as part of what is and knows that fighting against it with mental teeth gnashing only makes things worse and makes effective action less likely.

The meditation teacher and author Ajahn Brahm writes in his book *The Art of Disappearing*,

> Suffering is the nature of the world, the nature of the body, the nature of the mind. Things don't always go away the way you want them to . . . So don't force the issue and say, "This isn't right; it shouldn't be this way; I'm doing something wrong." . . . Detachment comes from the wisdom of recognizing the nature of suffering in life: you can't do much about it, so you leave it alone.[7]

An often referenced acceptance metaphor is about what happens if you suddenly find yourself in a pit of quicksand. I've thankfully never traipsed into any myself, but the common lore is that you should do the opposite of your reflex—instead of panicking, flailing, and struggling (which can have the effect of sending you deeper), it is much safer and more effective to lie back into the quicksand. The idea is to maximize your surface area and make yourself as buoyant as possible.

But here's the important question: does this "lying back" and "resting" in acceptance of the quicksand of your experience of pain and suffering actually fix the situation in and of itself? No, it doesn't. You're still in the quicksand. But here's the thing: how much more likely are you to detect and respond to a possible solution to get yourself out of that muck if you're resting and aware, versus flailing and chaotically trying to get control? You can't know for certain when a solution may present itself, but when it does, will acceptance be more or less likely to help you engage it?

AN OPEN INVITATION—TRY THIS

Making Pets of Your Peeves

In his text *A Guide to the Bodhisattva's Way of Life*, the eighth-century author Shantideva nudges readers to consider a list of "what if" scenarios that will challenge their mindful abiding. A modern take on this would be to list one's pet peeves. What are yours? Don't wait for life to trigger you.

Think for a moment about what annoys you most about other people. What are your biggest pet peeves regarding others' behavior? What are the things others do that really grate on you?

Imagine being trapped in a situation where you simply could not escape these obnoxious behaviors—you're literally up against them for an indefinite amount of time. How much are you up for this? Let's say you did have the option to slide out of these situations. How willing would you be to stay anyway, to press yourself into this annoying state of affairs?

Create an exhaustive list in your journal of all the things that trigger irritation and ill will in you—the things that irritate, vex, and lead you to reactive striking out. Take them and rank them from least to most upsetting. Now, are you willing to start applying one or more of the other skills in this section when these arise? Again, start with lower-ranked situations and work your way up. You want to build opening like a muscle. The idea is to show up to the harder-edge moments as a habit, a discipline, in your daily behavior.

The Dalai Lama distinguishes acceptance from passive resignation:[8]

> Nor, when I speak of acceptance, do I mean that we should not do everything in our power to solve our problems whenever they can be solved. But in the case of present suffering—that which we are already undergoing—acceptance can help ensure that the experience is not compounded by the additional burden of mental and emotional suffering.

His Holiness describes the real-life example of one of his monks, who was imprisoned by Chinese forces and reportedly tortured over a period of years. This was a situation the monk could not control, could not readily solve. And yet, through the practice of what in Tibetan is called *so-pa* (translates most closely as "patience"), through acceptance of this painful experience, this monk was observed to retain his calm, peaceful demeanor in the years following his release. By all means, when you're suffering and can do something to address the issue, do so. Acceptance is there for you when you can't. It's the aspect of what the Eastern traditions offer as a doable path.

AN OPEN INVITATION—TRY THIS

SNAPPing Your Fingers at Anger

Learning to rest in negative experiences that spark hostility and not adding to it with the mind's angst and agendas can be really helpful. True acceptance is an active, empowered choice to lie back and let the pain of hostility move through you. Rekindling our faithful acronym from chapter 2, ask yourself whether there were any opportunities for "SNAPPing awake" during a frustrating/angry episode today? Might there be any likely situations for doing so later today? Tomorrow?

Do the following when entering a situation that has sparked anger in the past:

1. **S**top, snap your fingers, and pause in what you're doing (the finger snapping is a cue for you to break your normal habit of reactivity).
2. **N**otice sensations in the body and the mind's reactive thoughts. How is the hostility manifesting in your chest, shoulders, arms, hands, and face? Tune into the flow of your thinking and track it for a moment. Notice the blame game, the focus on others' intentions there in your thoughts.
3. **A**llow the thoughts and bodily sensations all to be just as they are. Don't flinch away. Don't try to push them down. Simply choose to watch them as if watching Joe Pesci's gangster character in *Goodfellas* go on a rant.
4. **P**enetrate them all with slow, deep breathing. Take as many of these breaths as you feel you need.
5. **P**rompt yourself toward compassion for yourself and others (including those whose actions have triggered your hostility).

This mindful resting can also be done formally during meditation practice. Notice the various irritants—the itches, minor aches, and twitches popping up during sitting practice. If it's major, by all means don't torture yourself—adjust your posture. If it's not, are you willing to just notice the patient benefits coming from resting in moments of sitting with mind and body? What happens to your irritation when you do?

And to underscore the importance of an accepting, open stance in the face of current and aversive/hostile feelings once they've arrived on the scene, recent science is making it clear it's better to go this way. In addition to the greater emotional distress that comes with control or suppression reactions, people with higher levels of "experiential avoidance" (looking to move away from or control tough feelings or sensations) are much more likely to have behavioral health problems.[9] Also, another study asked experienced meditators and control participants to complete a Stroop task (in which people have to detect matches and mismatches in words and the color of their fonts, like "BLACK" or "RED"), which is a measure of mental control skills (or "executive function" skills).[10] The meditators (versus the controls) showed significantly greater executive function, or mental control, skills, and analyses suggested participants' increased emotional acceptance made the difference. Again, we're more able to effectively "see" what's happening around us without being as clouded by difficult emotions with practice of this acceptance component of opening.

When circumstances are what they are (which, by the way, they always are!), change is not possible now, and pain is here; our only real choice is whether we flick the switch of our awareness on or off. Acceptance means we're mindfully on. We're available for our life in that moment. There's a willing courage—a true strength in this. You will act when the situation allows, but for now, you will lie back and take a rest in what is.

If you need another example, how about consulting what any educated reader already knows of history's account of Mahatma Gandhi during the final years of British rule in India in the last century. Could he immediately solve the difficulties of British policies for the Indian people? Did he and many thousands suffer in those years? Was acceptance of hostile thoughts and feelings (and action when possible) or reactive flailing (e.g., with violence) more effective in the end?

AN OPEN INVITATION—TRY THIS

Your Anger Anchor

Create a personalized mantra to anchor your attention during a time of irritation or of anger. Choose words that resonate for you, but possibilities include

- "This *will* end"
- "This too shall pass"

- "I can't change what *is*"
- "There's possibility in pain"
- "I can hold this"
- "Opening leads to possibility"

Consider making this mantra a part of your daily routine. Have it written and in view while working. Make it into a bookmark. Embed it in a few of your e-mails or conversations. Sit with it at the beginning or close of a meditation session. Bring the mantra alive as you work with the energy of the pain of hostility.

Opening to the Pain of Hostility via Clarity Regarding Time and Impermanence

The Buddha is credited as having poetically said, "This existence of ours is as transient as autumn leaves. To watch the birth and death of beings is like looking at the movements of a dance. A lifetime is like a flash of lightning in the sky, rushing by like a torrent down a steep mountain."[11] The problem for all of us (and what contributes to a lot of our stress and difficulties) is that we don't allow ourselves to fully integrate this truth.

We shove against whatever aversive conditioned experience has just happened for us and end up seeing ourselves and the world through the lens of this conditioning. We tend to see things, particularly ourselves, in generally fixed, lasting terms. "I've always been angry, and I guess I always will be. You can't teach an old dog new tricks." Or "I do as a please. I'm beholden to no one." Simply put, and as we've discussed, that's karma. Our minds see and often our emotions and actions bear out this sense of solidity that can block our effectiveness and muffle our true voices and potential for happiness.

This fixed mind-set causes us to shove back because we lose connection with the essential truth that the Buddha outlined as a core component of reality—impermanence, the inevitable changing nature of all things. We know that things change, but somehow our minds trick us into forgetting or failing to feel deeply this knowledge on a daily basis. Especially when it comes to our bodies, our beating hearts, our named selves, we are generally unwilling to see the changing hue of the leaves of our lives. This is at the core of much of our suffering and is something that practice of opening works to ease. Opening practices spark insight into impermanence and foster a willingness to sidestep our inherently flawed addiction to conceptions of time.

In the well-researched mindfulness-based psychotherapeutic approach of Acceptance and Commitment Therapy (or ACT),[12] thoughts are given special treatment—particularly angry, rigid, restrictive thoughts that block people from taking action regarding things that matter. Concerning hostile thoughts, we might be talking about thoughts such as "This jerk did this to me on purpose!" or "This kind of unfair stuff is always happening to me!" Instead of these thoughts landing on the runway of your mind and taking up permanent residence, can you see them for what they really are—temporary? Can you simply have the thoughts? Try shifting your relationship to these "forever" thoughts by getting some distance with the following exercises for regarding them as less-than-solid gargoyles atop your mind.

AN OPEN INVITATION—TRY THIS

Allowing for Change in Angry Thinking

Consider a challenging person from your life—one who it seems will "never" change for the better and whose presence in your day tends to correlate with waves of hostility.

1. Add the preface "I'm having the thought that" to the fixed, hostile thought. Notice even the smallest shift in how stuck you are in your emotions when viewing the thought in this way. Do things stay exactly the same in your experience when you do, or do they change?

2. Put the thought across from you on an empty chair. Visualize it as having size, shape, movement, and so forth. What does it look like? How can it be "you" if it's sitting over there? Does it do anything—shift or change?

3. Take the one "nasty" word from the thought that has the most negative emotional charge for you. Say it out loud (or in your mind) as rapidly as you can for one full minute. What happens to your experience of this thought? When you mix up the timing of how you say it to yourself, does the meaning change? The impact on you?

Practicing within awareness of the fact of impermanence is a powerful antidote to anger, resentment, and "shoving" mental reactions. When we don't want to "have" something (or someone), the experience feels like a solid "it" that sits in our guts and seems like it will never leave. Learning to open to the dynamic, changing nature of our experience of hostility allows it to move through us before getting stuck in our minds and bodies. Such internal logjams lead to resentment and prime us for unhelpful reactivity.

Opening to the Pain of Hostility: Clarity Regarding Our "Nonselfness"

If you've ever driven in my hometown of Boston, you've probably noted the white-knuckle aspect of driving here, particularly on the busier roads. Aggressive, angst-ridden driving is the norm, and I've seen a far greater frequency of middle fingers aired here in traffic than in other cities I've visited. It's a rare commute to or from work for me to not experience someone cutting me off.

And what, pray tell, is a standard reaction to such fellow travelers? What do you do when it happens to you? If you're at all like me (and the rest of the populace), you often find yourself swelling with frustration and find your mind (and perhaps your mouth) churning out expletives, verbally eviscerating this jerk. It is entirely common, if not nearly universal, to have such reactions. Besides, this person is risking your and others' safety, in addition to delaying your getting to work or home, and at the very least this lowly worm is jarring you out of a rainbow and unicorn moment of daydreaming. This person deserves your scorn. *You*, on the other hand, are blameless and deserving of karmic redemption (if, as you'll remember from chapter 1, karma actually worked that way—which it doesn't). There's a distinct Grand Canyon of gap between you and this other driver: you, good; him, bad.

In many of the workshops I conduct with parents, educators, and clinicians, I often have them do an activity I first experienced in graduate school. I have pairs of people (often strangers, but it doesn't matter—it works even if they know each other) sit facing one another and do a simple task:

- Hold each other's gaze for just thirty seconds.
- Do *not* communicate anything.

The activity always unfolds in a similar way, with people chuckling, breaking eye contact and smiling, or looking about awkwardly, as if someone had just spiked the interpersonal punch bowl with something untoward and jarring. Everyone generally agrees they "failed" at the task—that it's basically impossible to *not* communicate when sitting face-to-face with another human being. And that's sort of the point: human communication is inevitable. We are always sending messages (verbal and nonverbal) to one another, and we are wired to do so quickly and intensively. Our brains are structured for nuanced and almost instant social messaging.

And by the way, people tend to report that this exercise not only feels awkward and unnatural (to hold back from the normal flow of interpersonal exchange), but that it can feel *invasive* to hold another's gaze. From an evolutionary perspective, you can imagine our primal cave-dwelling days and the need to quickly send messages to others in our vicinity to either back up (or get clubbed) or to come hither (and let's share a corner of the cave together). Our brains evolved the wiring to help these messages flow when such an emotional message is intended and is beneficial to survival and propagating the biological/genetic aspect of our patterned inheritance.

Deeply understanding this biologically based connectivity between us helps us build awareness. It helps us cultivate empathy, potentially even for those who provoke us into frustration, anger, and outright condemnation. Opening emerges from the deep recognition of our inherent interdependence, our tethering even to those taunting us. Regarding our social brain circuitry, Marco Iacoboni argues,

> Mirror neurons provide an inner imitation, or simulation, of the observed facial expression. They send signals through the insula to the limbic system, which provides the feeling of the observed emotion . . . Our brain produces a full simulation—even the motor component—of the observed painful experiences of other people.[13]

The London-based researcher Tanya Singer published a study in 2004 in which she had women lie in MRI scanners while their male partners sat in chairs nearby, hooked up to an electrode on the hand whereby experimenters could deliver shocks to them.[14] A colored arrow flashed on the women's monitors inside the scanner, letting them know which man among those present in the lab would receive an upcoming shock, as well as telling how severe it would be. Looking at the brain scans, when the women themselves were shocked, the areas of their brains processing tactile information lit up, as well as the emotional processing centers of the brain (such as the cingulate cortex). When the women knew their partners were going to be shocked, their brains *only* activated in the pain region, not the sensory/tactile area. What's important here is the realization that these women did not actually see the shocks being delivered or hear any cries of pain, yet their brains reacted with activation of emotional pain centers *anyway*. This is yet another piece of hard neuroscience pointing to how we're wired for mirroring one another and indicating that we recreate others' pain in our own brains in order to facilitate our understanding and ability to communicate and act.

So if we are wired to constantly and unconsciously mirror each other's intentions and emotions, why are we not immediately empathic with everyone? Why do I still (occasionally—much less than I used to!) pound my car's horn and grumble not-nice monikers when someone swerves abruptly in front of me? Why isn't openness to our hostility more the norm in these situations?

One argument I'll offer comes out of another branch of psychological science. Social psychology has long documented a phenomena referred to as either the "fundamental attribution error" or "correspondence bias."[15] The essence of this pervasive effect is that when we are observing someone else's behavior (often when it's assessed as negative), we process the action as intentional and caused by his or her internal attributes (e.g., their character, or lack thereof). When it's us doing the same behavior (and yes, I—and I'm betting you as well—have cut people off recently), we don't chalk it up to us being jerks, but instead we focus in on contextual accounts for why we did it (e.g., "running late" or "emergency" or "just following the flow of traffic"). Correspondence bias has been well researched and is fairly universal among people.

We seem to not only be wired to connect, but to disconnect as well when we're faced with another's noxious behavior. This, perhaps, is a major obstacle to our empathic, open propensity shining through more automatically with all (even the distasteful and surly) people. Arguably, such biases in perception may have evolved in us because they served us in our primordial and more physically dangerous saber-tooth-tiger-tinged days. We needed mental shortcuts of closure to make decisions that kept us more alive and available for reproduction than not. And so while this biological aspect of our patterning, our karma, may have served us then, it's less than ideal in our (relatively) less dangerous present-day circumstance. Even though mirror neurons are there to connect us (and remind us that we're not actually separate selves), our ancient biased brain architecture may detract from this natural, biologically based capacity for seeing the emotional realities driving others' actions (even the jerks in traffic).

AN OPEN INVITATION—TRY THIS

Enemy Mine

Consider an attitude of gratitude for those who hit your buttons and spark impatient reactivity. Who is someone who's aggravated you or gotten under your skin recently? Don't just silently regard them as your "teacher"; actually go up to them and let them know how you may have benefitted from interacting with them. Don't force it, and certainly don't be insincere. If you're truly connecting with gratitude for their role as your benefactor, find a direct, real, noncondescending way to let them know that (though things may have been hard for both of you) it seems to have led to something worthwhile for you. Let go of any desire for a thank you. Perhaps even do it anonymously. Here's the point: what happens in your experience and your practice of opening to hostile experience in later moments when you're willing to actually do a positive turn for this individual?

While the neuroscientific jury might still be out as to whether we're more wired for empathy or biased reactivity, Buddhist tradition falls down squarely toward the compassionate former. The meditation teacher Osho tells the tale of the young monk who came to the master, Bankei, and asked, "Master, I have uncontrollable anger. How can I be rid of it?"[16]

Bankei looked at his disciple compassionately and said, "Show me this temper of yours because it sounds fascinating!"

The monk paused in confusion. "Well," he said, "I haven't got it right now, so I can't show you."

His master smiled. "Well, bring it to me once you have it."

The story is meant to underscore our natural state of peace, our capacity for opening amid hostility. It's our karmic patterning that gets in the way. In the Bankei tale, and according to Buddhist teachings in general, if you can't produce something at any time, it's not part of your true nature. It's merely an artifact of conditioned existence, and with awareness, by embodying opening, the karmic "it" of angry, impulsive reactivity evaporates.

When someone cuts me off in traffic, it's karma; it's patterning; it's repetition of eons of correspondence bias that's grooved my brain and yours to blame and react with anger. It's then our turn to suffer under an outdated architectural design. We have a natural, biological basis for patient, compassionate connection. Our brains, if we open, can build the muscle (perhaps in places like the lateral prefrontal cortex) to ride out the old, karmic impulses, wait for what truly matters, or detour from angry reprisals. Michael Shaara captured this bimodal aspect of the human condition in the title of his wonderful novelistic account of the American Civil War, *The Killer Angels*.[17] Karmic patterning would have us "kill" out of angry reprisal and bias. The inherent potential in our brains would have us winging our way toward compassionate connection via the practice of open awareness.

Compass Check: Opening to Hostility as Our "True North"

When the thirteenth-century monk Atisha decided to travel from India to Tibet to learn the ancient compassion practices he'd heard were practiced there, he decided to bring a servant with him. Not just any servant—he brought a nasty, ill-tempered young man with him on the long journey and to stay with him during his time in Tibet. Why would he choose to bring someone along who could so easily get under peoples' skins? According to the story, he did so because he was hoping to deepen his practice of compassion. He was hoping to truly practice abiding aversion.

Though I have no idea if this old tale is fact or fiction, I myself know a bit about being connected to others where opportunities for opening are right there for the taking. I'm sure you have such relationships as well. One morning recently, my then five-year-old daughter was struggling getting out the door on time. I was going to be late for work, and I'm sure you can insert your own experience of time-infused frustration here. Celia was again having difficulty managing her anxiety, and even the scratchy feel of her clothes, and therefore it was all coming out with her new favorite word: no. Even though I teach mindful parenting as a clinician and public speaker, that morning I ended up screaming at Celia to put on her shoes and walk to the car. I knew it was only going to get worse when I got her to school and had to transition her inside. The meltdown to come felt of seismic proportions. Without any sounding of a singing bowl or whiff of a lit incense stick, a moment of mindfulness practice had presented itself—a chance to open.

Opening to hostility is foundational because with its cultivation, we become able to open to all the other obstacles as well. Without it, we perpetuate our habits of closing. Opening amid aversion, the "magnetic north" on our emotional compass, helps us orient when the world or others poke at us, prompting suffering, an angry/defensive rise of ego, and a sense of permanency-primed stuckness.

On the way to drop my daughter off at school, I took up my opportunity to open and touched on a few of the practices listed below. This intention and action to sidestep karma led to a fortunate spark of creativity. On the ride to school, I came up with a game I called "quiet creeper" and told Celia we would have a contest as to who could "creep" the slowest and quietest into school once we were out of the car. I said we were both squirrels, and whoever ran too fast or made too much noise would be caught, and the other person would "win all the nuts."

I'd never played "quiet creeper" before, and I still have no clear sense of where it came from, but it worked. She and I crept like squirrels into school, and she kissed me good-bye as if the early morning freak-out had never happened. I drove off that morning feeling grateful for having happened upon the idea (which never would have emerged if I'd dwelled in my fit of daddy rage) and was subsequently a bit more generous and yielding to my fellow drivers that morning. There was more energy to the ensuing hours at work, and I made better decisions with how to intervene with others in sessions. The well-being opening affords can be truly contagious.

An unattributed Zen proverb speaks of opening this way: "Sitting silently, doing nothing, the spring comes and the grass grows by itself." And I've found this to be true as a parent and as a clinician working with even my most challenging clients. Kids and clients need that silent sitting in the grass to feel engaged and even safe feeling that you're not going to add to their difficulties. When we react with frustration and anger, we give our karmic roulette wheel another spin and make it harder for them as well. Opening has directly translated into my children's smiling engagement (and I dare say "compliance"), as well as client trust and willingness to take the risk of healthy behavioral change in their lives.

An Open Invitation: Additional Contemplations for Personal Practice

Below are contemplations for cultivating opening with hostility. Meditating on each of the three universal aspects of suffering ensures you are building all the blocks of open presence. As your practice grows—as you increase your ability to open amid anger, resentment, and angst—a steadiness develops. We become more invested in *not* investing in temporary things with anger and upset derived of illusions of *always*—of permanency.

ACCEPTANCE IN THE FACE OF HOSTILITY

- When someone really angers you, instead of doing your normal reactive thing and flaring with anger, how about getting angry at the true source—the suffering or even hate inside this other person? Why add to this with the energy of your own anger?
- Does your indignation toward another person feel good? Does

it make things more doable and manageable? Does it boost or
block up the mind? How might letting it fester and fly out of us
negatively impact us and others? Basically, what are the costs of
feeding your hostile mind?

· How might you learn something from this "transgressor"?
Without intending to, how might the person be teaching you
about the edges, the boundaries of your capacity for opening?
You don't have to like the pain this person has set in motion for
you, but are you willing to be at all *grateful* for this opportunity to
expand your practice?

WORKING WITH TIME/IMPERMANENCE

· When you meditate, notice what happens to the breath when
annoyance or anger arises. Is each breath the same? What shifts?
Notice the flow of all sensory experience during meditation when
hostility shows up. Notice how things come, stay a bit, and then
notice their departure. Does this ever cease? Try concentrating
on just one part of your body (like a hand). Monitor the smallest
changes in sensation. See if you can stabilize your awareness on
the flow of these sensations amid aversion. Notice how much
things change the more you rest in awareness.

· Contemplate anything or anyone you are shoving at internally—
whether it be a grudge, a slight, a resentment toward a partner.
Where will this "object" you're focused on be in a thousand
years? What will happen to your experience of it even one year
from now? Exactly the same as now?

· Has a person who has hurt or upset you *always* done so in every
situation? Is a hurtful nature absolutely consistent, or does kindness ever slip out of such individuals? This doesn't mean such
folks should not be held responsible for the deleterious effects
of their choice, but the point here is permanence (or the lack
thereof). Is any "bad" person always so?

CLARIFYING THE TRUE NATURE OF SELF

· Notice your closing down tendencies as a meditator or seeker—a
practitioner looking to make something happen with meditation, to get somewhere. And if you don't mediate, notice how

many self-help books you own—the sense of yourself as "a work in progress." Can you directly experience the closing in the midst of your meditating or change efforts? Are you willing to forgo any destination and just continue planting seeds of opening in each moment of awareness of mind and body? Are you willing to drop the meditator, the self-improver, all together? What happens when you do?

I can't say it enough in this book: these are *practices*, not assumptions of perfection. The question for you is whether you're willing to show up to them on a daily basis and make a deposit in the direction of flexibility and well-being. This itself is where opening practice is useful. You don't get the payout if you're constantly dipping into the principal, if you're showing up to keep making the small deposits.

In working to open to hostility, are you willing to keep showing up to your practices and let the benefits build (exponentially) on their own over time? You (and I) cannot guarantee the results. It reminds me of the metaphor that mindfulness teachers such as Thich Nhat Hanh have referred to about the difference between the influence of a handful of salt in a small bowl of water versus the same amount of salt in a large river—if we cultivate a large enough "container" of awareness, we don't notice the saltiness. If we build enough skills of spaciousness and self-management, the anger, resentment, and unabated aspects of pain don't carry the same bitter taste for us. We won't suffer nearly as much. We must be willing to pick up and gently hold our bowl of patient, mindful, open capacity, regardless of what life dumps into it.

Sarah, my great-uncle's great unrequited love, never obtained the marriage to my uncle she'd expected. Who's to say, however, that her practice of opening yielded no returns? Ask the Dalai Lama about the results of his personal practice with the Chinese government. Ask yourself for that matter regarding your own dreams deferred and anger unrelenting.

Hurry up, open, and know that this new pattern does matter in ways you may never directly witness, let alone comprehend. Plant the seeds amid hostility, and willingly and lovingly walk forward anyway.

Into the next chapter we go where, not only do we not feel like leaping forward when we're hindered, we are so out of it we just want to lie down and take a nap.

CLOSING INQUIRY

If you continue to push out at that which threatens or in some way pokes, what truth might you miss out on?

5 Waking the Wilting Mind

Managing Sluggishness and Dullness

OPENING INQUIRY

When asked if he were a god or just another man, the Buddha is said to have looked at his inquirers and said, "I am awake." How much of your daily life is spent in a mind dimmed by fatigue or thickened by dullness? What might it look like to wake up inside a withered and wilted mind?

I had a run-in with over-the-counter "no doze" energy pills in college. Three final exams on the same day should have been outlawed, yet despite my inner protests, I found myself needing to pull an all-nighter to get myself ready. And while the pills were effective in keeping my eyelids open, they ran me over with the overdose of caffeine that left me near convulsing in my bed when I finally lay down to rest for a few minutes at four in the morning.

Staying awake seemed to require such brute force when I was in my late teens and early twenties. My studies often ran aground on sleepiness and fogginess in my dorm room or in the school library. I used all manner of props and strategies for buttressing my sagging energy so that I could squeeze yet another mnemonic acronym into my head: Ping-Pong or Nintendo video-game tournaments in the dorm living room with roommates, head-down power naps in study carrels until my pathetic pool of drool on the desktop would prompt me back to my own bed for sleep. And I could always find a willing companion for a late-evening jaunt to the local fast-food establishment for a triple cheese-burger, fries, and a shake as a well-deserved study-time snack.

And then there was my raging social anxiety and low self-regard for my intellectual prowess (despite a perfect 4.0 GPA). I shoved at myself from the inside and needed more and more on the outside to keep me from shutting down and closing off. There was much about my life patterns in college that would have led me to give a heartfelt and opposite answer to the question asked of the Buddha thousands of years ago.

"I am asleep. Or at least I wish I were."

No, I was not much different than many college students—I shared in the undergraduate curse of a vampire's sleep cycle, with sleep deprivation hitting me most during my afternoon classes. Between my poor sleep hygiene, diet, overinflated emphasis on socializing, and underinflated self-esteem, it was a perfect recipe for a foggy mind and diminished energy. I also was years away from learning my first lessons of meditation and its benefits. It would be some time before I would (in the words of Joseph Goldstein) "develop a mind so completely open that it can experience great pleasure and great pain with spaciousness, com-passion, awareness and energy."[1]

Sometimes our tiredness is a mere physical and mental consequence of simple causes (such as diet, exercise, and sleep), and at other times it is sloth and torpor (here aggregated as "wilting"), which is the focus of this chapter. For wilting the causes are deeper—manifestations of our unconscious wish to avoid experiencing unpleasant thoughts and feelings and/or conditioned habits of closing up our mental shops when faced with challenge and discomfort. According to Goldstein, this "mind that loves the snooze button" derives from a "pattern of retreating from difficulties [that] strengthens the tendencies toward laziness and inactivity, passivity and lethargy" and is often caused by "giving unwise or careless attention to certain mental states like discontent, boredom, laziness and drowsiness."[2]

The meditation teacher Gil Fronsdal suggests that this particular hindrance "often follows from excessive desire and ill will."[3] It is always important to remember the hindrances as deeply linked and mutually sparking one another. We'll delve into how to deal with this intertwined messiness of our reactive habits in the final chapter of this book, but for now it's sufficient just to notice these connections. When we've been chock-full of wanting stuff and experiences and resenting/battling with others who seem to stand in the way of our desires being gratified, our system learns to go offline—to wilt away.

Assuming you're not reading this chapter in a current episode of extreme wilting, let's begin with a quick tour of what Buddhism has to say about this hindrance. We'll then pause for a few nuggets of what scientific findings have concluded before we get down to the business of working with this hindrance that would have us fizzle out.

Asleep at the Dharma Wheel: What the Buddha Said about Sinking and Perking Up

Nasrudin wanted to steal some fruit from a stall, but the stallholder had a fox that kept watch. He overheard the man say to his fox: "Foxes are craftier than dogs, and I want you to guard the stall with cunning. There are always thieves about. When you see anyone doing anything, ask yourself why he is doing it and whether it can be related to the security of the stall."

When the man had gone away, the fox came to the front of the stall and looked at Nasrudin lurking on a lawn opposite. Nasrudin at once lay down and closed his eyes. The fox thought, "Sleeping is not doing anything."

As he watched, he too began to feel tired. He lay down and went to sleep.

Then Nasrudin crept past him and stole some fruit.[4]

As this tale suggests, sleep is *something* after all—it is a doing, and it's obviously very important to our well-being. But there were two aspects of sleeping in this story: Nasrudin's ruse of sleep in order to sneak forward and steal the fruit, and the wilting mind of the fox that allowed it to happen. It's the latter that we're concerned with here—the mind on molasses that keeps us from seeing clearly and doing with energy and daring.

In *The Path of Purification*, the Pali term for sloth and torpor is *thina-middha*—*thina* meaning "stiffness" and *middha* meaning "sluggishness."[5] In his commentary on this hindrance, Thiradhammo elaborates on thinna/ stiffness as a "paralysis due to lack of urgency and loss of vigor" and a "lack of driving power" and middha/sluggishness as "characteristic of unwieldiness," whose "function is to smother."[6] Basically, the Buddhist literature goes to great lengths to parse out a very difficult-to-describe yet universally felt state of being. We've all been there many times—the mind is wilting, slowing as if awareness is caught in a thickening mental muck. We don't want to "wield" this state and feel increasingly desperate to cave in to a complete tuning out, physically and mentally.

The Buddha, in the Pali canon, tells his monastics what sparks sloth and torpor: "There arises listlessness, lassitude, lazy stretching of the body, drowsiness after meals, mental sluggishness; frequently giving unwise attention to it—this is the nourishment for the arising of sloth and torpor that have not yet arisen and for the increase and strengthening of sloth and torpor that have already arisen"[7]

The Buddha wanted his monks on the alert for the conditions fostering each hindrance to awareness. Only with careful, committed attention to these ingredients of body and mind would a person move higher in concentration and stabilization of mindfulness. In addition, he wanted all practitioners on the lookout for opportunities to prevent sloth and torpor from arising or deepening.

"And what, bhikkus . . . prevents unarisen sloth and torpor from arising and arisen sloth and torpor from increasing and expanding? There are, bhikkus, the element of arousal, the element of endeavor, the element of exertion; frequently giving careful attention to them . . . prevents unarisen sloth and torpor from arising and arisen sloth and torpor from increasing and expanding."[8]

As we'll practice later in this chapter, there are common-sense (and less common) solutions to the wilting body-mind. But the key point here is the Buddha's admonition to go far beyond simple pick-me-ups with bright lights or cold-water face slaps. We ideally learn to look carefully at the causal conditions of both the rising and falling away of our wilting. Rousing the energy to do such investigation pays off doubly—in and of itself, the looking stirs and sparks the mind upward from sloth and torpor, and it gives us valuable intel for preventing such wilting in the future. Instead of downing a tiny bottle of sugary convenience-store energy in five seconds, we can learn to put in the five (and many more) hours of careful investigation of our sinking states of being and build a better mind going forward. With all the coffee I poured into myself during cram sessions in college, I missed a golden opportunity to turn my inner desk lamp on those all-too-frequent feelings of dimming out! If I had, maybe I'd be "wilt-free" by this point. And then again, I do believe I've seen video clips of folks like the Dalai Lama yawning from time to time.

Science and the Sinking Mind: The Jekyll and Hyde of Fatigue

You don't need statistics to know that it's dangerous to drive when you're overly fatigued. And yet, by the frequency of the accidents, perhaps we all could bear the reminder. In a large-scale study[9] with a sample of 14,268 crashes, it was estimated that 21 percent of these in which a person was killed involved a drowsy driver. If this statistic is extrapolated proportionally to all crashes nationally, 6,400 fatal crashes annually involve a fatigued driver. The wilting mind is not just something that blocks our progress as meditators; it can be lethal.

We've all had the feeling of drowsiness behind the wheel. Clearly, this book will not make a dent in these unfortunate numbers. A number of factors beyond our conditioned patterns of wilting (which this book addresses) may be at play in the more physical aspects of extreme fatigue.

According to the United Kingdom's National Health Service,[10] a number of medical and psychiatric conditions can engender significant fatigue. Here is a partial list:

- Celiac disease
- Anemia
- Chronic fatigue syndrome
- Sleep apnea
- Underactive thyroid
- Diabetes
- Anxiety disorders (like panic disorder)
- Clinical depression

It is important to consult your physician to rule these in or out so that your focus here in this book can be on the karmically conditioned thoughts, emotions, and behaviors that are sapping your energy and sending your eyelids earthward.

By way of example, I was once driving in semirural Ohio a few years back. After a state trooper's flashing lights in my rearview mirror snapped me out of my inner sagging, I pulled over to the side of the road.

The trooper eyed me from outside my driver's window, clearly looking for signs I'd been drinking. "You were over the center line quite a bit back there," he said. "Any alcohol for you today?"

I assumed I'd be doing some mindful walking on a line of the officer's choosing outside my car, but after we talked for a minute or so, it was clear he was letting me go with a warning.

"Sorry to hear about your grandmother," he said, nodding at me slightly before walking back toward his cruiser. I'd just told him that my grandmother had passed away several days prior and that I'd just left her funeral. Apparently, I'd become so absorbed in my emotional inner musing about things family—past and future—that my mind had sagged, and so did my hands at the wheel, leading to my sloppy (and dangerous) driving.

Basically (to use a bit of psychobabble), I was ruminating that day in the car. By this I mean I was cycling through a series of negatively toned thoughts—repeating, analyzing, judging them—and increasingly *not* taking in the actual sensory realities of my body and my surroundings. Research has linked this sort of pejorative mind wandering to lower levels of happiness and higher reports of psychological disturbance.[11] Rumination is especially linked with anxiety and depressive disorders and with a network of structures in the brain, commonly referred to as the "default mode network" (DMN).[12] These structures (such as the posterior cingulate cortex and the medial prefrontal cortex) appear to light up with activation when our inner experience is self-referentially focused.[13] Basically, it's when we're lost in thought about ourselves. As the researcher Jud Brewer and his colleagues indicate, this happens about half of the time in our waking experience.[14] Rumination is the negative, emotionally barbed variant of the wandering mind. Arguably, the DMN is active even as our minds are on the way toward serious sloth and torpor wilting—the wandering mind soon becomes the wilted mind.

What's exciting from the standpoint of our work in this book is how meditation has been shown to bring about *physical* changes in the default mode network—mindfulness practice has a structural impact on the areas of the brain where our minds' wilting meanderings arise. Brewer and his colleagues in the United States,[15] as well as Joon Hwan Jang and his colleagues at Seoul National University,[16] measured the degree of connectivity between areas of the DMN in thirty-five meditation practitioners versus thirty-three healthy control participants without any meditation experience. Using functional MRI scanning, these researchers found that meditation practitioners showed significantly greater linkage between these areas of the DMN in the medial prefrontal cortex of the brain. The DMN has been shown in previous studies to be most active when peoples' attention is focused away from the external world and into inner experience (thoughts, emotions, and bodily sensations). Basically, this study suggests that meditation experience is associated with an increased capacity for individuals to reduce mental activity (such as unhelpful mind—wandering/rumination) by accentuating their monitoring of internal bodily sensations and movement of energy throughout the body. Meditators appear to be more able to inhibit the process of rumination that leads to higher levels of stress, and this inhibition of excessive thinking may become more and more automatic (i.e., a new bioconditioned pattern) with continued mindfulness practice.

In addition to the wilting that comes from a mind that has become mired (and fatigued) by rumination, there is a wilting that occurs as a psychological self-protective mechanism against really intense experience. As Joseph Goldstein indicates, "there might be a strong and even traumatic emotion arising, and sometimes sloth and torpor arise as a defense against feeling it."[17]

As a therapist, I've worked with a number of clients who've experienced significant and terribly damaging trauma. From inpatient psychiatric patients to Vietnam combat veterans to adolescents in residential care, I've had frequent front-seat exposure to traumatic experience for those I've treated.

For one adolescent I worked with in a residential treatment program, I literally watched him fold himself over—wilt and go mute—in response to being asked to participate in a group therapy exposure session along with the other boys (all of whom had experienced significant trauma of one sort or another). This particular boy's trauma was more intense than most (chronic sexual assault from his uncle with threats of being killed if he told anyone).

This boy, Billy, was known for his energy and wit. He was every teacher's nightmare with his in-class callouts and spontaneous cutting up. His smile was impish and his mind always working on the next punch line. I loved that kid. He was the pick-me-up I often needed on my own wilting days at work—far more effective and worthwhile than my IV of coffee. Early on in my days as his therapy group leader, Billy even had the gall to smile at me and tell me that I had "a forehead big and flat enough to show a movie on." It's the rare kid who's willing to call me out on my Frankenstein's monster forehead (as my older brother had already done years before). I quietly respected him for it, even though I publicly sent him out of the group room for a time-out.

"It's your turn, Billy," I said. The boys were taking turns beginning to tell the story (what we in the field call a trauma narrative) of what happened to him over those days, weeks, and months in the attic of his mother's home. "You can do it, dude. Don't worry about getting anything wrong. You're right here in the room with us. That was then and this is now."

He mumbled a few words and proceeded to bend forward, placing his head on his knees. No matter what I or others said or did, he stayed that way for over fifteen minutes, completely unresponsive. Billy became a mannequin right in front of our eyes. He had truly and self-protectively wilted away. Less a pure falling asleep, it looked and felt more like a dissociative coma—a reflexive, brief emotional hibernation—he descended into.

Billy did not *choose* this reaction; it was his mind's learned pattern for staving off further pain, and it arose reflexively when the environment tripped the wires of traumatic memory.

We do not choose our karmic conditioning—it shows up in us moment to moment. Our choice is only in whether we see our patterns with the bright light of awareness. Patterning has a way of burning itself out if left alone in the spotlight of open knowing. There appears to be a causal flow of input and output in our bodies and minds. What comes into us by way of contact with the world, if not met with awareness, leads in lockstep to what comes out of us by way of reactive thinking, emotions, and behavior.

We need a balance of concentration of mind on the situation at hand with the energy flow in our bodies. Without this balance, we can (in the case of insufficient energy in the body, excessive rumination like my day in the car in Ohio, or a self-protective drawdown of energy in the case of trauma reactions like Billy's) slide away into hindering patterns of wilting.

As the parable goes, the Buddha was talking with one of his disciples who believed himself to be the most energetic in his practice of meditation, more so than all the others.

"And yet you have not found freedom, correct?" asked the Buddha.

"Yes, my lord," said his disciple.

"Tell me," said the Buddha. "Were you not once quite skilled at playing string music on the lute?"

"Yes, my lord."

"And tell me—when the strings of the lute were too tight, was the lute playable?"

"No, my lord."

"And when they were too loose?"

"Certainly not, my lord."

"And yet when the strings were adjusted to be not too loose and not too tight, you could play at perfect pitch, correct?"

"Yes, that's right, my lord."

"So it is with you," said the Buddha. "If the energy is applied too much, it leads to restlessness, and if not enough, it leads to lethargy. Therefore, you must keep your energy in balance, and you will make progress on the path toward freedom."

The meditation teacher and monastic Ajahn Thiradhammo says that managing our wilting minds requires a "careful balance of 'just enough'"—we need just the right mixture of concentration and amount of energy in our moments of practice, and then meditation will progress, and we will not be sidelined by this wilting pattern.[18] If we're willing and skillful at turning what energy of attention we have toward investigating what's showing up in our experience (thoughts and bodily sensations), then we might stumble upon insight into what's causing our dullness in the first place. Failing to discern our patterns of wilting can have some nasty consequences.

Consider a hapless trainee of mine toward the beginning of my days as a clinical supervisor (and no, this is not one of those embarrassing anecdotes about "that intern" that is really a story from the supervisor's own sordid list of clinical missteps). My intern waited until the very end of our supervision meeting to tell me there was "one more thing" she wanted to say. This is what therapists call door-knobbing—when a client waits until just before his or her hand is on the door to leave to drop the revelatory bomb that leaves you sitting by yourself in the emotional blast crater. The shaking in her voice said this piece of information was definitely not something she "wanted" to talk about. As I've learned in my career, and as we've discussed throughout this book, *wanting* to do and *willing* to do are quite distinct.

"I fell asleep on one of my clients," she said, her eyes on the carpet as if she were a guilty household dog looking at the spot of its transgression.

Typically, I've not been a nervous nelly as a supervisor—fixated and vigilant for any possible trainee misstep that might bring a notice of license revocation to me in the mail. But this comment from her served as a sudden pinch—a goosing of my anxiety button. It was the sudden association based on her choice of the phrase "*on* one of my clients" that did it. Flash to impulsive, immoral, and serious sanction-worthy assumptions of a therapist-client tryst under the negligent umbrella of my supervisory license.

"What did you say?" I asked.

"I fell asleep," she said.

"Just sleep?" I asked. And at that, my intern looked up at me, clearly confused—perhaps even more so by the avalanche of relief on my face.

So while it wasn't the career-ending big deal I momentarily assumed, it was still a hefty enough deal. Though I was proud of my intern's courageous honesty in supervision, I was disappointed that she'd allowed her inner wilting (which is indeed universal among therapists) to progress into flat-out, wanton snoozing. I was disappointed (and my intern mortified) because when my intern awoke, the client had left the session. And he never returned.

Therapists are—surprise, surprise—human. Yes, my trainee fell asleep on a client, and no, that's not a good thing. Yes, my intern needed to be accountable for the effects of her extremely wilted snooze-fest—its damaging impact on the client's trust in not just her as a professional, but for the treatment process in general. So yes, it's a big deal that her wilting got away from her, but she was not "bad" or beyond repair (both in terms of her alliance with that specific client and as a therapist in general).

As a side note (and since many readers of this book will, or have been, consumers of psychotherapy services), it's important to know that therapists are not gurus; they don't hold the keys to the good life. In fact, they (not me) are often seriously flawed. Indeed, therapists might have their hands full with their own emotional troubles—some of which might contribute to the inner landscape that leads to sloth and torpor. Studies suggest that approximately 10 percent of practicing therapists are clinically depressed.[19] Surveys of working psychotherapists indicate that between two-thirds and three-quarters of them reported experiencing moderately to severely impairing symptoms of anxiety or depression at some point during their careers.[20] Many professional helpers struggle against substance abuse,[21] and psychologists are one of the leading groups of professionals to attempt suicide.[22]

I have been very tired and let slip a yawn or two on occasion in session. If that were the greatest of my errors as a therapist, I'd be beyond grateful. And yet, learning to work with the wilting mind and rein in its far reaches, helps us and may help others with whom we interact.

As the meditation teachers Joseph Goldstein and Sharon Salzberg point out, "when tranquility isn't balanced with an equal alertness, it's easy to fall into a dreamy, drifty state."[23] It's that balance that we're aiming for in this chapter—that sense of more than just "becoming calm and relaxed, but about becoming calm, with alertness, healthy engagement and clarity."[24]

Whether it be during formal sitting meditation or sitting slumped over muffins at breakfast, we can learn from our wilting mind so that we understand what causes it, what makes it worse, and what brings us back to balance and a steady state of mental and physical energetic flow. So, as I suggested to my intern, we should put on our "curiosity caps" and learn from these sags of the mind without beating ourselves up.

The psychotherapist and mind guru Carl Jung put it well: "Nothing is so apt to challenge our self-awareness and alertness as being at war with oneself."[25] So let's get to work learning about our own unique reasons for wilting.

Opening by Exploring the Pain and Potential of Wilting

Buddhism would characterize sloth and torpor as "basically a lack of energy, and the fundamental dynamic is first deflation, followed by collapse."[26] The practitioner would ideally learn to recognize it before it becomes excessive or habitual, determine its cause, see clearly what factors seem to alleviate or prevent it, and then set about leveraging this hard-won information to create as stable and steady an energy foundation in the body-mind as possible. This foundation would allow the practitioner to climb higher into jhanic realms of concentration and ultimately enlightenment itself.

Coming out of the idealistic dharmic clouds and into the lowly hotel conference room, I have many times noticed what appears to be boredom overtaking the faces of attendees at workshops and seminars I've led. While I used to find myself deflated by this "clear" vote of no confidence in my abilities as a speaker, I now (usually) see the glazed-over look in folks' eyes as the result of that impossibly complex admixture of psychophysiological factors that we lump together with the term "boredom."

As Gil Fronsdal writes, though, "nothing is inherently boring; boredom is a judgment, an activity of the mind."[27] We need to do better than a simple, dismissive "I'm just bored." Our society regards boredom as a justifiable, external fact of certain situations. We blame our office cubicles, living rooms, and dinner dates for boring us and forsake any inner responsibility for the patterning within that is allowing for this maligned state of wilting to emerge in the first place. Instead of looking out at the world with a deflated, passive frown when bored, we could instead take such an experience as a call to curiosity. We could perk up just enough to begin asking what is happening inside and around us to create this experience. We could wonder what we might be wanting at that moment and thereby trip across another hindrance (like desire/wanting or hostility/wrestling), which may be draining our energy.

Curiosity is the key. Whether we're currently wilting or not, it can help us get better at delving into a deeper understanding of this hindrance pattern (and all of them) by building a habit of curious engagement with ourselves and the environment. Bill Morgan writes in his book *The Meditator's Dilemma*[28] how meditators in the West are often blocked in their practices by a dry, stiff, and achievement- and outcome-oriented approach to meditation. Borrowing from the developmental psychologist and theoretician D. W. Winnicott, Morgan discusses the benefits of consciously creating a wholesome, enlivening "holding environment" for one's meditation practice.

According to Morgan, our meditation can bloom if we are simply (yet elusively) willing to relax and invigorate our bodies and open our minds with gratitude and emotional warmth. Like a child's need for a consistent, supportive, welcoming, relaxed emotional climate from his or her caregivers, so do meditators need a holding environment with such qualities in order to flourish in their practice of meditation. And I believe we can take this further. We benefit from leaping toward our daily experience (whether in formal sitting meditation or while sitting waiting for an Uber) from a platform that truly supports and enlivens us. Let's take a look at ways for us to practice creating such a platform so that the imbalance of wilting becomes less likely—we're simply more curious and playfully engaged with our daily lives.

AN OPEN INVITATION—TRY THIS

Create Your Daily Holding Environment

Make a commitment to try doing the following on a daily basis for at least a short period of time (perhaps a few days to start). Pick a time of day and show up to the "construction site" of your inner holding environment for increased curiosity and willingness to open to awareness in general and to the goings on of your hindrance patterns in particular.

1. Hitch yourself to a dream. (Peruse a memory of a positive event, and notice what arises in your experience now. How does it affect you? Consider using some savoring breaths for widening a positive frame for the moment at hand.)

2. **Of**f your seat and shake it up. (Stand up and move around. Shake and stretch in no particular order or sequence. In fact, the more unpredictable the better. Notice what happens to your ability to take in more completely what's arriving at your sense doors.)
3. **Le**arn something? (Ask what this moment has to teach. What is fresh or easily missed? What is here that adds and expands?)
4. **Do** something unscripted (Be willing to break a stale habit, choose the road less traveled, and do something new, unexpected and dare I say spontaneous! Get the egg salad instead of the corned beef.)

Growing up in rural northeastern Ohio, I was not unfamiliar with fire-arms. My dad not only owned several, but he (a self-taught woodworker/hobbyist) even made a couple himself (along with the munitions for firing them). One in particular (an American frontier-era .50 caliber Hawken rifle) stands out in my memory due to the raised bruise it left on my shoulder when I failed to ensure it was firmly planted there before pulling the trigger and unleashing its massive recoil.

Though I'm not a gun enthusiast at present (I live in about as "blue" of a state as possible), I learned as a kid that you need to "aim small to miss small" when firing. What this means is that in firing (particularly at a moving target such as a woodland creature), the smaller the point on its surface that you're aiming at, the more likely you are to hit the target. Drill instructors in the military tell recruits to aim at buttons on uniforms, not the whole of the enemy charging in their direction.

Here, the closest thing to an enemy combatant is the dullness that's invaded the body and mind. And though you've probably practiced enough mindfulness thus far in this book to have learned how trying to overcome invading hindrances by force or control is less than effective, you can still take something away from this adage to aim small. When bringing mindfulness to bear on sloth and torpor, it can help to dial down to the smallest possible aspects of its manifestation in your body. Aim small for the places in the body that the wilting shows up, and you may learn a great deal about why you're dimming out in the first place, and you may find yourself perking up a bit in the process.

It can help, though, to not get lost in making your sagging, wilting sleepiness your "enemy." Instead of opposing and fighting our experience of dullness, we can learn to welcome it. Boredom can move from being an oppression to an opportunity—a challenge to invite into the microscope of conscious awareness. As Sharon Salzburg and Joseph Goldstein suggest in their guide to *vipassana*, or "insight meditation," there is immense benefit in gently bringing attention to the experience of sleepiness. In his eightfold path, the Buddha recommends that we each align with "right aim or intention" in our efforts—that (to use more modern vernacular) we have our "heads screwed on right" about why we're doing these practices in the first place. We're looking here to learn how to open to the experience of dullness in the body-mind. Are we willing to aim small and focus on "just this breath" as Salzburg and Goldstein recommend?[29] With a gentle noting of what's arising moment to moment as we wilt from the inside out, and if we position ourselves on a mental holding environment of relaxed, open curiosity, then the boring can become a boon to our path of mindful hurdle jumping.

At the first sign that you're sinking in mind and body, ask yourself: am I willing to lay myself "flat out"? With the body scanning practice below, you can walk your attention very slowly through these areas of the body, noticing the sensations as they arise, learning what you can about what's showing up there in response to recent and current circumstances, and you can sharpen the point of your awareness as you go.

AN OPEN INVITATION—TRY THIS

Lay Yourself FLAT OUT

Settle into awareness of your breathing after assuming a comfortable yet upright posture. In the beginning (and since you're working with sloth and torpor) do not lie down for this practice (even though the acronym is FLAT OUT!). Only after having practiced a number of times should you try it while reclined. A reclined position for exploring/scanning your body with mindfulness can be your goal. At some point, particularly if you've experienced some trouble falling asleep, doing so at bedtime will likely improve your ability to drift off with less struggle. For now though, we're looking to aim small and learn about how wilting emerges within the body. With awareness of the breathing established slowly, direct attention, in sequence, to each of these areas:

- **F**eet
- **L**egs
- **A**rms
- **T**orso

Allow your attention to hover and scan about at each body part for at least thirty seconds to one full minute.

And now, slowly and as if your attention were a feather, draw an

- **O**val around the mouth, and then move your attention up and
- **U**nder and around each of your eyes, and then up the scalp to the
- **T**op of the head

Repeat for as many cycles as you wish, looking to maintain slow, even breathing and as steadied a focus on each body part as possible. When thoughts/ distractions arise (and they surely will), gently come back to where you left off (or start over; no worries!).

In his exploration and scholarship of the Buddha's teachings in the Satipatthana Sutta[30] and its suggestions for meditation practice, Joseph Goldstein writes, "In working with the hindrances, the first step of satipatthana is not in actively opposing the hindrance or struggling with it, but in clearly recognizing and being mindful of it, and in recognizing the conditions related to its presence or absence." With gentle, continuous curiosity, we can learn what specific aspects of our bodies, our minds, and our sensory connections to the world and all that's arising there are prompting us to wilt. Dullness and the sinking mind are not a choice— they are the predictable effect of specific causal conditions.

When we bring playfulness, gentleness, and curiosity to our practice with this hindrance, we begin to see wilting as not a random event and not something we planned. It happens around, in, and through us, and we can more and more come to know its patterns.

Goldstein writes, "If the concentration is much stronger than the energy, we sometimes fall into what is called 'sinking mind' . . . It is a very pleasant, dreamlike state, in which there is a calm, floating feeling, but not much alertness."[31] It reminds me of what it felt like when I sat down to meditate in the days shortly after my daughter, Celia, was born. I, like most every new parent, was hopelessly mired in the throes of sleep deprivation. So while I brought a measure of focus to my sittings, it felt as though I were meditating in syrup. There was indeed a sweetness to the concentration within the meditation practice, but my low energy reserves left me bogged down. My mind was calm and had a drapes-fluttering-in-the-breeze quality, yet I was largely unaware of what was happening moment to moment.

In relaying his own encounters with sloth and torpor while meditating on retreat, Goldstein describes how he made a practice of his wilting body and mind. If that sagging feeling crept up on him while sitting, he would allow himself to lie down to rest. When he chose rest, his mind would "let go," and in that next moment he would do something I, as a meditator, personally consider to be "hard-core"—he would sit up abruptly. What he found was that doing so was usually sufficient to rejuvenate him.[32] Most of us are not as earnest about facing our own versions of sloth and torpor. In fact, instead of trying to work with and learn from our wilting, we blame ourselves (and others) for it (or when they struggle with it in our presence).

It's so hard not to blame someone for the wilting mind. Again, as a public speaker, I've often taken it as a personal affront when someone's head begins that sleepy "bobblehead doll" thing. To wax anger-poetic, their eyes' glaze sparks one's mind ablaze. But as we discussed in chapter 4, these reactive assumptions of blame are evolutionary artifacts readily explained by social cognitive science (i.e., correspondence bias) and are errors. The mind assumes intent and poor character as the cause of students' slumping and jerking upward when elbows slip from arm of chair, rather than seeing the full palette of contextual conditions—the pattern bringing such wilting into being.

Gil Fronsdal advises, "Mindfulness practice can help us understand how our evaluations and reactions lead to lethargy . . . We can see how the stories we tell ourselves drain our vitality."[33] So in our next practice, we look away from the body for a moment to our thinking mind itself. Let's shine that light of attention on what narratives about ourselves might be fueling our feeling out of gas.

AN OPEN INVITATION—TRY THIS

Sidestepping Blame for Your Inner Drain
(adapted from M. Abblett, 2013)[34]

Select a political pundit show (unfortunately, there are many to pick from), and prepare to watch it. Turn on the television, sit comfortably yet upright in a chair or on the floor (as always, a straight back is best—particularly if it's sloth and torpor we're looking to explore), and turn the volume all the way down. Now, do the following:

1. With your eyes closed, focus your attention on the flow of your breath in and out of your nostrils as you've done in many practices.

2. Now, for the next few minutes, shift your focus from your breath, and instead focus on any sounds you can notice in your immediate surroundings. What's here? Perhaps the ticking of a clock, air coming through vents, the hum of a refrigerator—whatever is nearby. As if you're a biologist doing so with butterflies, gently "collect" the sounds around you, noticing how they come to awareness and then pass away.

3. Once you are centered in this noticing and observing space, slowly turn up the volume on your set to a moderately loud setting. (A bit louder than you would typically set it is fine.) Close your eyes and continue noticing the sounds as they come. Notice the words and tone of the pundits in the program. Instead of focusing on the meaning, focus on the sensations in your body (the feel) that are prompted by the bickering, the arguing, the loud talk from these people. If you find yourself getting caught up in the content of what they are debating (understandable considering the insanity of the body politic in recent years), that is fine—gently, patiently, and compassionately come back in your awareness to noticing the sensation of experience in your body.

4. Watch as the words and their impact on your body come and go like passing clouds or like pounding rain that runs down your window, soon to disappear. Notice any thoughts too as they arise, and merely observe them, letting them come and go without grabbing onto them. How do you get tangled up in your thoughts? Don't wrestle with them—just see that you've gotten hooked by them and continue to watch.

5. In particular, notice any tendencies toward tuning out—distractibility or mental slumping. Notice what you say to yourself about yourself or others as you react in your *body* to the mundanity and insanity coming from the TV.

6. Continue listening and noticing for at least five to ten minutes. Let the sensations of sound and the ebb and flow of reactions within your body and mind pass through your awareness with as little ownership by you as possible. Are these reactions your choice? Did you plan to withdraw or wilt in some way?

After five minutes or so, open your eyes and spend a few minutes reflecting. What observations do you have of this activity? In particular, what do notice your mind doing when pressed against an angst-ridden, pressured, ego-filled exchange over a period of time? What did you learn about your own story regarding yourself and others in such situations? What pattern might exist here, and does it perhaps connect with any aspects of dimming in yourself when you're in the midst of challenging interpersonal situations? Who is to blame for your reactions? If not you, who? If not them (since in actuality "they" were not even in the room with you), then what do you make of the notion of blame altogether?

Let go of blame for your wilting, and focus instead on understanding and management of causal conditions.

If we can begin to break free of the habit of blaming ourselves or others for the tuning out that pours down on us like an odorless, tasteless sticky goo, then we might be able to tap an inquisitive finger to this murky mess and set about understanding it. There is no boredom, except should the mind make it so. You can get fascinated by a pencil, the creases of a dress, or way a child sleeps (even if that child just broke your favorite mug prior to a nap!).

As my friend and fellow mindfulness lecturer Tara Healey (the program director of Mindfulness-Based Learning at Harvard Pilgrim Healthcare) likes to relay, some people have made their careers stand out from the rest of the herd with their powers of mindful observation. She likes to mention the field biologist George Schaller and how he was able to gather information about Central African mountain gorillas (and other species in various locations) in the wild no other biologist could seem to. He did so with patient and curiosity-infused attention to the smallest details and a willingness to drop his preconceptions and conditioned mind-set. Schaller walked out into the wild and opened himself to the energy show of discovery.

If we're willing to get that curious about what's happening with our wilting body-minds, we'll learn quite a bit about what's draining our energy and/or what is the inner blockage that we're looking to tune out from. We can become a "Schaller eye-baller" and learn to see the details we've been missing. If we can learn to wake up from wilting, we can have impact where otherwise the opportunity to do so would elude our narrowed eyes. Schaller's work has, at least in part, led to the establishment of over twenty parks or preserves worldwide—a feat few biologists can cite. In the next practice activity, let's channel Schaller's curiosity and sense of wonder for discovery in the details.

AN OPEN INVITATION—TRY THIS

Big Banging This Moment

Scientists tell us it all started with a more than notable bang. So can your awareness if you open to curiosity as to what may be fresh and absolutely novel, no matter how mundane or routine the situation.

To practice "big banging" into new, open, and aware experience of your daily moments, select one or more of your daily routines—things as simple as brushing your teeth, walking your dog, or (though I know nothing of it) nagging your husband.

1. Before the start of the routine activity, ask: What am I *assuming* about this? What do I think about it and the role it plays in my life? Notice how definite your perspective on the activity feels—how constricted with certainty.
2. Begin the routine/activity. Settle into awareness of the bodily sensations and the sensory aspects of performing it. Do it more slowly than usual if possible in order to better notice the nuances of the routine.
3. Also, notice thoughts, emotional reactions, and judgments about yourself, the activity, and others.

4. Open to what's new and might have been missed about the activity, yourself, others, and anything else. What is here/now that otherwise would have passed you by?

Westerners spend much of their day sitting (not in meditation), hunched over a screen of some variety or another. How often do you walk into a room and find zombified folks sitting next to one another, but eerily smiling and reacting to indicators of digitized social media attention on their devices as opposed to the real humans within arm's reach?

In her remarkable book *Reclaiming Conversation*, the MIT professor Sherry Turkle discusses research pointing to how a quarter of teens in the United States are connected to a device within five minutes of waking up each morning, and most teens send at least one hundred text messages per day.[35] Most alarming to me is Turkle's citing of another scientific finding: over the past twenty years our society has seen a 40 percent decline (most of it occurring over the past decade) in indicators of empathy in people, and researchers are linking this trend with the rise of digital communication technologies. Our devices take us away from the sources of stimulation (e.g., one another, nature, exercise, etc.) that evolution intended for us to find energizing and conducive to well-being. Instead, we fit an electronic straitjacket on our attention, locking ourselves increasingly in our thoughts and mindless ruminating. "Why did she unfriend me on Facebook?" we wonder. "How come that post on Twitter did not get retweeted?" "I haven't posted anything in the last five minutes, so what does that say about me?" From preteens to presidents, we're tethered to electronic technology, which may be draining our own energy.

In the next practice, we take heed of Ajahn Thiradhammo's recommendation that "if you have over-emphasized or over-energized mental activity, it can be very helpful to try to shift awareness to the body."[36]

AN OPEN INVITATION—TRY THIS

SNAPPing Your Fingers at Sluggishness

Let's return to our "universal" opening practice. Try sitting and breathing through a wave of wilting without allowing yourself to tune out altogether or mindlessly stimulate yourself from the outside (à la TV, YouTube, or social media). Are you willing to "surf" the waves of wilting by SNAPPing awake?

1. **S**top as soon as you can after you've noticed the onset of significant dullness or droopiness of the body and mind.
2. **N**otice how wilting is showing up in your body. Take your attention and lightly touch each sensation as if with a feather. Visualize "tickling" each sensation with your awareness—no need to shove at them, just a gentle mental touch. Notice the inner monologues of thought—the "I'm so bored" or "I can't think at all right now" or "I can't handle this"—and again gently come back to the body and tickle any sensations that are present as if they're bubbles floating around inside. Touch (don't stab) them with your feather ever so gently.
3. **A**llow the bodily sensations to flow in and through you just as they are. You may not like them, but are you willing to just watch them? Even though the "weight" of the wilting may increase, are you willing to stay with it a bit longer than is your habit, noticing and giving the sensations permission to manifest just as they are?
4. **P**enetrate down through the sensations with one or more slow, deep belly breaths. You're not forcing the feelings of wilting away with the breath, but instead you're breathing space in and around them. You're loosening and lightening that heavy, drooping set of sensations.
5. **P**rompt your awareness toward self-kindness for the effort you've placed into riding the current of this wilting, even if you feel the need to break away from this practice.

Repeat these steps as much as you're willing until you experience the changes in the manifestation of sloth and torpor. What have you learned as you SNAPPed awake, if only for a few seconds?

In his *Book of Virtues*,[37] the colonial-era patriot and wit Benjamin Franklin suggested we each benefit from cultivating specific positive character attributes. (He suggested thirteen, including qualities like silence, order, resolution, and industry.) He even recommended we (and did so himself as a young twenty-something) keep a daily record of our progress in avoiding "slips," or violations of each of these.

As a psychologist, I love the idea of monitoring things oneself (and recommend you do so as well in your journal—using one yet?). This is where curiosity cultivation can be so useful. Instead of beating yourself up for yet again doing the karmic hindering dance that steps on your life's toes, you can get curious about how you might open up and investigate your moment-to-moment experience and do things that matter despite the chaos, uncertainty, or—for our purposes in this chapter—the wilting of the moment.

One of Franklin's virtues—in fact the first on his list—was temperance. He advised that we "eat not to dullness; drink not to elevation." So here are multiple hindrances in the crosshairs of your consciousness—desire/wanting and dullness/wilting. When we eat, drink, use, peruse, and primp or in any way consume to excess, we are facilitating imbalance and a hindrance-fest for ourselves. The Buddha admonished all his followers to remember to find the "middle way" forward. Though he was most certainly not a Buddhist, Ben Franklin appears to have valued a similar pragmatic, experientially focused middle-of-the-road approach to self-management in life.

With the practices in this section, hopefully you've renewed a sense of energetic curiosity in your experience of sloth and torpor. Curiosity may have killed cats, but it saves us from falling asleep within our deepest selves by perking us up to the novelties of a given moment. Take the breathing we did in these practices—the point is to go beyond breathing as usual and learn to see the breath as the dynamic, always-available tool for exploration that it truly is. The breath should ideally be regarded "as something we're studying and investigating versus something rote we're doing."[38] Curiosity can help us find the truth in our "sleepy" selves.

Bedar, the Watchman, caught the Mulla Nasrudin prying open the window of his own bedroom from the outside, in the depths of night.

"What are you doing, Nasrudin? Locked out?"

"Hush! They say I walk in my sleep. I am trying to surprise myself and find out."

Now that we've rested in acceptance of wilting (hopefully without immediately nodding off on a client), and now that we've unearthed insight into how we've developed habit patterns of closing our eyes and hearts, we can work to more skillfully address the causes of this hindrance. In particular, we can take our increased understanding and do things internally in our experience and externally in our actions to generate and notice changes in our patterns of wilting across time and learn to let go of the self-protective armor that weighs us down. Remember, there are times when it's perfectly OK to lie down and take a well-earned nap. Learning to distinguish these times of self-care from the times when you're wilting due to avoidance is the key skill from this first section. Now that we see this hindering pattern more clearly, we'll move toward some habit change by working with our experience of time itself.

Opening to Wilting by Rip Van Winking at Time and Impermanence

For centuries in Japan, Shinto practitioners have engaged in a purification ritual called *misogi*, which involved dousing oneself in sacred (often very cold) waters. Legend has it that samurai warriors would use this method on occasion to enliven their body and spirit prior to battle. Though I've never traveled to Kyoto to dip myself in the frigid waters of Kiyomizu Temple's "Sound of Wings" waterfall, I have tried a "samurai shower" in my less-than-sacred bathroom at home on occasion.

What I noticed from such frigid dousings is an immediate shift in my experience of energy in body and mind. And if I'm aware and watching, I also notice how this jolt to my system ripples out and opens me up in the hours that follow. Joseph Goldstein writes, "The great power of mindfulness here, as with desire or anger, is that we can be with all these states when they arise, and when we can stay aware of them until they disappear."[39]

Here, we escalate our practice with sloth and torpor by moving from mere watching (acceptance) of how this hindrance shows up in our experience to now actively intervening with our wilting. And here's where the Western mind gets a bit more interested. "Finally, we're doing more than this passive meditation stuff," it says. "Now we're *doing* something!"

True, and yet it's an escalation because we're not just going to mindlessly intervene (as with, for example, energy drinks, coffee, or cigarettes); we're doing specific, healthy things *and* maintaining the watching, noticing, mindfulness we've been practicing throughout this book. It's a powerful combination. Particularly when the wilting within our body-mind is on the mild side, it can help to give our systems a nudge toward more energy.

There are no diets or workouts or ultimately even practices for transcending the hindrances, including sloth and torpor. It boils down to a fundamental shift in awareness—a mind-set of opening versus closing. And when we see ourselves and the world with open eyes, we see the unshakable truth of certain changes to our daily habits around the intake and output of energy.

You have endless book and online options elsewhere around the energetics of nutrition, yet with the wilting body-mind, it bears repeating the following:

- Eat and drink libation in moderation (think Ben Franklin's virtues).
- Avoid processed and fried foods as well as high fat (particularly trans fat).
- Eat whole grains and healthy sources of protein (leafy greens, nuts, legumes).
- Have minimal consumption of sugar, caffeine (this one hits home for me), and red meat.
- Increase your intake of water and fruit/vegetables.
- Slow down and eat with a modicum of mindfulness in order to allow your biological messages of fullness to catch up to your greedy mouth.

Yes, yes, you're thinking. *I know this.* And yet, are you (author included) deeply seeing the mindless, reactive consuming you're doing? Note that I didn't cite any nutrition experts for the reminders above. They are so often repeated in the online, print, and television media that they are right at the ready as I type out this chapter. We know these facts but don't consciously install them, via experience, into lived, embodied wisdom.

Energy (including the energy of pain) wants to move freely through our body-mind system, and when we pack in so much gunk, it's no wonder energy gets trapped and we find ourselves prone to serious wilting. And for God's sake do we all need to move more! The average American sits and watches an average of 19.6 hours of TV per week, and this follows an average of eight hours of sitting at the office per day.[40] The fact that many of us have a natural slump due to our hunching over computers, and based on how the term "text claw" has made its way into the lexicon (it's that ubiquitous smartphone-texting hand posture), it's time for us to put down the screens, stand up, and give energy a chance to move through us.

Our bodies are built for movement, yet our societal context and years of conditioning call for us to wilt into sofas and video-gaming chairs. I'm going to stop short of venturing specific intensive physical movement practices or exercises (I'd prefer to avoid the liability lawsuits), but please don't take the brevity of this section as a commentary on the amount of your waking life that should ideally be dedicated to moving your derriere.[41]

Join a kung fu class. (I'll join you.) Take up Zumba. Walk the dog less for the excretory necessity of doing so and more for your own energetic dewilting. Stand up from your desk at regular intervals, and drop to the carpet and burpee all over the place! Hurdle jumping is contagious and so worry less about how you look to others, and know that your example will perhaps help others get their energy (what the Chinese traditionally refer to as qi) flowing as well. Challenge yourself to move throughout the day, break up your sedentary habits, and find yourself stimulated with a more steady flow of energy. Cue yourself to mix it up with movement and exercise with reminders on your phone (finally a healthy use for it!) and the strategic placement of fitness equipment around your office and home. Make it harder for movement opportunities to recede to the dank corners of your basement or garage. To be frank, you need to "goose" yourself into a steady energetic state. In fact, let's use the practice below as a cue to get energy moving.

AN OPEN INVITATION—TRY THIS

PINCH Me

With this set of practices, we can remember to experiment with different methods for perking ourselves up. This is more than what you get from an energy drink, however; this is an opportunity to intervene in one's energy system and notice changes that occur from one moment to the next. Instead of a mere jolt, you're also jotting a mental note of what happens to the body-mind when a bit of nudging is applied.

1. **P**ull gently (but not too gently!) at your earlobes. Pinch and hold them for five to ten seconds, and pay attention to what happens to the sensations there and in other parts of your body when you do so.

2. **I**nvestigate sensations that show up in specific areas of the body as if you're peering into them with the focus and intensity of a powerful microscope. What are the nuances and minute details of each sensation? Give your earlobes another pinch and pay close attention to the rise, apex, and fall of feeling there. What's happening to your degree of open awareness versus wilting and sluggishness?

3. **N**ap! By all means, if it's possible where you are, lean back (or slump forward if you're at a desk) and take a quick nap. Do so! As we've discussed, this is crucial when driving long distances, but it's also quite helpful to set at timer for fifteen or twenty minutes and let your brain do what it needs to do to power up a bit. There's no shame in doing so; just make sure you're not drooling on that crucial report on your desk!

4. **C**hant it up. You don't need to be a monastic (or even deign to play one on TV) to reap the benefits of chanting aloud if the situation permits. Without being concerned about hitting the right notes or saying the "right" or "spiritual" words, try one of the classics, like the Tibetan OM MANI PADME HUNG. What's good about this mantra is that it's conducive to notes that vibrate in your body—which might (particularly if you're paying attention) stimulate your system toward a parting of your mental fog. For God's sake, try chanting my last name if you want—it doesn't really matter what the word is (though the latter suggestion would be great subconscious marketing for yours truly!). For stimulation's sake, try chanting words that lead to either inspiration or perspiration. (Think children, diplomas, mother-in-laws, legal proceedings, and bosses, and you'll catch my drift—I'll let you sort these into categories.)

5. **H**op over habits of sluggishness with movement. Get up and move about in nonroutine ways. Don't stroll in your habitual fashion or stretch in the way you always do. Try shaking it out, as if your body were a live wire or a puppet being trounced by a hyperactive child holding your strings. Do

some burpees or make like you're Bruce Lee around your office or living room. (Use common sense as to office or romantic mates in the vicinity.)

The obvious point with these PINCH suggestions is to spark energy into your body-mind. But again, don't just do so blindly. Light the lamp of your attention to these actions as much as you can so that you bear witness to the changes and brighten your awareness in the process.

The Buddha told his adherents that increased understanding of the essential decaying nature of all things is helpful in avoiding the conditions of sloth and torpor.[42] "In a monk who is accustomed to see the suffering in impermanence and who is frequently engaged in this contemplation, there will be established in him such a keen sense of the danger of laziness, idleness, lassitude, indolence and thoughtfulness, as if he were threatened by a murderer with drawn sword."[43]

When our sense of urgency for the short span of our lives is kindled, we find ourselves increasingly aware of the variables that dim our access to as much awareness and engagement in life as we can muster. Who—save the Long John Silvers, Zorros, and musketeers of the world—wants to be prodded by a drawn sword? So with the next practice, consider yourself "on guard" and perhaps a bit stoked toward an uptick of awareness via our essential transience of being.

AN OPEN INVITATION—TRY THIS

Eulogy Mine-ing

As odd (and macabre) as it may seem, see what happens if you take some time and actually visualize your own (eventual/inevitable) headstone or grave marker. Instead of the usual (and wilting-conducive) surname and dates of your life entry and exit, imagine that the stone is etched with words that summarize what you would most deeply wish your eulogy to have reflected. Spend some time journaling as if you were "mine-ing" down deep for the core qualities representing your life. Instead of simple achievements, you will likely end up with words and phrases gravitating toward things such as love, creativity, commitment, courage, showing up, friendship, and so forth. Attach names of key people and places you've been that call up these qualities in a visceral way.

In a session of meditation, sit and visualize these words carved into the stone marker of your life. Watch what happens to the flow of energy and thought through your system. Feel your headstone and the impact of its etchings on your sense of urgency and engagement with the life of this very moment.

Stand up and do something that manifests one or more of the words on your headstone (except the death date of course).

In the traditional Pali canon, monastics were advised of six methods for sidestepping sloth and torpor and its diminishing impact on progress as a meditator.[44] You don't have to be a Buddhist monk to benefit from these reminders. Whether formally meditating or not, when the mind is wilting, it may help stabilize your energy to peruse this list and make necessary adjustments. Consider this a "preflight checklist" of sorts, similar to what airline pilots use before takeoff. You know where I'm going with that analogy, so instead of me embarrassing myself (and perhaps sparking a condition of pun-induced wilting in you), I won't drone on about how checklists help planes take off more efficiently. I won't inundate you with associations to the efficiency, diligence, and friendly sky flying of professional pilots who are careful to consistently tick off their to-do lists.

No, I won't bore you, but pilots and I are not the only ones who like lists—the Buddha is famous for them. Here's his list of how to prevent and address sloth and torpor:

- Knowing that overeating is a cause of it
- Changing the bodily posture
- Thinking of the perception of light
- Staying in the open air
- "Noble friendship"
- "Suitable conversation"

Here's a helpful mnemonic device for you to use whenever the mind is sagging:

AN OPEN INVITATION—TRY THIS

Say PLEASE

1. **P**osture: Are you slouching or going rigid in a way that's sapping your vitality and making your body an inefficient conductor of energy? Sit or stand upright (without going rigid) and notice the immediate shift in your experience.

2. **L**ight: Part a curtain, open a blind or go for a quick walk outside. Just don't stare at the sun! It will wake you up, but will lead to an unnecessary ophthalmology appointment.

3. **E**ating: There are many resources and endless online guidance for this life domain, but suffice it to say you should be aiming for the "middle way" on your plate . . . Eat as if you're Goldilocks (both in terms of volume, speed, and nature of the food itself) and you'll find yourself less likely to wilt away from awareness.

4. **A**ir: Consider getting some fresh air outside. Maybe try some conscious, energy breathing (see "Firing Up the Breath" practice below).

5. **S**upport system: You are who you spend time with. Who are those you name as friends, and what inputs do they provide your system with that impact your energy and levels of openness to what's happening? Insert yourself into situations of true friendship and positive support.

6. **E**ngagement: And don't just stand there with these "noble" folks—look for avenues to offer and receive interaction, conversation with them that fuels, rather than depletes you. Offer and receive what inspires, and walk away from what deflates.

In addition to the above, it goes without saying (though I'm doing it, just like I did around nutrition) that it's advisable for each of us to attend to our sleep patterns. (I've always found the term "hygiene" strange regarding sleep—it always cues me to floss my teeth, which on the nights I've neglected to do so only adds to my restless to-do list, further damning my sleep prospects.)

Instead of a recitation of the standard sleep improvement tips, I'll offer instead a nudge in the direction of habit patterns I myself have found useful. Again, our society is brimming with stimulation. Our minds become so restlessly, greedily, or angrily jammed up (à la other hindrances); we find ourselves unable to let go into the restful sleep we need for energy in the day to come.

Try ending each day with one minute of journaling. Write the words "What went well?" on the top of your journal page (or the back of a receipt—it doesn't matter), and etch out the mundane to magnificent aspects of your day for which you can nudge your consciousness with an inner echo of gratitude. Much of our daily life is spent in routine, reflex, and conditioned neutrality. And yet we breathe, we move about, we influence and are influenced, and we (dare I say) are aware—there's nothing mundane in that when the actual odds against these facts are apprehended.

So much comes and goes in every minute of our daily life, much of it unnoticed. To open into habits of leaping the hurdles to happiness is to increasingly not just find the devil in the details, but to let him poke the hell out of you and find yourself vibrating with energetic awareness. And if you're not noticing much change in the moment you're currently in, try doing the following breathing practice. I challenge you to remain mired in the mundane!

AN OPEN INVITATION—TRY THIS

Firing Up the Breath

1. Sit upright and comfortably.
2. Take a deep breath, inhaling through the nose, letting the breath fill and expand the belly. Exhale through the nose, and as you do, pull your belly in toward the spine until all the air is expelled.
3. Inhale once more, and exhale approximately half of the air from your lungs, and then quickly exhale the rest with a snort. As you exhale, pull the belly in again toward the spine. Keep the belly relaxed.
4. Continue inhaling and exhaling without pausing. Breathe steadily and at an even pace (at about one cycle of inhalation/exhalation per second), pulling the belly in toward the spine on the exhale, in order for it to act like a bellows, expelling the air. Let the belly out with each inhale in order to fill the lungs with air again.
5. Rest your attention on the breathing, returning after any mind wandering.

6. Aim initially for thirty seconds to a minute of breathing in this way, expanding out to two or three minutes with practice.
7. Notice how you feel immediately after and how your energetic state has shifted.

Note: If you become dizzy/light-headed, stop the practice. Be sure to consult with medical practitioners if this happens with any frequency or intensity in case this practice is contraindicated for you.

You've looked for and prompted changes in your body and mind to awaken energy. Now let's see how wilting comes from the illusion of separation—of there being a "me" that is distinct from the world we live in, others around us, and the situations at hand. When we see ourselves as solid, separate, and in "possession" of our lives, we weigh ourselves down and prompt future wilting to arise.

Opening to Wilting: Clarity Regarding Our "Nonselfness"

In the last section's eulogy activity, you may have had a rude awakening of sorts. The urgency of our death goes from being a faintly acknowledged fact—a sort of quiet whisper of our own eventual undoing—to a current-moment, intensely felt experience. It is this urgency of our limited time (and its constant passing) that can help bring us into more direct contact with the values and activities that are most central in our lives. Faced with our headstone, we're also staring directly into the illusion that the "me" we tried to prop up for as many years as possible is not really the "I" we thought we saw with. In the light of open awareness, we can perk up from our conditioned wilting and see through the illusion of separation and walk forward with more meaningful, enlivened steps.

The master had preached for many years that life was but an illusion. Then, when his son died, he wept. His students came to him and said, "Master, how can you weep so when you have told us so many times that all things in this life are an illusion?"

"Yes," said the master, wiping away his tears while they continued to course down his cheeks, "but he was such a beautiful illusion!"[45]

Your "energy level" is not your own. By buying into the illusion that it's "yours," you end up wasting energy in shoring up your make-believe boundaries of "me / not mine," which could be flowing more freely into others and creative, productive outlets. It's like dumping billions of energetic dollars on building walls on fantasy borders to keep out the bad hombres, when you could have been investing in opening up to compassion, connection, and creative impact with others (including the hombres).

Let's try another practice for loosening our bondage to the ultimate addiction—the selfhood we cling to and that wears us out and wilts us away into mindlessness.

AN OPEN INVITATION—TRY THIS

The Ultimate Inquiry

For this practice, I will use fewer words and direct you to your experience (instead of your thinking mind). Enter and open slowly to each question. Do not "think" for answers—feel them. Witness the answers arising in your direct experience. Do not move to the next question until you've experienced the previous fully.

1. What is here? (Include all sensations, images, verbal thoughts.)
2. When is it?
3. (Answer with eyes closed.) Where is it in the body?
4. Is it? How do you know with eyes closed? (Other than via flickerings of sensation or memory.)
5. What is here now?
6. And now?
7. And now?

Realize deeply, fully: there is no "where," no "who," not even a "when."

There's just *this*.

Rest in this. Watch this. You *are* this.

In many mindfulness talks I give, I often show a brief video clip called "What Is a Moment?" put together by the director William Hoffman for

WNYC Radio and National Public Radio's Radio Lab initiative.[46] In the clip, the viewer is presented with very brief (two- or three-second) clips of seemingly randomly placed, generally mundane moments from peoples' lives—licking an ice cream cone, someone running after a bus, lovers kissing in Times Square, kids playing kickball, a scalpel making its mark in an operating room—things that happen all over the world at any given moment.

I've shown this clip (and by the way—there's even a segment with someone clipping toenails!) to hundreds of folks. The response is pretty consistent when the video ends. The room is always very quiet. Some people have tears in their eyes. People say that it was "very meaningful" or that "this is what it's all about." Why? What is going on here?

Life is a series of moments. Our minds—our conditioned, patterned inner stories—like to place these moments on a timeline, give them labels, evaluate their worth, and discard the undesirables. And yet, as this video so poignantly presents, these stories are essentially fictions— they are attempts to make our separation and permanency-hungry egos happy. And the stories we tell others (and ourselves) as to what our lives are about often leave us feeling insufficient. They feel stale and fall flat. Certain stories we might ruminate about or traumatic ones we're shoving at can lead us to play defense, our minds dulling and dimming.

No, people have tears in their eyes from watching this video because they are reminded of the truth—that our lives are a series of moments. Regardless of the content, if we thread our life moments consistently with our awareness, we perk up, come awake, and feel as though we're actually living. We are moved when we let go of the story of "me." The puzzle is solved when we toss all the momentary pieces up in the air and let them be unto themselves—the jewels of nonselfishness. As the meditation teacher Rupert Spira indicates, the moments of our lives are like beads of a necklace.[47] And what holds the necklace together? It's not the story, the word-based judgments of the mind. It's our true self—the awareness that pierces each and every moment if we're willing to claim that moment *as* ourselves.

The next activity is adapted from the "mirror time" intervention as described by Michael Mahoney.[48] The goal is to get some distance from the "you" that may be less than palatable—the identity you are less than enamored with and may (on occasion) find yourself dimming out when the world cues its aspects out from the shadows.

AN OPEN INVITATION—TRY THIS

The Most Wakeful One of All

Select a time when you won't be disturbed and place yourself in front of a mirror. (If one is not available, your reflection in a window will do.) With your eyes closed, take a few deep breaths to center and calm yourself. With your eyes still closed, consider an invitation to open to full awareness of yourself—all that you are and have done—effective, ineffective, well intended, and reactively destructive. Are you willing to see what's there? When you're ready, open your eyes.

1. What do you notice as you first look in the mirror? What shows up first and foremost in your thoughts? What is the tenor, the tone, of your feelings?

2. Look gently into your own eyes. What do you see? Notice the thoughts, evaluations, conclusions that emerge. Again, notice the tone of your emotional response.

3. What urges to move, blink, speak, or shift facial expression do you notice? What does your mind do when you notice these? Can you just notice any impulses, seeing if they pass? Notice any urges to distract or wilt away.

4. Allow yourself to close and then reopen your eyes. What shifts? What shows up in your mind? Allow yourself to exaggerate and expand whatever expression you find on your face. What emerges now? How do you regard this extreme?

5. Close your eyes once again. Think of your various daily roles (e.g., family member, partner, colleague, friend, etc.). Consider a recent situation when you felt more than effective and respected—one in which what you did mattered. Open your eyes and look at yourself. What do you notice about this person? What does this individual in the mirror have to say? What happens to your energy level or sense of mental engagement?

6. Close your eyes once more. Think of a recent episode when you felt less than competent and/or rejected or devalued in some way—when you believed your actions were truly unhelpful, if not destructive. Open your eyes and look at yourself. What do you notice about this person? What does this person have to say? Are you willing to let him or her remain? What's happening to your energy and engagement now?

7. With your eyes gently open, take in everything that you've seen and experienced while at the mirror during this activity. Notice how it's all there—the worst and the wonderful. Are you willing to hold it all? Even to embrace it?

8. Consider saying something akin to the following to yourself as you end the exercise: "May I learn to allow all that comes. May I learn to hold both the good and the bad with openness and thereby continue to grow."

Journal about anything that seems important from participating in this exercise. Be on the lookout for evidence of clenched conclusions or judgments about yourself. Watch for emotions you find yourself eager to sidestep, especially the dullness and deadening of your energy.

We are not going to be perfect at leaping over our inner hurdles. When we fall short (and become more hindered and reactive), we may beat ourselves up, thereby benefitting from a dose of self-compassion. And yet, even here, we can slide into a sense of ourselves as "solid" and separate. We can find ourselves wilting away from awareness because we're feeling like "I" deserve to check out for a while. Our wilting, which can look like self-compassion, can really be a disguise because we're not aware of how we're ducking the full brunt of our discomfort with ourselves.

A few years ago, I participated in a daylong silent meditation retreat at a local meditation center. It was a good day of practice, and I left the retreat feeling open, at ease, and energized in general and about my practice of meditation in particular. "I deserved this retreat," I told myself. "It has been stressful, and I needed to focus on my practice," I said. "I needed to get going again with deepening meditation for myself." With all of these sentiments, I'd thoroughly installed a subtle virus in my system that would sap my willingness to stay open to discomfort.

Late that afternoon, I picked up my daughter, Celia, and drove her to an appointment in the Longwood area of Boston—the hospital district renowned for its snarled traffic and pedestrian chaos. We were late for our appointment, and the drive was taking what seemed like forever. A more than familiar restlessness and irritable angst crept up my insides as I gripped the wheel.

"Oh come on!" I yelled when the car in front cut me off brazenly.

We got caught at a stoplight because of some Sir Speedy's selfishness, and I sat as a wave of wilting tugged at me, my mind thickening with increasingly narrowed thoughts.

It was a full multihindrance onslaught, and I was awash in deep karmic conditioning.

The light turned green, yet we weren't going anywhere. More selfish foes had decided to run their own red lights and were now blocking the intersection.

"You've got to be goddamn kidding me!" I yelled.

My daughter, as she'd done before from her beginner's-mind Zen-master's perch from her car seat behind me, interrupted: "Daddy, it won't help to yell because they can't hear you," she said. "The other cars will move when they can. Yelling won't make them move."

This episode in the car, so quick on the heels of my retreat, had seemingly taken a nibble out of my interlude in *nibbana* (the Pali term for nirvana). And yet, there was a lesson here for me that I'm only now in this moment of writing seeing with open clarity. According to Ajahn Thiradhammo, "spiritual practice never lives up to our self-imposed expectations, and holding those expectations usually results in disappointment, discouragement and loss of energy."[49] I had built up my meditation retreat as a means to an end (i.e., "progress" as a meditator) and then felt defeated that a mental-torpor-and-hostility combo attack in the car had agitated and deflated me—and over something as simple as traffic. The wilting was my reactive way of closing down and away from the pain of my unmet expectations for lasting progress as a meditator, as well as the stress I'd been experiencing in my life at the time.

My daughter said it best though when she innocently reminded me that things will move "when they can." We wilt inside when we don't find ourselves marching forward linearly and in lockstep, be it as meditators, hedge-fund managers, or whatever role we find ourselves expecting within.

We must not sink so low as to succumb to postretreat letdowns or some other variant of multihindrance pileups that, in true falling-domino fashion, lead to a wilted, self-protecting (i.e., "self"-affirming) mind. Are we instead willing to open?

Compass Check: Opening to the Wilting Within

Gil Fronsdal points out that "chronic sloth and torpor may represent a lack of meaning or purpose in life."[50] Hopefully, the exercises above cued up some reasons in your life that make exploring and hurdling these hindrances worth it. You don't have to develop the spiritual fervor of a monastic to address the downside of the hindrances in your life. You might, however, benefit from putting increased attention to how you might up the ante as to your life's most meaningful pursuits. The final contemplations of this chapter are meant to help you do just that—and hopefully the energy they provide is a tad more sustaining than a cheap extra shot of espresso in your three-p.m. store-bought coffee.

An Open Invitation: Additional Contemplations for Personal Practice

Below are contemplations for cultivating opening to your experience of conditioned wilting. Try these in the midst of at least a mild episode of mental dullness. See what happens as you experience the *meaning* of these words even while your mind is (for some reason that perhaps your work in this chapter has brought to light) dimming things for you.

ACCEPTANCE IN THE FACE OF WILTING

- Aim small, miss small. What exactly is happening in this mind and body right now? What is the smallest, sharpest, clearest evidence of energy in your body-mind? What happens with the simple, certain, and ongoing watching of it?

WORKING WITH TIME/IMPERMANENCE

- Watch ballet dancers as they rest on pointed toes, and notice the truth of no perpetual balance, but instead an ongoing, skillful balanc*ing*—feet moving rapidly, slightly, microadjusting to the changes in weight and momentum.
- What is excessive in your treatment of your body in recent days, weeks, or even months? How much has wanting or wrestling with your experience been happening unchecked?
- Let go of any self-criticism for, yet again, getting unbalanced, as if perfect ongoing balance were ever really possible.

- Using practices in this chapter, how might you resume an on-going dance of balancing across time and situations?
- Are you willing to stay aware and notice changes?
- The Buddha held out four reminders to practitioners to help create energy and engagement in walking the path of awakening. The last of these is the "preciousness of this human birth"—how incredibly unlikely and rare it is for conditions of matter and the moment to come together such that a human is born (versus a beetle, whether it be the crawling or nostalgic vehicle varieties). Beetles fall short of the capabilities required for awareness, yet human beings have the raw ingredients of awakening at our disposal, though we tend to dispose of them during our short life spans. Consider the truth of this fact for a moment. Consider how privileged this very moment of awareness is. What sounds most important for your next moment—a couch-potato session in your living room in front of the TV or a session of sitting meditation? Even if you're wilting, what happens to your energy level when deeply considering this?

CLARIFYING THE TRUE NATURE OF SELF

- Go outside and watch the sky. Day or night, it doesn't really matter. How "awake" is it? No matter the weather, how's the sky doing in "holding" all of it? As you look with wonder and curiosity, how awake are *you*? No matter the wilting showing up in this moment (or whatever else is here/now), how are you doing holding it all? Are you weather or sky? What happens to the wilting when regarded in this way?

There was once a Zen master who was much feared for his harsh manner of teaching. One day, one of his students, while striking the time of day on the temple gong, missed a beat because he'd become drowsy and distracted. Unbeknownst to the student, the master was standing behind him and struck him with his staff. The shock of the blow stopped the student's heart and he died.

"Surely this master is cruel and should be punished," said one of the townsfolk. "He killed his disciple."

"Perhaps there's another perspective," said another. "Perhaps the master noted how his student had lost his wakefulness and seized the opportunity to usher his pupil into awakening just prior to the moment of death."

Would that we all had such a master behind us willing to do what is necessary (despite likely manslaughter charges) to restore us to alertness at the greatest moment of opportunity.

CLOSING INQUIRY

What might happen if, the next time you felt yourself sagging, you allowed yourself to briefly "close"—to withdraw, glaze over, doodle on your notepaper, or even begin drifting off to sleep? And, like Joseph Goldstein did during long meditation retreats, intentionally come sitting upright again just after you'd allowed that briefest "indulgence" of wilting? What might you learn in such moments of opening when the mind, out of long habit, assumes a complete wilting is in store? Are you willing to practice a rapid close and open?

6 Worrywarts

Restlessness and Leaping Forward

Does all your worrying about the future and beating yourself up over the past ever, in and of itself, open things up in your life in the here and now?

I was in graduate school when I happened upon a flyer for a literary panel discussion that was to feature some lions of the literary world— among them novelist Kurt Vonnegut (one of my absolute favorites). I sat in the auditorium and listened to the discussion with great interest (at the time, I had my own fantasies of literary greatness), and at the end the moderator allowed members of the audience with burning questions to approach microphones set up in the aisles.

An awkward-looking English Department grad student walked up to the microphone. *I'm way better than him*, I told myself. I knew I could write him into the ground.

"I have a question for you, Mr. Vonnegut," he stammered, clearly nervous. "I've admired your writing for years, and I also want to write satirical novels like yours," he said. The poor guy was embarrassing himself. No one could write like Vonnegut—especially satire. I settled back into my chair with smug satisfaction. "I was wondering if you might have any advice for me as I move forward."

No question in there anywhere. I felt a wave of condescension for my long-haired friend—this collie of a creative writing student who pushed his glasses up on his nose while waiting for Vonnegut's reply. I wished for a power outage. Maybe someone would faint. Perhaps a fire alarm would rip the room and relieve this guy of further humiliation.

Kurt Vonnegut sat forward slowly. He was thin and looked like he might break in half if he came forward too quickly to the microphone sitting on the table in front of him. He smiled at the young man, but only a bit. He knew something very powerful, very deep that we could all benefit from. We all waited for his wise, lengthy description of what it took to become truly great as a writer.

"You will fail," he said. And that was it. He sat back and waited for the moderator to move things along.

I couldn't have agreed with Vonnegut more. That guy would surely fail. Me? No way—I would follow my restless itch to leave graduate school (I had already dropped out of law school prior to entering training to become a psychologist) and head on over to a doctoral program in creative writing and stake my claim on future literary glory.

There seemed to be multiple aspects to my restless struggling at the time and through much of my childhood and into my adult years. They include:

- Physical and mental agitation / excessive energy
- Excessive worrying about the future
- Excessive remorse over past wrongs

In traditional Buddhist texts, the hindrance of restlessness is referred to in Pali as *uddhacca*, which translates as "to shake"[1] and is generally experienced by most of us as having both psychological and physical aspects. It's that "jumping out of the skin" feeling—that uncomfortable, antsy, gotta-be-elsewhere-and-other-than-this urge that whips up the mind and body and prompts all manner of ducking-and-covering maneuvers, be they too many coffee breaks or too many relationship breakups.

The future-leaning, worrying aspect of restlessness is not all bad, nor is remorse (*kukkucca* in Pali). Both aspects can prompt us to take stock of our actions and life situation. They can give us a psychophysiological flick toward taking corrective, repairing action or planned, artful dodging of perils to come. In these senses, a certain amount of restlessness is helpful—it's a major component of our in-the-moment motivation for healthy change.

The problem is when restlessness overwhelms and blocks us. The Buddha spoke of a pool of water (representing the mind), with restlessness being the whipped-up waters leading to muddiness, which inhibit clearly seeing to the bottom.[2] When restlessness gets this wild inside us, we don't see ourselves or the world accurately. We distort and react in order to stave off this internal "shaking," and we are hindered in our ability to relax into our essential being. We have a harder time focusing, and our efficiency in daily life takes a hit. Our brains juice up with the stress hormone cortisol in an ancient attempt at reducing threat, and we're left feeling drained and depleted.

Imagine yourself on a bus, and you're late for an important meeting. This bus route is new to you, and there are a lot of stops, and it's getting increasingly crowded. It seems like you are inching forward and that walking might get you there faster.

You call up to the driver and ask how many more stops until you reach yours. He says not to worry, that your stop is only three more ahead. And yet, you find your thoughts (and blood pressure) amping up even more when the driver waits for an elderly man to amble very slowly up into the bus.

"How much longer till we're there?" you ask. "I can't miss my meeting."

This time, the driver just glances at you in his rearview mirror without saying anything. The passenger next to you says, "We all have somewhere to be you know."

Your thoughts race faster, and your pulse is palpable at your temples. Sweat is making its way out in all the usual places.

And now imagine that this bus is whatever "vehicle" you're in during a given day that is not yours to drive, to control. It's most every situation you're in—the contexts where you are much more passenger than driver—and you're just along for the ride.

How much does your increasing blood pressure and rush of thoughts actually move the "bus" any faster? Get you there any sooner?

And now imagine that you're trying to meditate on this bus. Consider the all-too-common experience in meditation wherein you're hoping to "get somewhere" with your sitting—perhaps, dare I say, to that end-of-the-samsaric-line depot called "enlightenment." Or maybe your meditation is a cacophony of monkey-on-methamphetamine thoughts and images. These are the sits when your eye pops open to check the clock, timer, or some evidence of sweet relief from the angst.

The meditation teacher Gil Fronsdal referred to this (and all) the hindrances as "like wandering through a maze staring at the ground. Being mindful is like standing above the maze to get an overview."[3] Thus the goal of this chapter: to give a sense not only of what restlessness is from both the Buddhist and scientific perspectives, but also what one might do in daily life to help the pond to settle, to nudge corrective and skillful responses that come from a clear view of one's true reflection. You don't need to have full-blown panic attacks for restlessness to get in the way. You need only not want to have the angsty energy bouncing around in mind and body, and you are, for all intents and purposes, hindered.

Ants in Our Pants: Why It's Hard to Stay Put

If there's a hindrance requiring clarity of view (from both contemplative and scientific perspectives), restlessness may be it. According to the meditation teacher Joseph Goldstein, restlessness arises when we're less than wise about our habits of consumption—what we allow into our minds and bodies.[4]

I (and likely you) find myself represented in data reported by the Pew Research Center regarding the use of mobile technology.[5]

- 67 percent of cell owners check their phone for messages and alerts even when the phone is not alerting them.
- 44 percent of cell owners sleep with their phone next to the bed so they don't miss out on the next dollop of dopamine in the brain from receiving the "ding" of a new text or e-mail.
- 71 percent of teens use more than one social networking site.

Though I can claim ignorance around things like Instagram or Snapchat, I also find myself among the 50 percent of the population who have taken a selfie. From that mundane arm's-reach shot of you, a friend, and the sunset at the beach to a famous actor's celebrity-crammed Oscars

pic, selfies and the phones we're addicted to remind us of our fundamental modern challenge in being OK without constant stimulation—of
staying with our experience, particularly when it's uncomfortable.

Traditionally, Buddhism refers to various "personality types"—patterns of conditioned responses to pleasant, unpleasant, and neutral
aspects of our environments.[6] One of these is the "delusional" type, and
while it does not refer to a psychotic disconnection from reality, it does
refer to folks with a confused and easily distracted disposition. It appears
that the delusional personality has restlessness as its hindering cousin
and in a modern context might most closely map with the widely known
(and increasingly diagnosed) attention deficit hyperactivity disorder
(ADHD).

According to the Centers for Disease Control and Prevention, the
percentage of children with an ADHD diagnosis continues to increase,
from 7.8 percent in 2003 to 9.5 percent in 2007 and to 11.0 percent
in 2011.[7] While there may be multiple reasons for this increase (e.g.,
true increase in prevalence of ADHD in the population, increased accuracy of diagnostic procedures, and/or increased societal focus on the
condition), the data (and my own restless iPhone checking) must lead
us to ask whether we are a society suffering in the midst of a restlessness epidemic. ADHD may indeed have a genetic predisposition, but
the ways in which we condition ourselves through our lifestyle choices
and technology use may be contributing to our essential antsiness and
anxious distractibility.

In *The Path of Purification*, the Buddha describes restlessness as having
the "characteristic of disquiet, like water whipped by the wind. Its function is unsteadiness, like a flag or banner whipped by the wind. It is
manifested as turmoil, like ashes flung up by pelting with stones."[8] This
latter image is particularly gripping. Nothing says "I need a change of
scenery" like whipping up sparks by chucking rocks into a campfire.
The Pali canon suggests that the primary cause of this agitation of the
body-mind is frequently giving attention to unsettledness of mind
(*avupasantacittassa*).[9] We "nourish" restlessness by giving unwise attention
to it when it's present, and we therefore make it more likely it will pop
up again in the future.

Research data are increasingly clear on this latter point. Rumination
(or repetitive and passive thinking about negative emotions) has been

shown to predict the chronic nature of depressive disorders as well as anxiety symptoms.[10] Another study showed that people who show a ruminative style of responding to being in a low mood were more likely to later show higher levels of depression symptoms in kids and adults.[11]

As a clinician, I've been trained to spot and address the unhealthy mental habit of repetitive and negatively toned inner chatter that broils our minds and bodies from the inside. And it's not just my patients who ruminate—it's me (hypothetically) telling myself over and over that I'm an "absolute failure" as a therapist for getting sidelined by selfish day-dreaming during a session or eviscerating a future version of myself based on a minor faux pas at a dinner party. Rumination is the run-on self-talk of the mind that has agitated energy as both its fuel and its output. Ruminative worry and remorse are toxic to our well-being and clarity of mind.

And research suggests part of the path forward relative to this aspect of restlessness. In a 2010 study examining the levels of reported self-compassion, rumination, worry, anxiety, and depression in 271 nonclinical undergraduate students, results suggested that people with higher levels of reported self-compassion are less likely to report depression and anxiety.[12] The data showed that self-compassion may play the role of buffering the effects of rumination. In some of the practices that follow in this chapter, we learn how to unhook from rumination and cut our-selves (and others) the slack requisite for increasing clarity and ease of being.

In addition to self-compassion, what the restless mind needs is a counterbalance to its imbalanced and excessive energy. In Buddhism, the antidote to restlessness as a hindrance to awareness in one's med-itation practice is to cultivate three specific factors of enlightenment: concentration, tranquility, and equanimity.[13] When we build these com-plementary muscles of concentrative focus, inner calm, and virtuous action without an agenda, restlessness abates and clarity naturally emerges. We see our accurate reflection in the still, clear waters.

It should be fairly obvious that when we don't care well for our bodies by not sleeping, eating, or moving our bodies adequately, these create energy imbalances that lead to restlessness. Similarly, when we behave unethically, these actions stir our minds and bodies with the muddy raw ingredients of remorse. When our parents told us to "clean up our act" as teenagers (or as adults), they were not just making an offhand swipe at our misdeeds; they were (likely unintentionally) taking aim at the very heart of our well-being.

As Gil Fronsdal points out in his book *Unhindered*, restlessness links to all the other hindrances.[14] If our loves are unrequited (i.e., desire frustrated), then restlessness can arise. If we suppress (and ruminate about) our pent-up rage for that guy Dave from two towns over who stole the (hypothetical) girl's heart from us in fifth grade, then restlessness comes to the fore. Understanding how restlessness manifests for us as individuals and what might be causing it can be key to informing skillful practice responses in order to sidestep further unhelpful karma.

Restlessness is the "check engine light" on our psychophysiological dashboard. It lets us know the system is out of whack and that it needs some balancing. Agitation is therefore not our enemy; ideally, we see it as a wake-up call and mindfulness bell for practice. It asks us to either get busy opening up or get busy closing down.

As the Taoist scholar Solala Towler relays the tale, things had gone from bad to worse for the ancient emperor.[15] It seemed that no matter how the emperor ruled, things turned out badly. Famine, war, conflict in the royal household—nothing was going right. Many of the people began gossiping that perhaps the emperor had lost the gods' favor.

The emperor became impatient because none of his aides or advisors were of any help. He was desperate to arrive at a workable path forward for his kingdom. The future seemed bleak. The emperor traveled far into the mountains and met with a great sage. All else had failed, so the emperor had nothing to lose by taking the master's counsel.

The sage ignored the emperor for quite a long time. The emperor became impatient and frustrated that the old man did not notice him, did not know who he was, or did not care to help. With his mind frenzied with the familiar feel of worry and desperation, the emperor yelled to his aides to prepare the way for a return to the palace. "There's no wisdom to be had here!" he called.

The old sage looked to the emperor. "All I have to teach is what I've learned about managing my own life," he said weakly. "I know nothing of empires and their dominion."

"I don't care about your life," said the emperor. "Don't you realize how much I'm responsible for? How much is at stake with my every decision? The people count on me, and all you have to offer is how I might spend my days sitting alone by a stream in the mountains?"

The sage waited, smiling calmly and silently at the emperor. "I see before me a man full of worry—a man who has shouldered all that is not in his control and has made this burden his prison. How, if your life is in shambles, can you expect to rule an entire country?"

At this, the emperor felt as though a weight had been removed from the inside. Though the responsibilities of his role remained, he somehow held them differently—lightly. It was his nature he needed to rule, not his kingdom. And at that he became the wise ruling emperor destined, at the end of his life, to sit by the side of the Jade Emperor himself.

As a psychologist, I've worked a great deal with parents whose children struggle with significant emotional and behavioral challenges—some who had adopted children out of early living situations of extreme abuse and deprivation. One parent sat with me in my office during one session and, after sharing her stories of her teenage son's angry holes in living room walls and f-bombs exploding without warning around her mother's Thanksgiving table, she looked at me with eyes weighted and wet with restless pain. "This is not what I signed up for," she said after a long pause. "I've done a great deal toward him I'm not proud of, and I'm terrified that he'll end up in prison—I'm trapped."

And in that moment of truth—a crossroads in my work with this mom—I lingered in my own restless angst. I worried I was not up to the task of helping this mother and son. I found myself wondering if they'd be better off with a better therapist. Restlessness can be contagious; the energy passing between us like friction-rendered static sparks at the moment of contact. My patient and I needed practices to help us ride the uncomfortable currents of rumination and bodily clenching and churning. We needed help opening to restlessness and letting it teach us what we in our lives needed in order to more fully open. In the next section, we move forward by practicing how to steady ourselves and ride the uncomfortable yet necessary teaching restlessness brings.

Opening by Abiding the Monkey Business

In addition to what you'll find in sitting meditation practice, if you want to discover your current restlessness status, sign up for a session at a local "float tank" spa (assuming you are in luck and have one in the vicinity). What is a float tank? The more common term for them is "sensory deprivation chamber," and they have evolved into a relatively new spa sensation—literally immersing yourself in highly buoyant, treated water in a chamber that cuts out all light and sound. You effortlessly float, and without the light and sound, you are pretty close to devoid of external stimulation for the thirty to ninety minutes or more you waft your cares away.

I've done it a few times myself and now "hint" to folks that it's always a great gift certificate option for yours truly. Except for my last float (where a small paper cut on my finger led to an annoying burning sensation due to the acidity of the treated water), I've emerged from these sessions feeling as though I'd slept for ten hours. I also was temporarily acutely aware of the subtle sounds and sights around me and the bodily sensations within. Take away our typical sensory gateways, and we suddenly become sensitized to how much we're desensitized by the constant onslaught of stimulation in our daily lives.

The psychiatrist Eric Berne of transactional analysis fame referred to this state as "stimulus hunger" and argued that when sensory apparatus are insufficiently stimulated, human beings experience distress or numbness.[16] More recently, the longtime meditator and Brown University researcher Willoughby Britton has conducted research on the potential hazards for some people pursuing intensive (i.e., long-term retreat) meditation practice.[17] Britton's archival data tells of the rare, but too frequent and intense to be dismissed, negative experiences some have had in which the extremes of quiet and reduced sensory stimulation have perhaps sparked exacerbation or onset of intense anxiety or even psychotic disturbances. Britton's work advises calm amid all the revolutionary fervor about the benefits and apparent "risk-free" qualities of meditation. The restless mind becomes amplified (at least initially) when we take away its food source of external stimulation. For some, the mental wolf can get unruly when left unfed. Those charged with teaching or supporting others in their practice of meditation should be trained to recognize and assist practitioners experiencing the far reaches of restless distress.

According to the author Joseph Goldstein, restlessness is essentially "an imbalance of concentration and energy. Restlessness often comes from an excess of energy and not enough concentration or steadiness of mind to hold it."[18] Whether we've intentionally created "stimulus hunger" for ourselves or not, our restlessness is a sign that our energy is in need of balancing. When we develop and stabilize our skills of concentration, restlessness becomes more manageable. The author, psychologist, and meditation teacher Bill Morgan argues that in meditation "concentration practices . . . have not been emphasized much in the west . . . the ability to stay with unfolding experience in a calm and continuous way. This is the province of concentration, which is the backbone of mindfulness."[19]

Concentration—the ability for attention to remain connected to a chosen object (physical or mental)—and the avenues for cultivating it have filled many volumes, and a comprehensive survey of these is beyond the scope of this book. Suffice it to say, get started if you haven't already with the practices below or others that help your mind learn to (in puppy-in-training fashion) "stay." We may think we already have this skill, which is again a key to sidestepping restlessness, but then again, we likely have room to grow.

The meditation teacher and author Osho relays the following tale of one of the Buddha's monks.[20] The Buddha was staying in the city of Vaishali where the beautiful courtesan Amrapali lived. She was the prostitute of the very rich—the most powerful men in society at the time. One day she was sitting on her terrace when she saw a young man who happened to not only be extremely handsome, but was also a Buddhist monk. She was lovestruck by him and determined to win his heart.

She invited the monk to stay at her house. "I will ask my master," the monk said, and he went to ask the Buddha for his counsel. The Buddha condoned the visit, much to the chagrin and jealousy of the many other monks who were present. "Surely, he will succumb to her," they said.

The Buddha smiled and bid them to consider the eyes of the young monk. "There is no lust in him. I trust in his awareness."

Four months later the monk returned, knelt, and touched the Buddha's feet. Following him was Amrapali, now dressed in Buddhist nun's robes. She too touched the Buddha's feet. "I did all I could to seduce your monk," she said to him. "And it was me who was seduced—by his presence and compassion," she said.

Many Western readers of this book likely default to their "head" rather than their "body" when faced with anxiety about the future or remorse over the past. When I ask audiences at talks to respond to a "stressful" video clip, over 90 percent of the comments are strands of abstractions and conjecture around motivations, conceptualizations, and consequences.

For example, I love to show groups of therapists a specific clip from the classic 1960s movie *Who's Afraid of Virginia Woolf?* In the scene, a drunk, agitated Elizabeth Taylor (who won an Academy Award for her portrayal of a very unhappy wife of a college professor, played by her onetime real-life husband Richard Burton) is unleashing on her husband in a flurry of demeaning, history-laden marital jabs, and Burton ends up smashing his bottle of booze on the mantle in anger. All of this takes place in front of the unwitting young couple who were unlucky enough to have been invited over for dinner. The scene is intense, and I ask workshop participants to imagine they are there in the room at the time. I suggest they imagine that the scene is not occurring in a living room, but in their therapy office. It's a couples or family therapy session. Lucky them to have this case on their roster!

Very few people respond to the prompt "Tell me what's showing up for you after watching this" with comments like "clenching in my gut" or "tension in my jaw." We are well trained (particularly us wordy therapist types) to go "verbal," when it's in our bodies where the deepest truths of our reactions to stressful situations lie. To counter the monkey mind of our bouncing, agitated thoughts about past and future, it can be a crucial skill to learn to drill down with concentration into our direct experience of our bodies. With enough concentration, as Gil Fronsdal suggests, the body can become "a wide container where energy is allowed to bounce around like a ricocheting ping pong ball."[21]

How have you felt about anyone in a position of authority telling you to "just take a breath and calm down"? I'm betting you have less than fond recollections of such individuals in those moments. I don't want to replicate your early history of redirection from parental-figure types (which I'm betting had more to do with *their* hindering patterns than your own). In the practice below, I'm suggesting you render your breathing less as a sledgehammer for your stress and more as an ever-present vehicle for riding into and through your patterns of restlessness. This practice, if done consistently, can build your mental muscle of concentration, and the deep, penetrating breathing can do much to help you ride out periods of restless agitation.

AN OPEN INVITATION—TRY THIS

Penetrating Breaths

1. Begin this practice by acknowledging the mere presence of restlessness—give a soft, slight internal nod to the thoughts, images, and sensations of remorse and/or worry.
2. Rest in sensations of the breath. Let your attention drop gently onto wherever you feel the breath (e.g., nostrils, belly, or perhaps the toes for the more light on their feet).
3. Penetrate the sense of restlessness in both the body and mind on inhale. Visualize the breath coming into and through the restlessness. The breath is not forcing the energy away, but rather it's moving into it.
4. Acknowledge the restlessness just as it is on exhale. Don't try to shove all the energy out with a sigh or exasperated puffing. Note the sensations and word images as if touching them with a feather.
5. Continue following the breath, circulating between penetration into the space of awareness with the in-breath and acknowledging what remains on the exhale.
6. Don't force or control. Just follow the restlessness just as it is, and simply penetrate through it with the breath. Allow awareness to seep into and around these thoughts, sensations, and images.
7. Take inventory of what remains after your allotted meditation time. What is there to be witnessed, felt, acknowledged "behind" the restlessness?

The penetrating breaths practice can be a useful companion on the path of opening to and learning from restlessness. The "remains" of restlessness are perhaps hanging around because there's something powerful to be integrated. Painful emotions linger when they're due the respect of full witnessing. This is why I'm suggesting you "acknowledge" the restlessness. This lets your system know you're willing to respect what may be thumping and call for awareness from below. Ask a mechanic, and he or she will tell you that sometimes a car's knocking is simply a less-than-clean tank of gas or it's your car letting you know that something more egregious is about to explode out the bottom.

The pain of loss, rejection, trauma, and even oblivion itself has a way of finding a voice from underneath restlessness. Sometimes all that's needed for these injuries to heal is our compassionate, unwavering attention. Bringing compassionate awareness to the thoughts and bodily sensations of pain allows them to peacefully pass away.

But what to do if the restlessness is at the extremes? If the anxiety or remorse are flooding through any attempt at penetrating breaths or another concentration practice you've been using? It's here that it may help to break down your practice even further in order to create the footing necessary to get moving into and through this hindrance.

I once had a friend who told me that in the minutes leading up to and during a panic attack, her thoughts became a "tsunami of doom" and her body curdled with nausea. This was no gentle nudge to correct a misstep or to set a phone alert so as not to forget the rent payment. This was a mind ensnared in the extremes of restlessness. My friend needed help for seeing her thoughts, bodily sensations, and the world around her with the open, wide-angle lens of mindfulness.

As a socially anxious college student myself sitting in class, terrified of being called on by my professor, if you'd told me to "gently rest my awareness" on the physical sensations of the fear-sparked knot in my throat, I would have laughed at you. This assumes, of course, I could even squeeze any air out. Mindfulness instructions often suggest for practitioners to place attention on their bodily sensations, to "let go of judgment" and to "rest" or "simply notice" their experiences "just as they are." They often include well-intended reminders like "there's no wrong reaction or experience"—no way to mess meditation up. These kind sentiments can make the practice of mindfulness all the more daunting for those whose anxiety is regularly at fever pitch. According to my patient, "When your body is raging with anxiety, it feels so condescending, and you feel like such a failure when you can't even meditate." The far reaches of anxious restlessness are no mere itch of agitation—it can be a seemingly impassable obstacle to the promised land of calm in meditation.

What my anxiety-stricken friend realized about her mindfulness practice was crucial for her and is a very important point for those who suffer from acute levels of anxiety. What is your *intention* for practicing mindfulness? What she learned is that you can't control or force your way into awareness of anxiety and at the same time access nonjudgmental awareness regarding excruciating restless sensations you are then experiencing in your body. To the degree there is a pressured goal of "making anxiety go away," more likely practitioners will criticize themselves as meditative failures and either write off mindfulness altogether or, worse yet, add to a growing sense of self-loathing.

It is imperative to approach mindfulness with a revised perspective, a renewed intention.

While it's certainly understandable to want to reduce one's restless suffering, it's important to learn to view mindfulness as a process of gradually opening to experience, versus suddenly damming up the flow. Basically, have an intention to be free of the constricting effects of restlessness, but learn to release the immediate agenda for making it be the case in every moment of practice.

Mindfulness practices come closer to the reach of people experiencing extremes of suffering by embedding a dollop of self-compassion, or self-directed kindness, into any meditation practice session. Individuals suffering from acute restlessness (either anxiety or remorse) need help easing into more traditional, formal meditation practices; they need help in recognizing the minisuccesses along the way. People need much more than the unintended condescension to "just let go"—they need the validation of the urgency their extreme distress creates for their mindfulness practice, as well as a structure for accessing practice when pain is most of what they've known.

When mountain climbing, it is crucial to anchor your rope as you ascend a sheer rock face—to literally secure yourself as you inch upward with a successive series of stakes or bolts. Those climbing through episodes of anxious suffering need an anchoring structure as well.

Instead of just launching into thirty minutes of mindfulness of the breath, it can help to create a series of self-compassionate anchors as you practice. Such a structure can help create the space for noticing gradual progress and can help minimize the self-berating banter so common for those whose extreme restlessness seems to place meditation out of reach.

AN OPEN INVITATION—TRY THIS

A Practice for Acute Restlessness

1. Sit upright in as comfortable a position as possible. The eyes can be open or closed—whichever is more comfortable.
2. Silently begin with a recognition of the reality of restlessness. Make the words your own, but quietly say something like: "I've suffered a great deal. This pain is real and intense." Place your attention on the words, and repeat them quietly a few times.
3. Place your attention on a single breath. Feel the air coming in, and feel it leave the body.
4. Silently repeat the phrase above and consider adding the following: "In this discomfort, I'm caring for myself."
5. Now try placing your attention on two full cycles of the breath, feeling the sensations of the air coming and going.
6. Add the following self-compassion anchor: "This is hard, and right now I'm giving myself permission to understand that."
7. Expand the practice out to mindfulness of three to five cycles of breath.
8. Say to yourself: "Though the pain continues, may my practice and care for myself continue as well."
9. Continue in this way, allowing self-compassion to anchor your practice of mindfulness. Let it be a scaffold on which to stand in self-acceptance, and let it help you disarm the inner voice of criticism and failure.

And yet, sometimes restless energy is not some neglected, forlorn chronic pain. Sometimes it's just a high-fat burger and fries having its way with you. When this is the case (which sometimes requires some patient and penetrating breath witnessing to discern the difference), you might try some simple adjustments. For example, we can simply try opening our eyes when lost in the feverish flow of thought. I think this is wise whether one is formally meditating or meandering down a busy sidewalk (particularly in the latter circumstance, with respect to speeding buses, taxis, etc.). Open up to awareness of more than just the vibrating, restless energy of body and sensation. There's always more to be had than the hindered mind would have be so.

When the mind is swirling with restless, agitated energy, it can be very helpful to shift out of your thinking and mentalizing and direct and express energy in your body. Taking a brief detour into mindful movement can help settle the energy of the mind and allow for more clarity in the mind. In addition (particularly during periods when the agitation is particularly strong), making physical movement the exclusive focus of your mindfulness practice is a wise choice. Whether for five seconds or five months, moving into the body when restlessness is prevalent will do much to open you beyond the constraints of this hindrance.

We all have an amazing mental "zoom lens" like that of a camera. Though our capacity for thinking into the past and future is often the source of our suffering, if we wield this power wisely, we can direct our attention to zoom in on a particular object (like the breath) or out toward "what else" is there inside and outside our bodies that might help us relate to restlessness more skillfully.

Jack Kornfield relays the tale of a monk who struggled to adjust his lens to accurately see outside of his expectation and deeply into what was right there in the moment:[22]

A young Zen monk and his master were strolling through the gardens of the monastery. Though he had practiced ardently, the young man still had not come to any deep understanding of Zen. Finally he turned to the master and asked, "Please, master, tell me something of this enlightenment."

The master pointed. "See that bamboo over there? See how short it is?"

The monk replied, "Yes."

"See that bamboo over there? See how tall it is?"

And the monk replied, "Yes."

And the master said, "Just that is enlightenment."

With our amazing mental apparatus, we can zoom "in" and "out" and become aware of the restlessness as a whole and in part. Joseph Goldstein muses, "Sometimes I picture this hindrance as a Jackson Pollock painting and mindfulness is the frame we put around it."[23] Here, let's revisit our core SNAPPing awake practice and see how it might help us see the "bamboo" of our restlessness, just as it is.

AN OPEN INVITATION—TRY THIS

SNAPPing Your Fingers at Worry and Remorse

When our minds are caught up in thoughts of past (remorse) or future (worry) and it goes beyond a simple, natural mental "nudge" toward corrective action (which is fine), we can become bound up and suffer as a result. Our clarity, connections to others, and capacity for effective action are diminished. It can help to practice SNAPPing awake by expanding our awareness and building our mindfulness muscle for gently holding all the agitation showing up until it passes harmlessly away on its own. This open monitoring is in contrast to the previous concentration-on-an-object practices for addressing restlessness.

The far reaches of restlessness have a circular, stuck, loop-like feel to them. It can feel like a wildly spinning carousel of angst you can't seem to get off of. Do the following when the energy of restlessness has ensnared you:

1. **S**top and pause in what you're doing.
2. **N**otice sensations in the body and past thoughts of your "badness" or the woeful worries about the future. How is the restless energy showing up in your chest, shoulders, arms, hands, and face? Notice when your mind is, versus when it's not, in the present.
3. **A**llow the bodily sensations to be just as they are. Let them bounce around like balls on a billiard table without grabbing onto them or trying to direct their path. Don't flinch away. Let go of trying to "clear" the table.
4. **P**enetrate them all with one (or more) slow, deep belly breaths. Take as many of these breaths as you feel you need.
5. **P**rompt yourself toward wise action for addressing the remains of the restlessness (perhaps doing some walking meditation, stretching, or

taking another action that flows naturally and flexibly from the awareness you've opened up to).

6. Finish with a flourish and perhaps a snap of your fingers. It's a cue that you've acknowledged the message of this restless moment, and you've responded with clarity.

In SNAPPing awake it can also be helpful to accentuate the noticing stage by labeling the restlessness when it arises (in addition to its bodily and thought components). Joseph Goldstein finds it helpful to note the arising of hindrances using their Pali word equivalents.[24] Doing so helps the practitioner get some distance from all the associative baggage of connotations of words like "restlessness" in English. If Pali is not in your language wheelhouse, you might also consider using a w-word equivalent like "worrying": "Worrying is here" could be the noticing technique, or simply "worrying." The word really does not matter, but instead it's the mental act of observing that counts. The film character and chocolatier Willy Wonka has always struck me as a restless soul. Feel free to notice your restlessness as "Wonka" or the "Willies," and it will work just the same.

Mirth to the side, these practices (and this book in general) are about learning to learn from discomfort. With mindfulness, we peer behind karma's curtain into the messages we're most in need of getting. Again, the restlessness is the karmic engine light letting you know something is amiss. That something may be "big" (like an unresolved trauma or loss) or "little" (like too many lunchtime French fries or an embarrassing slip over the water cooler at work), yet with practice, we can learn to quit shoving at or ignoring our restlessness. We can take it as a cue to open up and practice.

Opening to Restlessness via Clarity Regarding Time and Impermanence

In ancient times the beautiful woman Mi Tzu-hsia was the favorite of the lord of Wei.[25] According to the law of Wei, anyone who rode in the king's carriage without permission would be punished by amputation of the foot. When Mi Tzu-hsia's mother fell ill, someone brought the news to her in the middle of the night. So she took the king's carriage and went out, and the king only praised her for it. "Such devotion!" he said. "For her mother's sake she risked the punishment of amputation!"

Another day she was lingering with the lord of Wei in the fruit garden. She took a peach, which she found so sweet that instead of finishing it, she handed it to the lord to taste. "How she loves me," said the lord of Wei, "forgetting her own pleasure to share with me!"

But when Mi Tzu-hsia's beauty began to fade, the king's affection cooled. And when she offended the king, he said, "Didn't she once take my carriage without permission? And didn't she once give me a peach that she had already chewed on?"

Oh, how things change! And though we "know" this, we don't typically allow ourselves to know it in our deepest experience, particularly in the physicality of our bodies. We "think" change—impermanence—but we don't maintain contact with the feeling of it. In working with our patterns of restlessness, it's helpful to apply close attention to the changing face of the manifestations of worry and remorse in our bodies and minds. Exactly how does it feel to shift from restlessness to calm and from calm to restlessness? We often miss these transitions, only paying attention when the agitation reaches its peak. The causes of our anxious angst often reveal themselves in these subtle changes.

The Zen teacher Thich Nhat Hanh refers to how unlikely most people are to pay attention to their "non-toothache."[26] What he means is that we typically don't notice our inner experience when things are going well or when things are balanced and calm. We notice the pain of our toothaches—when things have gone significantly awry. As Ajahn Thiradhammo suggests in his book on the hindrances,[27] restlessness can be remedied by giving focused attention to periods of calm in the mind and body (*vupasamo* in Pali). He recommends that we tune into these states, which are more likely to arise when we're in calm environments and when we're around peaceful people and doing relaxing activities.

In deeply considering impermanence, we learn to skillfully monitor the ebb and flow of our inner states. Instead of our states of restlessness feeling as though they randomly descended upon us like some biblical plague, we can learn to discern the causes of angst and calm the flow predictably from specific conditions (both inside us and without).

Watching change as it occurs allows us to take stock of the determinants of both our aches and our smooth-sailing states. In the activity below, we practice improving our skills for anticipating the changing conditions of our restless patterns.

I have always been a big fan of David Letterman's "Top Ten Lists" from his late-night comedy shows. There's something about taking the headlines—the news—from real life and placing them in a rank-ordered list of the ludicrous. In the activity below, learn to make a practice of creating a list of your worries and wrongs, and hold them aloft for awareness to have a chuckle at the self taking itself too seriously.

AN OPEN INVITATION—TRY THIS

Reciting Your Top Ten Worries, Wrongs, and Things Unwound

1. Take out your journal or smartphone and create a rank-ordered (from least to most) list of your top ten pent-up frustrations, fences unmended, issues unresolved, unmet expectations, or anticipated snags. These are the things you find yourself either regretting/beating yourself up for having done or worrying that they may transpire. Whatever they are, jot them down in the order of their vexation.

2. Make another rank-ordered list of your top ten calming, relaxed ease-inducing activities, people in your life, and situations you've experienced. These are the people, places, and things that lead to your best states of calm and "going with the flow."

3. Find a comfortable, stable seated position and observe the next several breaths.

4. Bring your attention to the sensation of breathing, noting the rising of the in-breath and falling of the out-breath for a few moments.

5. Without pausing to analyze or reflect, read each list (starting with the worries and wrongs) steadily from number 10 to 1 without pausing and at a slow, yet consistent cadence. You might actually try reading the lists aloud, but be sure to do so without pausing.

6. If you find yourself getting distracted or pulled into analysis or a loop of thinking, simply bring yourself back to your lists where you remember leaving off, and continue your slow, steady pace of reading off the lists.

7. Speed up the pace and now read/say each list as rapidly as you can.

8. What do you notice in your experience of the items in your lists? What is your body telling you about these regrets and worries? What specific sensations do you notice in your body when focusing in on the calm/relaxing people or situations? What do you notice changing with concentration and repetition? What happens to the emotional "sting" of number 1 on your worry list when you read it and move on to number 10 again without hesitation?

9. Spend a few more moments noticing any changes in your thoughts and bodily sensations.

10. Use your journal over time to continue noticing the specific experiences in your body and mind when any of the "negative" or "positive" items on your lists arise. See if you can get better (and faster) at recognizing both the inner state and the accompanying outer conditions for experiences of restlessness and of calm.

Another aspect of practicing with restlessness is the importance of learning to let go of debating with the universe for sending difficulties your way. Pain is every human being's birthright, yet we often spend a great deal of mental and emotional energy bargaining with reality when less than ideal situations show up in our lives: bosses who block our career advancement; Uncle Harry, who wrecks every holiday meal; our spouse, who seems increasingly inconsiderate of all we do to keep the household afloat. We go round and round in our heads making promises to ourselves, resolving a litany of changes, and gorging on fantasized futures of bliss and expectations fulfilled.

A traditional fable from Ireland fictionalizes this angle of human restlessness.[28] There was once an old man who had three sons, and he wanted to make something of them but didn't have the money or connections to make it happen on his own. His worry for his family's future was intolerable, so he sold himself to the devil to raise money to pay for the best education for his sons. "I will give you the money," said the devil, "but only if you agree to give me your soul after seven years have passed." The man accepted the offer, and the deal was struck. He made one a priest, the other a doctor, and the third one a lawyer.

At the end of seven years, the devil showed up to claim the old man and his soul and take him down to hell. So when the devil came, the old man's son who was the priest began to pray and beg and appeal for mercy for his father. The devil relented and gave the man a few more years. "But make no mistake," said the devil, "I will return and take your soul once the three years have expired."

When that was up and the devil came again, the physician son was there, and he appealed for a few more years because of all he had helped his father do to improve his physical health. The devil again relented. And when the devil came a third time to claim the old fellow, the lawyer was there. The lawyer says to the devil: "You've been giving allowances to my father twice already, and I know you can't be expected to do it again. But," he said, "as a last request, will you give him at least a bit more time—only while that butt of a candle is still there?"

The candle was burning on the table.

The devil, knowing the man's soul would soon be his, smiled and said he would. It was only a butt of a candle and wouldn't be but a few minutes of burning before it and the man's life were snuffed out.

At that the lawyer picked up the butt of a candle and blew it out and put it in his pocket. And that was that! The devil had to keep to his bargain and go without the old man, for the lawyer held on to the butt of the candle.

Unfortunately, not even the slickest lawyer can negotiate our inner angst away. The "devil" of our peace-choking restlessness is truly in the details. And the details are the specific patterns of thinking we each entertain that keep dredging up the past and promising betterment in the future. And when it's rumination about our past failures, missteps, and transgressions with others, we can be especially fixed in our thinking. We are bad or less than because of what we did. There's a solidity to this broken-record time-locked thinking that eclipses our view of the bright spots of our daily lives.

When we don't feed our restless remorse with belief, analysis, and emotional intensity, does it grow stronger or weaker with the passage of time? The practice below is adapted from Glen Schneider's wonderful little book *Ten Breaths to Happiness*.[29] This practice helps us open to joy and can do much to move through remorse over past unskillful actions and step back onto a path of clarity and skillful connection with ourselves and others.

AN OPEN INVITATION—TRY THIS

Sidestepping Remorse with Savoring Breaths

1. Find a comfortable, stable seated position.
2. Bring your attention to the sensation of breathing, noting the rising of the in-breath and falling of the out-breath for a few moments.
3. Notice the presence of thoughts and emotional body sensations related to the remorse that's been stirring for you.
4. Give yourself permission to allow this remorse to shift into the background temporarily. You'll get back to it later.
5. Either recall a very pleasant/happy memory or (better yet) go look at/ listen to/touch something beautiful, inspiring, or that matters to you deeply in some way. Again, you'll get back to your remorse later.
6. Once the pleasant/positive memory or object is here, keep it in view as you place a hand over your heart. Feel the warmth and the sensation of your heart's beating.
7. As you continue to notice the positive object, begin drawing its positive qualities on the in-breath.
8. Relax into your bodily sensations on the out-breath, really giving yourself permission to feel what happens in your body when you bring this positive aspect in.
9. Savor the object and rest in the sensations of the body for ten full cycles of breath, expanding your awareness out to your entire body, as well as what happens to your mind as you cultivate the joy of this moment.
10. After the tenth breath, feel free to turn back to the remorse if you want. If it's left at this point, well, I guess you'll have to make do without it for now.

The past is truly dead. None of us can travel even five seconds into the past, yet we live with thoughts (happening in the now) that have such excruciating energy about the past that they certainly presume a desire to go back to our past in order to create a future we might begin to feel worthy of. In addition to the obscuring effect of illusions of time that fuel our restlessness, there's also the mistaken sense of a solid "me" who owns this past and the future.

As the metaphor goes, there was once a small wave who was unhappy.[30] "I'm so miserable," it moaned. "The other waves are so big and powerful while I'm so small and weak. Why is life so unfair!"

Another passing wave heard the small one bemoaning his lot and decided to linger. "You only think so because you haven't seen your own original nature clearly. You think you're a wave, and you think you're suffering. In reality, you're neither."

"What?" the small wave protested. "I'm not a wave? But it's so obvious—I have a crest. I have wake and, by the way, have you seen my swell—small though it may be?"

"What you're calling a wave is merely a temporary form you assume. You're really just water! When you fully understand that, you will no longer be confused, and you'll be free of your misery."

"Well, if I'm water, then what about you?" asked the small wave.

"I'm water too. I'm temporarily a wave, somewhat larger than you, but that doesn't change the fact that I'm really only and always water! You and I are essentially the same."

Opening to Restlessness: Clarity Regarding Our "Nonselfness"

It would be a mistake to consider your self to be a problem. Yes, getting mired in what is ultimately an illusion (or more accurately a universally held delusion) limits awareness and capacity for a truly open, awakened life. And yet having a self is not a mistake or evidence of something being broken. It is merely a statement of the fact of the limitation of how far biological evolution has taken our brains. The human brain evolved the grooves and connections to make selfhood a necessity. In a world more physically dangerous than our current one, saber-toothed tigers and bloodthirsty rivals would have ended our time on evolution's stage without the ability to say, "Hey, this life is mine—back off!"[31]

Psychological science is pretty clear[32] on this fact: without the development of a sense of self—an identity of personage that separates us from the world and from others—we would not adequately develop from incoherent, babbling babes into the discerning, thinking, and filial-feeling adults capable of not only building careers, homes, and families, but of building the conditions of awakening itself (and the "loss" of self it entails). Let me be direct—we need the self in order to let go of it! A newborn infant may be truly anchored in the present moment, but (like our dogs, cats, and assorted other pets) it is not aware; there is no capacity for knowing the fact of its essential thinglessness and timelessness.

Without going too far into the neuroscience and sociobiology of selfhood, let me bring us back to the restlessness that brought you this far in the chapter. We have to learn to let go of much of the thinking that, while it may have served the purpose of species survival, no longer serves us in our restless, angst-ridden present. Tens of thousands of years ago we needed ruminations of past and future to keep us scanning the world around us for threat and for avenues of repairing our connections with others in order to avoid the certain death of banishment.[33] But when we're holding our smartphones, getting lost in flights of past and future fantasy, this same biological reality keeps us locked in the restless illusion. We need to learn to let go of the beliefs—the thought patterns— sustaining this hindrance of restlessness so that we can see deeper into the reality of our lives, so that we can see more ways forward with one another than mere self-interest provides.

The 1970s television detective Colombo, played by actor Peter Falk, was famous for his brilliant illusions of confusion when investigating a crime. He disarmed the guilty into giving over evidence of their culpability by portraying himself as too dim to possibly pose a threat. He played to the classic assumption of narcissism in suspects such that they would "want" to explain their malfeasance as if they were professors of criminal justice. With the following activity, you're going to do the same thing with your inherently arrogant egoic self—that narrative "I" that (after the fact of a pain-pricking situation) makes rigid judgments and proclamations along the timeline.

Our constructed self likes to blame itself (bizarre, right?) for having done some unskillful/hurtful deed in the past (therefore the stuckness of remorse) or project coming attractions of calamity via the worry that lights up as future talk in the mind. It can help sidestep the stuckness of restlessness to channel Peter Falk when it comes to dialoguing with ourselves—the minds we've evolved that, though they saved us eons ago, bind us up here and now.

AN OPEN INVITATION—TRY THIS

Playing Colombo with Your Inner Critic

Conjure a current or recent snippet of your mental chatter—remorse over the past or worry of the future. Imagine sitting down across a table from this thought process. You're Colombo, and you're a bit slow on the uptake, but you're curious.

1. Ask your inner critic: "So what is this person [you] up against because of [things you did in the past or might do in the future that you're fixated on]? What makes this a big deal?"
2. Note what shows up in your experience in response to this. Don't analyze it. Instead, just notice.
3. Now ask the critic: "You seem to have a good read on this person [you]. How will your focus on how they caused [your past or future action] impact things? What are you trying to do for them?"
4. Notice what arises.
5. Ask: "Would it be too much of me to suggest that you are hammering this person with guilt and/or anxiety because you want them to avoid getting zapped with pain in the future? Of causing pain for others too? Is that too much of a stretch?"
6. Sit with this last question a bit. What does your critic do in response?
7. Just when the critic thinks Colombo will end the awkward questioning and walk away (and just like on the show), he pauses, taps a finger quizzically to his cheek, and says: "Oh, and one more thing . . . How about since this person understands you've been trying to protect them by reminding them of their past or future pain, and since they seem more focused on the present moment rather than the past or future . . . How about you and I head on down to the station? You're under arrest for hijacking this person [you] in the present with restlessness about the past and future."

This activity may be tongue-in-cheek, but the quagmire of restlessness over past or future actions gives rise to the very real question of whether we actually serve ourselves (and others) with all the inner self-interrogating. Healthy regret that leads to corrective, more skillful action is absolutely appropriate. Healthy anticipation of challenges ahead helps us plan and prepare. But is self-lashing, agitated restlessness moving things forward or keeping you stuck? Don't just buy into my perspective. Be a detective and collect the evidence yourself from your own felt experience.

Earlier in the chapter, we inventoried your top ten lists of calming and agitating activities. The Buddha—fond of lists as he was—had his own top ten list of "unwholesome actions." These are the behaviors that, if propagated in one's life, would likely stir the mental muck of restlessness in one's experience. They will ring a bell to any reader familiar with another famous "top ten list" of moral behavior commandments:

THE UNWHOLESOMES

1. Killing
2. Stealing
3. Sexual misconduct
4. Lying
5. Harsh talk
6. Backbiting
7. Useless talk
8. Covetousness
9. Ill will
10. Wrong view of self

Joseph Goldstein suggests, "We can reflect on these and become mindful of how each one becomes the cause for mental disturbance."[34] It is fairly obvious that the more we fix our attention on how these behaviors ripple out like noxious fumes into the rest of our (and others') lives, the less attractive these behaviors become. Mindfulness shines the light on them as they hunker down in the dark corners of our mental lives.

The compassion researcher and author Paul Gilbert writes, "Different patterns in our brain turn different systems on and off. You can't feel relaxed and frightened or angry and loving at the same time. You can switch between them, of course, but you can't feel them simultaneously. One pattern negates another."[35] The more we cultivate mindfulness of the causes of our restlessness, the more we are likely to avoid them. The more we build our habits of virtuous action, the less likely we are to do the unwholesome things in the first place. We set our brains up to be much less likely to spark the flames of restlessness. Better yet, the more we learn to let go of our proprietary self-delusion, the less burdened we'll be altogether.

One day the master gave his disciple an empty sack and a basket of potatoes.[36]

"Think of all the things you've done or said against others in the recent past—especially those things about which you're ashamed. For each, inscribe the name of the person harmed by your words or deeds and put it in the sack."

Soon the disciple's sack was heavy with the weight of shame-laden potatoes.

"Carry the sack with you everywhere for one week," the master said.

At first, the task was not so burdensome because the disciple was quite strong. But after a while, the burden became immense and very disruptive to his daily life. Even though the actual weight of the potatoes did not change, the bag required increasingly more effort to carry about.

After the week was over, the master summoned his disciple. "What say you about this task I gave you?"

"When we're unable to forgive ourselves, the negative feelings become an immense burden we carry with us everywhere, weighing down everything in our lives."

"Yes," the master said, smiling. "So how might we lighten the load?"

"I can forgive myself!" the student cried, pleased with his insight.

"Yes, you can," said the master. "Very well then—go ahead and remove all the potatoes." At this the disciple happily discarded the now rotting potatoes, smiling at the empty sack in his hands.

"But," called the master, "have you done or said anything in the past week since we last met that may have injured another?"

The disciple blushed and immediately recalled many such transgressions. His heart fell at the expectation of carrying yet another large load of potatoes for another week. "I'll start filling my bag anew," said the student.

"Or you can just drop the bag altogether," said the master. "There's forgiving yourself to ease the load, and then there's letting go of the container itself. Learn to live from this emptiness, and you're not only less likely to react to others in ways that harm them; you won't see yourself as something needing to carry around anything at all in order to be happy."

In his comprehensive meditation manual, *The Mind Illuminated*, Culadasa (John Yates) reminds us that "there is no self-control of the mind, and therefore nobody to blame! . . . No 'you' 'me' or 'I' at the helm to be responsible for having 'wandered away.'"[37] Truly, we need to cut ourselves some slack because there's actually no self to have cut into us in the first place. Yes, we need "self" in order to navigate our daily lives— it clearly serves a purpose. But so does the Tooth Fairy when it comes to helping kids navigate the discomfort of losing teeth. Let's all agree that it's important to use illusions as tools, but let's not be so naive as to believe the illusion as reality. And it's crucial that we not believe that we *are* the illusion! Restlessness abates when we go behind the wizard's curtain and see no one actually there.

AN OPEN INVITATION—TRY THIS

The "I's" Don't Have It

It's rare to have a conversation in which we don't refer to ourselves at least once, if not many times. In order to learn to let go of the worry about "our" future or the mistakes of the past, it's important to learn to focus less on ourselves and more on what we're actually doing and whom it might benefit (other than us!).

1. Pick a recent situation of worry or regret from your daily life. It can be a big deal (like an impending court hearing) or a little deal (a faux pas during a work interaction). Either by writing it down or just speaking out loud, the challenge here is to describe the situation without mentioning yourself at all.

2. If you're alone, try writing a quick description of your situation without using self words ("I," "me," "mine," "myself," "my"). Set a timer for three minutes, and see if you can fully describe the situation without any of these words. If you're doing the activity with someone else, try telling the story without the self words. Have the other person buzz you if you slip and use one. See how long you can go into the three minutes without tripping over a self word.

3. Notice what it's like to tell the story of a past mistake or anticipated

negative event with your "I's" closed. What's it like to focus on things other than your own needs or perspective? What if you focused less on "number 1" when speaking with others about situations as they arise? Would it help or hurt things in your daily life?

4. (Optional) Try this same activity, but instead of talking without self words, do it without referring to any place other than where you are right now. So no words about things that aren't immediately present in your surroundings!

5. (Optional) Same activity, but talk to others (or yourself!) without any mention of words about the past or the future. Everything has to be about now (the present moment).

6. If a given situation you're considering is not about you, how might regarding it in this "self-less" manner be of benefit? Is regret as likely to descend into shame? Is worry as likely to escalate into panic and reactivity? What might be the ripple effects of keeping your "I's" shut? Spend some time journaling about this.

If you want to quiet the rumbling of restlessness in your system, cultivate contentment. I recently worked with a teenaged patient whose restlessness was apparent from the first moment she sat across from me. Arms folded across her chest and scowl on face, she clearly was anticipating that our first session would be like that of all her foregoing experiences with shrinks—lots of questions and admonishments to use "coping strategies" to get her behavior under better control.

"I don't want to be here," she said.

"I don't want to be anywhere either when I feel like people are trying to get me to talk about things," I said.

She looked up from the carpet where her eyes had been hiding and met mine. "Yeah, that's all my last therapist did—try to get me to talk about stuff. I hated it."

"Well then, instead of me hitting you with questions, maybe you can help me with one I've been struggling with." I proceeded to tell her about an upcoming trip to visit family I hadn't seen in a while. I told her about a possible difficult time I'd have with a family member with whom I hadn't seen eye to eye.

This grumbling, antsy adolescent soon sat up and began chatting with me. I'd given her an opportunity to be helpful—truly kind toward another human being—and she lightened, and the anxiety and irritability that was her defensive strong suit melted away. Again, the brain can't be agitated and relaxed at the same time. When you arrange conditions in favor of positivity, competence, and contribution, restlessness tends to evaporate.

My young patient has continued to freely offer her compassionate helpfulness to me, other children, and members of her family. She even told me at one point that she might shift her career plans—from physician to psychologist. She smiled in gratitude at me as she said it.

Virtue can indeed be the best medicine for the restless mind. Compassionate, other-oriented, healthy behaviors clear away the gritty residue of past restless karma and make way for more clarity and awareness.

Once upon a time, a young man said good-bye to his parents and embarked on a holy pilgrimage. On his way, he encountered a monk.[38]

"Where are you going?" the monk asked. The man replied that he was going to the holy city.

"Going to the holy city cannot compare to seeking the Buddha himself," said the monk.

The man agreed, because though the holy city was a worthwhile pilgrimage, it was nothing compared to the Buddha himself for sending one on the way to enlightenment. "Yes! How do I find the Buddha? Tell me where I need to go to find him."

The monk smiled and pointed back in the direction from which the man had come. "He is at your own home at this very moment," said the monk. "When you arrive there, you will recognize him as the one under the blanket."

The man, puzzled and amazed, hurried home and burst through his front door. "Where is he?" he asked of his wife. "Where is the awakened one?"

At that moment, the man's young son had wandered out from his bedroom where he'd been sleeping. The commotion had summoned him from his slumber such that he still was wrapped in his favorite, well-worn blanket.

Upon seeing his father returned home, the boy's face lit up with absolute wonder and delight. And in seeing that, the man recalled the monk's words and awakened to wonder himself.

We need not look far for the best opportunities to clear away our unhelpful karma—the restlessness of ghosts of past or future. It's there at home with a child you can love unconditionally, at work with a colleague to whom you can give away the glory, or to a store clerk who deserves to hear that his or her hard work is appreciated. Give without self, and get the jackpot of an uncluttered mind.

Compass Check: Opening to Restlessness

The therapist, meditation teacher, and author Bill Morgan writes, "Striving is pandemic in our culture . . . the push to achieve . . . This misunderstanding and unconscious striving run deep in the West, but they are terribly counterproductive in meditation."[39] I've argued in this chapter that the striving mind blocks us in daily life, not just in meditation. It hinders us from the clear seeing necessary for flexibility in our family, work, and relationship decisions and actions.

The essence of restlessness is a habitual unwillingness to rest in the incompletions, discomforts, and jagged edges of the now. The mind, via thought, conjures more or other than and all loose ends tied. The mind wants the symmetry of a crusts-cut-off-your-sandwich daily existence, and reality offers its many textures and degrees of fresh and stale. We then get distracted, impulsive, agitated, worried, and down on ourselves for what was or might be less than what Mom would render in perfection with my lunchtime peanut butter and jelly. At the extremes, we become paralyzed with shame and flooded with anxiety.

In this chapter, we looked at how both scientific studies and centuries of contemplative tradition converge on what is most helpful when the mind "shakes" with restlessness. In short, when we learn to sidestep rumination and drop down more squarely into our bodily experience, when we build our concentration, and when we develop compassionate habits toward ourselves and others, restlessness abates.

The pool grows clear, and we can see our true selves reflected. And upon seeing ourselves so brightly and compassionately framed there, we may even find a smile emerging on the water's surface, like a small bow ready to fire off its next wisely aimed arrow.

An Open Invitation: Additional Contemplations for Personal Practice

Below are additional contemplations for your practice with restlessness. Use these in conjunction with the foregoing practices to penetrate into the heart of the energy that often prompts you to move out and away. Use these to help you sit still despite the impulse to distract and distance.

ACCEPTANCE IN THE FACE OF RESTLESSNESS AND REMORSE

- Consider the impact of who you associate with on a daily basis on your experience of restlessness. Whose energy is out of balance and perhaps bouncing up against your own in unhelpful ways? Who are the restless souls you associate with? How might you lessen their impact, and who might you associate with who manages themselves with a stabler, more balanced way of being? How might you harness the "contagion" of others' energy to assist in balancing your own?
- Consider a past failing or mistake about which remorse is strong for you. Consider the following:
  - What were *all* of the possible causes of this failure? Remember how every behavior, every event has innumerable contributing factors, so just when you think you've identified all the causes, ask: what am I missing that could have contributed to my misstep? While we are each responsible for the effects, the consequences of our actions, no action is chosen in a vacuum.
  - How might you make amends for this failing? If you cannot address the specific people involved, how might you take action to cause new effects to issue out to others that make such wrongs less likely to occur for yourself and others?

MANAGING RESTLESSNESS BY WORKING WITH TIME/IMPERMANENCE

- Are you willing to harness the psychologist Carol Dweck's concept of a "growth" (versus a "fixed") mind-set[40] when it comes to managing restlessness? Is your current experience of restlessness a static "thing" that will carry forward indefinitely just as it is? Or is it a set of sensations and thoughts that, while challenging and uncomfortable, will shift and transform if you merely watch them closely? What works best for you: seeing your anxiety and remorse as permanent or transitory? How might treating your restlessness as a fixed "thing" have been a defensive or protective move on your part? Are you willing to hang out with the uncertainty of it being less than a personal possession you can carry around in daily life?

· How might you be approaching daily life with a "what if," "if only," or "when I" perspective? What happens to your experience of restlessness when you do? Does this mind-set help or hinder?

PENETRATING THE WANDERING MIND BY CLARIFYING THE TRUE NATURE OF SELF

· Ask yourself: Am I still looking to get somewhere as a meditator? Who is it I believe will be benefiting from my practice? What exactly will be added to this "me" by meditating "well"? What happens to your felt experience of restlessness the more you hang out with these questions?

· What happens to restlessness when you drop your agenda of being right or winning and take a one-down stance with others? By doing so, you're willingly letting go of claiming an outcome as your own and instead making it clear to others that your higher priority is your relationship with them. When you drop your ego, what rises up in its place?

My highly anxious friend needed help in breaking free of her thought threads of restlessness. Just when she would come to a crossroads of choice in her life—a moment of truth calling for a leap forward with work, relationship, or the concerns and needs of her family life—she would fall back into the habits of restless flailing. She would get lost in the old narratives of "what if" and "won't be good enough."

For my friend, restlessness could escalate into a straitjacket of panic and throat-closing anxiety. Though the intensity varies greatly, all of us know the constriction restlessness creates in our lives. It can bind us from pursuing its opposite—healthy risking. Once we've listened deeply to the present moment—the sensations, feelings, and thoughts happening here and now—and once we've looked with clarity at what matters most for ourselves, we should not hesitate to leap. We should truly get ready, get set, and then go. Unfortunately, many of us do a lot of aiming and not enough firing.

My hope for you (and for myself) is that the practices in this chapter help you to shift from restlessness to healthy risking. Don't allow your conditioned mental chatter to drown out your true voice. That voice would have you leaping. So let's help one another leapfrog our way forward to unhindered, conscious daily lives.

In the coming chapter, we dive into perhaps the deepest and most ensnaring hindrance—the quicksand of doubt. All hindering roads have the potential to lead to doubt; and falling in, it can pull down your spiritual practice and sap your freedom of movement in daily life. And yet, working with doubt can lead to some of the grandest openings of all.

CLOSING INQUIRY

Are you willing to let all your angst-ridden worries and fantasies, as well as the ghosts of the past, die now in the present moment? In doing so, are you willing to have what already is?

7   Becoming a Know-(*Nothing*)-It-All,

Working with Doubt

Bertrand Russell once said, "The trouble with the world is that the stupid are cocksure and the intelligent are full of doubt."[1] When it comes to your history with doubting, which company do you keep?

I've often wondered whether I drove Sally out of therapy. My colleagues at the time told me I hadn't. "She's resistant to change," they said. "You can't make her want to fight her depression. At some point she has to want to help herself." I listened and nodded but silently knew the truth lay elsewhere; it was deep and dark, and I kept it to myself.

Sally was a thirty-something single woman who lived with her multitude of pets in a one-bedroom apartment. She had few friends and was plagued by highly conflict-ridden relationships with her family members. She took solace in eating (and was therefore dangerously obese) but had no hobbies or apparent aspirations. She'd been living off disability checks for years and had no desire to obtain work, even though she seemed physically capable of doing so. Sally clearly met criteria for a major depressive disorder. I saw her for about a year, and it felt to me like we'd gone nowhere in treatment in all that time.

Sessions were filled with Sally's complaints and grievances. So-and-so had been rude to her on the phone. Her mother had barked at her for not getting a job. Even her cat bore the brunt of her low mood; the poor thing had dared ignore her when she'd called out to it. Her demeanor was dour and negative, and I felt drained at the end of most therapy hours. Her depression was "infecting" me.

At each meeting, I used my best reflective-listening skills; I tried to focus my attention and responses to the feelings behind what Sally was telling me. Somehow, I always felt strained and unproductive. Her complaining, crying, and powerlessness did not stop despite my efforts. I consoled myself with musings about how this failed therapy would indeed be *her* fault.

One week, while planning our next session, I considered that a mere supportive therapy stance was unhelpful because it was not teaching Sally the thinking and behavioral skills she needed to get on top of her depression. She needed an evidence-based, cognitive-behavioral course of therapy. I decided to switch gears, stop trying to focus so much on Sally's version of her life story, and nudge her into writing a *new* story—one based on sound coping skills. I smiled to myself, confident, locked and loaded for my next session with Sally with this research-support treatment plan tucked under my arm.

I entered the therapy room with charts for her to complete as "homework" where she would have to rate her mood and thought patterns on a daily basis, and I had planned a series of behavioral "experiments" for her to engage in to prove to herself that she had the power to beat her depression. I tried to get Sally to test out one of these experiments in that very session. After describing the rationale for this new approach to our therapy, I (rather dramatically and not unlike something out of Stanley Milgram's obedience studies of the 1950s) handed Sally the classified section of the local newspaper. "Our experiment for today is for you to look through this paper and come up with possible jobs you might apply for."

There was a long pause as she held the folded newspaper as deadweight on her lap, as if it were a stone tablet etched with something damning and commanding. She suddenly threw the paper on the ground between us. "No!" she said, tears in her eyes. "You look at it—you tell me if there's a single job in there someone like me could actually do!" I sat in dismay and watched a thirty-five-year-old woman throw what, at the time, felt like a tantrum in my office.

The change in focus made complete sense. My former approach was only fueling Sally's depression. I was, in effect, rewarding Sally's complaining and depressive moods by giving them so much attention during sessions. I basically needed to give her a kick in the pants to attempt some change. My hope was that the results of her efforts would be self-reinforcing; she'd feel good for trying, and her depression would begin to lift. The only problem was that the shift in the treatment plan was motivated more by *my* needs than by Sally's. Dammit, she was "making" me doubt my skills as a therapist, and it was her fault I was feeling so incompetent and ineffective. I needed to do something about it—my uncomfortable feelings, that is. By God, I would be effective even if it meant that I ended up sitting alone in my office during our appointed session time.

And that is what happened. Sally dropped out of treatment after a couple more sessions. I was not wrong for pursuing a new, evidence-based plan for Sally's treatment. I was wrong for not relating to my own feelings of doubt. My error was failing to walk into this new approach *with* Sally instead of trying to yank her into it in order to dispel the pain of uncertainty.

Joseph Goldstein said it best: "Unnoticed, doubt is the most dangerous of the hindrances because it can bring our practice to a standstill."[2] Not only can it bring meditation practice to a halt, but it almost led me to repeat my childhood quitting pattern and bow out as a therapist before I'd even really gotten started.

In this chapter, we delve into doubt. The other hindrances may agitate, distract, or slow us down. Doubt is a killer—it can bring our willingness into a state of complete withering.

"Doubt as a hindrance is a mental preoccupation involving indecision, uncertainty, and lack of confidence."[3] When we can't decide, don't know which way to turn, and lose faith in ourselves, we're mired in existential quicksand. In the coming pages, we'll explore how we might lie back into the muck with less struggling and perhaps even learn how what would trap us and pull us down might actually lead toward wakefulness and empowerment. So let's take a swim in some quicksand with an initial exercise.

AN OPEN INVITATION—TRY THIS

Your Un-Inspiring List

If you're anything like me, it shouldn't take much digging here in this exercise to spark some doubt-laden material for you to work with in this chapter. As we've all heard, it's universal to at some point become "plagued" by doubt. Let's let the locusts of uncertainty in by listing at least ten things about your current life—your relationships, meditation practice, work, family, finances, and so forth—that you are to some degree stymied, confused, blocked, wary of, or, in some fashion, unhorsed by.

List topics and agitators of doubt in your journal. Don't worry or analyze, but instead aim for a full objective inventory of the blockages of heart, mind, and forward movement in your life. Don't dwell and ruminate; simply note an item and briskly move on.

Now take a moment and simply notice. How are you feeling after creating this list? Are you eager to read more, or are you wanting to somehow go offline (perhaps by going online)? What feels more desirable upon perusing the items above: Facebook or facing *this* book?

Stirring Your Pot of Doubt

One of the more interesting and eye-catching objects in my private-practice office is a mason jar filled with blue water. Both kid and adult clients are apt to pick it up (particularly when doubt is popping up for them and they're looking for a distraction). "What's this?" they ask.

"It's my mindfulness jar," I say. They then, predictably, want to know "how it works."

Cue the teaching moment. Either I take a charged, self-defeating thought I've been working on with them or perhaps take the opportunity to elicit a sampling from their doubt-o-meter and then say: "This jar is your mind. See how clear and blue it looks?

"Well, this is how it feels once those thoughts get cranking and revved up." I proceed to give it a vigorous shake until the glitter resting at its bottom begins whirling blizzard-like on the inside. With the mason jar, what is essentially a snow globe has the look and feel of the craziest of deep-woods moonshine concoctions.

I then lean forward and hold the jar sideways across both the client's eyes. "When your mind is swirling with doubt and angsty thoughts like this, how clearly can you see what's actually in front of you? How effective are you going to be managing things?"

Even little kids get the point. I can then proceed to teach them mindfulness practices to put the jar at arm's distance and, with practice, let the glittery thoughts settle. You should see my office. I have many such not accidentally placed teaching doodads. This particular one is not new though. The Buddha clued us into it thousands of years ago.

The Buddha used the metaphor of a pot of water to describe the mental experience of the hindrance of doubt.[4] He taught that doubt is similar to the inability to see one's face reflected in the surface of the pot's water after it has been stirred up and clouded with muddy sediment.

In Pali, the term for doubt is *vicikiccha*, which translates as "perplexity or uncertainty."[5] Who among us has not earned an unofficial doctorate in vicikiccha—been beyond-belief, confused or wishy-washy, unable to move forward? The back-and-forth flitting of the squirrel in my yard out the window at this moment hasn't come close to the jittery, flip-flopping I've felt at various points in my life. We would do well to cultivate gratitude here for the practices we're discussing in this chapter, and the many millions of beings (like the Buddha) who paid them forward with their own practice of mindfulness to "unstick" us from doubt.

According to the Pali canon, there are some specific factors that aid in leaving doubt behind:[6]

- Firming one's conviction in the three jewels of the Buddha, dharma, and sangha.
- Practice and reflection regarding the factors of concentrative absorption (*jhananga* in Pali).
- Investigation of reality and the factors of enlightenment (*bojjhanga*).

It's in these three areas of practice that we'll drill down with practices in this chapter: how to create anchors of certainty, how to build confidence through concentration, and how to deeply investigate into experience instead of relying on the veiled whisperings of the doubting mind.

The dharma traditions also provide helpful guidance in making distinctions about types of doubting—hindering doubt versus questioning doubt. "Hindering doubt is not the same as 'questioning' doubt. Doubt as a hindrance leads to inaction, sometimes to giving up. Questioning doubt inspires action and the impulse to understand."[7] Even Shakespeare got into the act when it came to making doubt distinctions. He said the "modest doubt is called the beacon of the wise."[8] When doubt nudges us to ask questions and push ourselves and others closer to the unarguable truth of our experience, that is indeed healthy. We're less likely to end up buying junk on late-night infomercials and bidding our families farewell as we take flight to meet up with our newfound cult bunkmates.

And speaking of cults and wholesale clubs, questioning doubt helps keep us moving and trusting our own experience versus the authority or charisma of a leader or influential "someone" in our lives.

Two men were lost in a forest in the depth of night.[9] It was a dangerous wood, full of wild beasts, dense foliage, with thick darkness all around. One man was a philosopher and the other a mystic. Suddenly, there was a storm, a crashing of the clouds and intense lightning.

The philosopher looked at the sky; the mystic looked at the path. In that moment of lightning, the path was before him, illuminated. The philosopher looked at the lightning and started wondering, "What is happening?" and missed the path.

"Don't look at the sky and lightning," called the mystic. "Look to your next step on the path. If you look to the light for the answer, you will miss it, because the lightning will not continue."

Learn to look at the path and step forward, and do not pause searching the sky for the flash of light from those who illuminate it.

It's the deeply and personally skeptical form of doubt that's the real hurdle to overcome. "Skeptical doubt closes us off, removes us from experience, and keeps us from actually practicing, from actually living."[10] Instead of relating to our experience directly, we allow the mind to mediate with doubts, and it pushes us to the sidelines of our lives. We're ushered over to warm the bench (as happened to my neurotic

Little League mind many times) instead of learning to get ourselves into the game. Doubt of this variety makes us focus on the bad feelings that crop up along with it. We pursue more runaway thought trains trying to analyze our options and (all in our minds, mind you) end up consuming our mental and emotional resources, which could have been helped by us swing away at the plate. (Clearly, I'm hoping one of my dear readers has invented a time machine, so I can go back and regard doubt differently during my baseball days.)

"The great seduction of doubt is that it comes masquerading as wisdom."[11] Doubt mind is a rampage of thoughts that are aiming to keep you safe from the pain of failure, rejection, and loss of some sort or another. They co-opt your intelligence and can sound quite convincing. As we'll see later in the chapter, they can even drill into you with the power and situational command of a military drill instructor.

Six Degrees of Separation: Science and the Doubting Mind

We should all give ourselves a hearty "there, there" hug and cut ourselves some slack for how much we doubt. If you take seriously what scientific research suggests, we may actually be wired for it.

Overt evidence of a biological basis for doubt comes from neuro-scientific findings by researchers at the University of Iowa College of Medicine.[12] Erik Asp and his colleagues presented eight different consumer advertisements to eighteen patients who had suffered localized damage to the ventromedial prefrontal cortex (vmPFC) of the brain, as well as to two other group of patients (some with damage in the brain but outside this specific area and the other group a set of healthy control patients). Based on foregoing studies, the researchers suspected that the vmPFC plays a role in facilitating self-protective skepticism (e.g., for misleading ads). Results of the study showed that patients with vmPFC damage were significantly more likely to be swayed to purchase products from these ads than were patients with other forms of brain damage or healthy individuals.

We should be grateful that evolution handed us the vmPFC's ability to facilitate a healthy, questioning, clarity-seeking mindscape. And if you happen (hypothetically of course) to have a wife who is more than a little frustrated with your Amazon purchasing of less-than-sensible products, then direct her to this study. "See, honey, it's not me; it's my insufficient vmPFC!" Without the brain's ability to engage in this scanning of other information passing through the mind's eye, we are more at risk for self- and other sabotage. We're also simply less willing to seek out the truth of reality—a necessary ingredient not only for greater well-being and effectiveness in living, but also for humankind's expansion of knowledge.

Dr. Niamh Connolly, an Irish neuroscientist, said the following about her own experience of doubt in a post on Science.com:[13]

> As scientists, we have to interpret our data, extract meaning, form hypotheses, and support them . . . What should I include? What can I omit? How long should I continue to prove myself wrong? . . . Will all my papers be rejected? Will I ever feel like an expert? . . . I've come to think that this basic uncertainty will never go away. And maybe it shouldn't. It is part of who I am and the work I do. So I will embrace this uncertainty and use it to guide me, rather than allowing it to hold me back. Doubt will help me question things that others might not and, hence, hopefully to see things in new ways. It will allow me to be more fluid and more open to alternatives. Fundamental doubts, I'd like to think, can lead to fundamental insights.

Dr. Connolly has clearly opened to doubt, and as a scientist (and I'd venture as a person in general), she has learned to sidestep the unhealthy strictures of skeptical self-doubt and harnessed the power of questioning, clarity-seeking doubt. And yet, despite what self-help gurus would have you believe about being "unlimited," there are clear limits to human perceptual abilities that should give us pause—both in terms of checking our excessive expectations and cutting ourselves some slack when we drop balls in daily life.

Biologically, our bandwidths for accurately seeing the full range of reality are not as wide as you might think (or wish for yourself).[14] Even though about one-quarter of our brain's terrain is devoted to visual processing, our binocular vision affords us only a 200-degree horizontal view of the world; whereas a pigeon's monocular vision gives it an almost 360-degree view. Also, the anatomy of our eyeballs is such that (due to the location of the optic nerve at the back of each eye) we actually have a blind spot in our field of vision. We don't see it because our brain automatically fills in the hole with information gathered from both eyes. What you see right now is, at least in part, an illusion. The human eye only sees wavelengths of light between 390 and 750 nanometers, whereas many animals can see in a far broader spectrum to which we are blind. And this is only considering the sense of vision. We are limited indeed in what we can even perceive of the universe's full truths.

Our perceptual apparatus is not only limited in how much information it can take in at any given moment, but the content of our perceptions and behavior itself is also distorted by aspects of the environment around us. Speaking of visual limits, imagine being asked to watch a video clip of two teams (one wearing white and the other black) running in and among one another, each team passing a basketball as quickly as possible between their teammates. If you were asked to accurately count how many passes the white team made in about ten seconds of passing, do you think you'd be able to do it?

Even if you were able to provide the correct number of passes to the experimenters in this research study, you'd still be very likely (about half of you) to miss the most relevant detail in the video clip— the moonwalking man in a gorilla suit who moved fluidly through the mass of basketball players during the clip! About half of all research participants do not see this at all! This research documents how humans often exhibit inattentional blindness for objects that are complex and are part of fluid, changing scenes.[15] In the rush of things, and particularly when we've narrowed in on a specific expectation (e.g., "I think I'm going to drop the ball"), we (or I, in the case of that day in the outfield during a Little League game) will drop it and miss the other details that could have shifted the outcome if we'd only noticed them.

Doubt may also be "contagious" among members in social networks. Though doubt itself may not be among the emotional or behavioral constellations studied thus far, an extensive number of studies have demonstrated how emotional and behavioral patterns can be contagious for people who are merely connected in terms of interpersonal interaction to some nature or degree.[16] These results include how things as disparate as obesity, smoking, depression, cooperative actions, happiness, tastes in movies, or even degrees of altruism are more likely just by virtue of being connected to others who exhibit these patterns. Such results are nothing new. Social psychology has a long history of documenting the malleability of our thoughts, emotions, and behavior when we place ourselves in certain contexts.

Research repeatedly highlights how we are always part of a larger system of interacting influences and how no behavior occurs in complete isolation. Runners will run faster when they believe they are being observed.[17] A group of coworkers will make riskier decisions as a group than individuals would have made.[18] People will often say that something is true even when it is clearly false simply because the rest of the group appears to be in a consensus.[19] A group can staunchly defend a bad decision, clinging to the belief that they are correct, even punishing those within the group who appear to disagree.[20] People in crowd settings can exhibit very serious antisocial and destructive behavior they would be very unlikely to exhibit on their own.[21] Ordinary people placed in situations where their role or an authority figure calls for them to punish others, even severely, will often do so.[22]

You might think such findings apply to many, but not all, people, and therefore you might be able to maintain your own course of behavior and see your every intention through to completion despite the pressures of a group. If you were asked to sit at a control panel and "teach" another person in an adjoining room to correctly answer questions by administering electric shocks for incorrect answers, of course you would refuse. We like (and perhaps need) to feel as though we are always fully at the helm of our own behavior, yet time and time again, research evidence and daily life seem to suggest otherwise. Our actions seem much more the result of our social context. As a result, we need to push ourselves to step back and see the system of influences on ourselves and others before we rush to judgment.

To date, I have led hundreds of group and family therapy sessions. Groups and families seem to develop their own "tone," a sort of emotional and behavioral fingerprint that results in patterns of interactions within the relationships. One parent may be chronically "distant" during therapy sessions. A group member may be the savior of others. A child within a family session may be the identified source of all the family's woes. A group member may be a mutineer who seeks to rally other members to stage a coup against the therapist. And these families and groups often can seem very different, have a noticeably shifted tone, if one or more members are absent at a given session. Families and groups in therapy can develop a sense of cohesiveness over the course of treatment, a sense of mutual responsibility and belongingness that, in and of itself, has been shown to positively influence the outcome of treatment.

My training and experiences as a therapist working with groups of interacting people have demonstrated to me again and again the immense value of consciously choosing to assess things from a systemic perspective. I've learned to ask myself questions to help me step back, like:

- What underlying messages are these people sending to each other and to me?
- What is the pattern communicating?
- What does so-and-so really want and need, and how are they trying to take care of these things in this interaction?
- Who else, other than who is currently present, may be influencing this person's behavior and attitudes?
- How is this person expressing influences of other family members, their friend or professional network, their community?
- If I had to do a complete accounting of all the forces affecting things right now, what might they be? What might I be missing?

The goal of this process of questioning is not that your immediate answers are absolutely correct but, rather, that you're breaking free of snap judgments, which may be based on distortions and prejudices, and you're considering and generating alternatives. Creativity and change come from such a perspective. This would be a healthy, questioning form of doubt.

So what's the takeaway from this brief survey of doubt-relevant research? Doubting is inherent to the human brain, and therefore we should give ourselves a bit of breathing room for how readily doubt seeps into our minds. In addition, our brain-based perceptual lenses are limited in scope and readily distorted by factors in our environments, and therefore . . . we should learn to doubt the certainty and absolute conclusions our doubting mind (particularly at the extremes) creates. To doubt is human, and to question with the goal of clarity is approaching the divine. Just don't take your doubts so damn seriously—particularly the intense, skeptical kind, which, if given mindless berth, will be one of the highest hurdles to happiness in your life.

In the next section, we shift toward methods for working with and making a practice of the experience of doubt. In order to begin, it helps to first be able to recognize that you're stuck in doubt—it has a way of sneaking up on you, and so sniffing it out is key. Here are some clues that doubt has descended—that your head is firmly dunked in the Buddha's stirred-up pot of water:

- Tension or clenching in the body before, during, or after an activity, endeavor, project, or relationship interaction
- A sense of indecisiveness about what action to take in a given situation
- The experience of "holding back"—not gentle and aware, but rigid and closed up
- Lots of self-talk (i.e., lots of "I/me/my/mine") is cropping up, often followed with words like "can't" or "won't"
- A feeling of wanting someone or something to just "decide for you"—a discomfort with not knowing what to do, think, or feel about something or a situation

Opening by Exploring Doubt

I've not always been the on-the-mark, Sigmund Freud-had-nothing-on-me psychotherapist you've likely assumed me to be throughout this book. In fact, it's been a long road of learning to open up to a healthy, questioning doubt of my "rightness" as a therapist, while also not allowing the deeper, unhealthy doubt to drive me out of the profession altogether. Thankfully, I've learned to (not always, but more than before) abide by Mark Twain's recommendation: when in doubt, tell the truth. The truth is, many in my profession don't doubt *enough*.

Julius was no stately Caesar, no regal leader of the populace. In fact, Julius hadn't held a job since his discharge from the army after a psychotic break while on active duty. No, Julius was not what most would call a contributing member of society. He received monthly disability checks from the government and was what we called a "frequent flyer" on the inpatient unit at the hospital where I worked. And over the eight months I worked in this unit, each time Julius was admitted, he would be assigned to me. Somehow I was supposed to help him—help him lose his frequent flyer status.

The diagnosis of bipolar disorder leapt out of Julius's file like a stain left by the dirty yet dutiful fingers of some previous clinician. He was prone to "grandiosity" and "flight of ideas." His emotions were historically highly unstable, and he had been arrested numerous times for threatening people on the street. He was homeless and had no connections with family members, not for over ten years. Julius lived at a homeless shelter and spent his days walking the streets, scowling at the world and mumbling to himself about grievances and affronts no one would ever know or understand. Julius frequently quit taking his medications, became manic, and would do something extreme or threatening that would lead to an arrest, a quick realization of his psychological impairments, and an ambulance trip to the hospital emergency room, where he was just a step away from our inpatient unit. His behavior upon arrival at the ER was always so egregious that he quickly earned himself "three hots and a cot" on the unit.

Julius was a large man, over six feet tall, and had a head wild with long tendrils of dreadlocks. He made me extremely nervous, particularly when he was volatile. In session, he would sometimes spark with anger and begin yelling at me about the injustices of the world. When he was unmedicated, Julius's speech often made little logical sense. "Word salad" had been an abstract concept to me as a psychology student until I met Julius. To listen to Julius talk was to become ensnared in his twisted mix of words and emotions. It was as if the "script" for his comments had undergone a random scrambling prior to his monologues, yet after I spent some time with Julius, I began to discern some patterns. In particular, I was struck by his "clang associations" (an aspect of his disorder in which spoken words rhymed though they did not appear logically related to one another). His speech sometimes had the feel of poetry.

Julius indeed had a way of reaching out from behind his significant mental disorder to try to express his basic human needs.

It's impossible for me to effectively mimic Julius's speech pattern, but it might have gone something like this. While sitting with legs crossed in session and an intensely angry scowl creasing his broad, unshaven face, he'd say, "*My paycheck will make you lose the shoes because the news will stack on my back with the dead law of them all.*" At first, Julius simply knocked me back with the intensity of his anger, his resentment for a life he'd lost, while it seemed little wonder he'd lost it due to the extent of his mental illness. Didn't he see that he was ill? That he needed to take and keep taking his medications? Didn't he want to get better?

Once he'd arrived on the unit and settled into a single room (he was too volatile for the larger dorm space), he would soon begin his routine of coffee and artistic renderings. Julius, while symptomatic with mania, would sit in the day room on the unit and produce page after page of sketches and drawings, renderings of nurses, doctors, and fellow patients, sympathetic outlines of those with whom he shared his psychotic space. Though intense and potentially dangerous to himself and others, Julius glimpsed something during his periods of intensity. His creativity flooded out on the current of his rage.

Julius's angry intensity left me feeling a bit shell-shocked. I felt helpless and incompetent as his therapist and case manager. No matter what I tried, he always came back and was always as impaired as he'd been the time before. And yet, looking back, I think Julius liked me. Again, he never threatened me, and he usually asked for me once he arrived on the unit. He once offered to make me coffee before a session.

And then we'd medicate him, stabilize his behavior and his mental status with powerful mood-stabilizing drugs. Over a period of a few days, Julius's rage and intensity would abate. He'd sleep more and no longer could be heard yelling from inside his bedroom. The clang associations would disappear, to be replaced by calm, logical chats during our therapy sessions. His tone and volume would be no different than what I might experience during a casual Starbucks conversation on a Sunday afternoon. He'd talk about wanting to move forward with his life, break out of the pattern of homelessness he'd been trapped in for so long, maybe get a job at some point, a decent place to live—maybe even call up his mother to see if he could drop by on Thanksgiving.

But he also stopped drawing and painting. His speech was slow and monotone. His words lost their passion and poetry. Julius told me once that, though he knew himself to be ill, by making him take medication, we'd "taken away his fire." He meant his vibrance, his life-affirming hue. He seemed very sad once we'd stabilized him on medication, like someone had died. It began to make sense to me why Julius was a frequent flyer. He was indeed trapped, locked into a pattern whereby he struggled to find himself, and only while "crazy" did he seem to feel he'd found something worthwhile—until our medications banished this passionate, creative, alive aspect.

Did Julius need treatment? Yes, he needed his medications. He would likely have died or seriously hurt himself without them. Did we help him learn how to strike a balance between stability and vibrance? No, to do so, we'd have needed to be willing to call our own assumptions about "normal" and "abnormal" into question. We would have ideally allowed for less certainty in our conclusions and more room for understanding Julius's needs—how his symptoms at times served him. We took away his defenses without helping him learn how to manage things on his own. We failed to give him the skills he needed to maintain a stable and potentially vibrant daily life.

Julius would enter our unit, and we would force him to take medications to stabilize his behavior. His manic behavior was indeed dangerous, but it was also what made him feel creative and alive. We'd manipulate his neurochemistry until his mania and his vibrance ebbed away. Julius was stripped of what he used to sort out his experience of the world, but we never found a way to help him find another way, another more "acceptable" avenue for expressing himself and getting what he needed for himself.

I left the hospital not long after another of Julius's stints on the inpatient unit. Yes, he needed the medication, but maybe we failed to really listen to him before forcing it on him; maybe he would have been more likely to want to stay stable on his medication if we'd helped him find a way of accessing the aspects of himself that only uncontrolled mania had previously unleashed.

Julius needed us to look behind his intense angry scowls, listen beyond his word salad and clang associations, and hear the man who wanted to connect to others and to something meaningful to give himself hope. I don't know what happened for Julius, but I hope someone learned to really listen to him after turning down the dial on their own rigid claim on truth. I hope someone gave him the tools he needed to find his way out of his frequent-flyer pattern. He deserved a chance to paint—maybe caricatures of tourists instead of fellow patients and nurses on inpatient wards.

As we've discussed, we *need* doubt—the questioning, asking, clarifying kind. What we need less of is the skeptical form. We suffer when hindered by doubt that weighs the body and mind and cripples action, crushes self-worth and confidence. We now turn toward exploring this less than healthy aspect of doubt.

AN OPEN INVITATION—TRY THIS

Your Inner Crystal Ball

Consult the "un-inspiring list" from the beginning of the chapter—the likely sources of doubt in your life currently. Queue up three (or more) anchors or specific, concrete sensory details about a person involved in your list—particularly if the person is challenging to deal with in some way. With the person firmly in mind, ask yourself: what is it that this person needs to do (or not do) for things to move forward for them (and you perhaps)? List your top five to-do or not-do thoughts on a piece of paper.

Look over your list. These things make complete sense, don't they? This is sound judgment. Of course these are reasonable. You likely know this person well, and you're certain that if he or she could start doing or not doing these things, things would improve.

Take a pen—the darker and thicker the ink, the better. Don't use a pencil—this needs to be permanent. Look at your top-five list above, and one by one, cross out each item. Pause and consider each one as you cross it out. These things are gone!

I've consulted my crystal ball, and I've seen the future—down the tracks of your interactions with this person. These things are not ever going to happen. Close your eyes and use mindfulness to observe your experience of the reality that these things will never happen. What shows up in your thoughts and feelings? Do you notice any tugging toward reactivity?

You crossed out your needs for your person. You deleted them and were left with nothing to guide you. Hello, doubt! It's likely here for you right now. What is doubt leading you to want to do?

For now, just notice all of this—the thoughts, the sensations and emotion, the impulses to turn away, react, whatever. Just watch the herky-jerky play in your body and mind.

While it may not be much fun to sit with whatever arises when you face doubt squarely, as I hope you'll see, the effort is well worth it. In guiding meditators, Joseph Goldstein and Sharon Salzberg write, "Doubt is an inability to make a commitment, or to take the risk of finding out for yourself where a certain path might lead. Doubt is especially detrimental when it keeps us from truly listening."[23] This is why this uncomfortable straight dealing with doubt is important—it gives us more capacity to decide in our daily lives from a foundation of clarity and confidence. We can learn to wield our lens of attention in ways that put doubt into more accurate (and less hindering) focus.

The philosopher Alan Watts referred to our acquired ability (through mindfulness practice) of adjusting our "level of magnification" for viewing reality.[24] Instead of assuming it's valid the way our minds habitually filter our daily routines of breakfast bickerings, office-cooler chilly receptions, and bedtime rebuffings from spouses, we can "move in" and "move out" to more micro- and macroperspectives in order to see things with clarity. We can move in closer with mindfulness and notice our spouse's quivering pain of loss on their face, or we can mentally move "back" and see how what feels stuck and emotionally "solid" is slowly and subtly changing. Doubt would have us failing to do so. Mindfulness is what gives us the ability to adjust the lens—in fact it is the lens adjusting itself moment to moment with clarity.

So as we explore the heart of doubtful darkness, we're learning to apply sustained attention but gently so. We learn to see doubt just as it is—impersonal, time-bound patterns of conditioned thought, memory, and feeling. As Goldstein and Salzberg argue, "when you're not identified with and caught up in the moods of your mind, you can see with clarity and acceptance: 'This is doubt; this is its nature. This is how it affects my body. This is how it affects my energy.' You don't need to get un-centered, unsettled, or tossed about as doubt comes and goes."[25]

The path of hindrance hurdle leaping asks if we're willing to relate to our discomforts, failures, and situational obstacles with acceptance and, in doing so, not allow doubt to take root.

Mulla Nasrudin decided to start a flower garden.[26] He prepared the soil and planted the seeds of many beautiful flowers. But when they came up, his garden was filled not just with his chosen flowers but also overrun by dandelions. He sought out advice from gardeners all over and tried every method known to get rid of them but to no avail. Finally, he walked all the way to the capital to speak to the royal gardener at the sheik's palace. The wise old man had counseled many gardeners before and suggested a variety of remedies to expel the dandelions, but Mulla had tried them all. They sat together in silence for some time, and finally the gardener looked at Nasrudin and said, "Well, then I suggest you learn to love them."

Exploring doubt means that we see clearly how it shows up in our bodies and minds with such specificity and careful attention that we can learn how we might live in and through triggering situations, relationships, and experiences. Doubt can't have its way with us as much (and shut down our lives) if we put it under the microscope of mindfulness. Gil Fronsdal wrote, "It can be helpful to feel what it is like to be in a human body that is experiencing doubt."[27] I think how Fronsdal states this is important. Instead of talking about "our" doubt, he says that we should feel "what it is like to be in *a human body*." As we'll discuss more in a later section, doubt is not the personal matter it purports to be.

AN OPEN INVITATION—TRY THIS

Your Body of Evidence

Learning to dabble in your bodily experience of doubt and not succumb to it and its conditioned agendas can be really helpful.

Do the following to SNAPP awake when doubt seeps up inside you and tugs at you physically with its message of dismay:

1. **S**top and pause in what you're doing. Close your eyes and take a slow, full breath.
2. **N**otice the various and even the smallest sensations in the body. How is

doubting manifesting in your chest, shoulders, arms, hands, and face? Tune into the flow of your body's energy and sensations, and scan them from head to toe for a moment. Notice the blame game, the focus on others' intentions there in your thoughts.

3. **A**llow the sensations all to be just as they are. Don't flinch away. Don't try to push them down. Simply choose to watch them as if watching the *Peanuts* cartoon character Charlie Brown doubting himself yet again.

4. **P**enetrate them all with slow, deep breathing. Take as many of these breaths as you feel you need.

5. **P**rompt yourself toward compassion for yourself and others (including those whose actions have triggered your bodily experience of doubt). How many others in the world right now are experiencing the pain of doubt? May all of you be free of it.

When thoughts arise and sweep you up into analysis, judgment (of others or yourself), or attempts to solve the situation, try resting in how the doubt *feels* in the body. Stay with the sensations just as they are in the body, and let yourself *not know* in the mind. Let yourself *know* clearly what is happening in your body, just as it is.

Where specifically in the body is doubt manifesting? Where is it strong and where subtle? Relax into the physical present moment of doubt instead of the future it wants you to think your way into.

Pause for a moment and consider this quote from Ajahn Thiradhammo: "Knowing the conventional meaning of the word 'enlightened' is not the same as having an ultimate direct experience of it."[28]

Doubt is a conventional and conditioned "knowing" (actually *not*) and takes us away from our true, unconditioned, unhindered selves. We can come back home by seeing through doubt's murkiness by letting the silt settle. By watching carefully, doubt, like the glitter in in my mindfulness jar, takes its rightful place at the bottom.

Opening Up Doubt via Clarity Regarding Time and Impermanence

Once a man was about to cross the sea.[29] Bibhishan wrote Rama's name on a leaf, tied it in a corner of the man's wearing cloth, and said to him: "Don't be afraid. Have faith and walk on the water. But look here, the moment you lose faith, you will be drowned." The man was walking easily on the water. Suddenly he had an intense desire to see what was tied in his cloth. He opened it and found only a leaf with the name of Rama written on it. "What is this?" he thought. "Just the name of Rama!" As soon as this thought entered his mind, he sank under the water.

Our minds expect far too much of ourselves and the world. We'd be much better off in many ways if we could somehow adopt our household furry friends' degree of expectation. Any dog I've lived with seemed perfectly content with the smallest of sensory "snacks"—and even if he or she'd been outside in a cold rain (due to my dereliction of duty in reopening the door from the backyard), no worries! My dog was perfectly happy to see me and proved it with wagging tail and licking tongue.

We, on the other hand, have forebrains affording us the beautiful curse of expectation. And we use it to labor toward long-term goals such as painting ceilings of cathedrals, curing polio, and planting flags into the surface of the moon. The horrible downside is that we solidify our sense of future by making it a "thing" looming mirage-like on the horizon, and then we doubt we'll ever get "there"—wherever or (more accurately) *whenever* that is (but in actuality *isn't*).

The psychologist and meditation teacher Bill Morgan refers to the "progress trap" that meditators fall into.[30] We expect meditation to get us "somewhere," to have something to "possess" or put on a psychological trophy shelf for ourselves. (Who wouldn't want a golden enlightenment medal to wear around their neck on retreat—retreat bookings here in the West might skyrocket with the mere mention of such a prize!)

Just like the GPS system that gives me guidance when I'm driving in an unfamiliar area, our minds evolved to anticipate threats and to access the "stuff" of survival. The problem is when we plaster our faces to our mental GPS systems, believing erroneously that the Google Maps screen (and the robotic voice announcing our lefts and rights) is the ultimate authority—that it *is* reality itself! We crash our cars as a result. Over the millennia, we've gotten increasingly confused and believe our mind's (GPS's) future-related agendas are infallible and essentially who we are.

Imagine if your car's system whispered to you something like the following:

"Really? You must not care about getting there on time if you *take* that exit."

"Just who do you think you are tailgating like that? A poor excuse for a driver, that's who!"

These are the voices of doubt. As Goldstein and Salzberg suggest about working with doubt, "the most important thing is to recognize it as doubt, because it's so seductive. When you don't become involved in the story, a wonderful transformation can happen. Doubt itself becomes the object of your awareness."[31] We need to get more curious than a dog sniffing out, say, a peanut butter granola bar in my backpack and listen to the voice of doubt, its accompanying sensations in the body, and the conditions that spark and sustain it. We need to sniff around like a mindful hound on a peanutty mission and not identify with the GPS voices of "I can't" or "I'll never." That's why dogs are great at sniffing out the truth inside ne'er-do-wells' luggage—they don't have doubts as to their capacity to do so to block them.

AN OPEN INVITATION—TRY THIS

Tripping On Your Agendas

Think for a moment about some event coming up that matters a great deal to you. In particular, select one that you've been struggling with internally—doubting yourself, others, or obtaining some deeply desired result in your life. Whether it's a fiftieth wedding anniversary celebration or a romantic escape to a beach-lined locale, pick a real source of doubt for yourself.

1. Sitting, centered and with eyes closed, visualize this future event. Make it vivid, and let yourself go viscerally into whatever arises. Don't try to do anything other than let the event have its way with you. What are you expecting to happen? What do you want and need to happen? What's at stake? Stay with the scene until doubt has reared up within you.

2. Practice merely noting the *presence* of doubt. Label the experience with the acknowledgment "doubt is here" or "doubting . . . doubting . . . doubting." Notice what shows up in your experience as you do so.

3. Notice what *else* is here and now. What changes in the intensity and feeling tone of doubt as you continue watching? Bear witness to the ebb and flow of doubt.

4. What's happening in and around you as the doubt comes, stays, and then ultimately goes? Mentally nod to all of this as it changes in your experience.

5. Let go of the visualized scene, and rest in the sensations of your breathing for a few moments. Take inventory of what you've learned about how permanent and solid doubt and its contents are.

With doubt, we flinch away from circumstances that pose some threat of discomfort, loss, or some aspect of pain. In our mindless moments, we doubt as if this mental and emotional activity will somehow mystically (as if by some universal "secret") vibrate out into the universe and shift the course of events. We assume doubt will *do* something, that our doubting in and of itself will somehow—magically—move the world around us. The truth is, it doesn't—not like we'd like it to. With mindfulness, we see clearly the nonimpact of doubting thoughts on reality. If we keep awareness open, we experience the pointless waste of skeptical doubt, particularly doubt about ourselves.

Doubt, if allowed to grow unchecked, can inhibit our willingness and readiness to make necessary changes (if it's sufficiently and pessimistically skeptical), and it can serve as a helpful strategy and tool in the change process itself (in the case of merely questioning/clarifying doubt). The trick is to home in on the changing nature of conditions. We are most likely to make the healthy changes that benefit our lives (and others) when we embrace the truth of change itself.

My mother always told me to stop cracking my knuckles. She said that if I didn't, I'd end up with arthritis by the time I was thirty. Well, I'm older than that, and I don't have arthritis. Evidently, as I learned just recently, there is no link between knuckle cracking and arthritis. There is, however, a link between the sound of this sudden popping in one's joints and looks of disdain from others in the vicinity. Basically, I just have a bad habit that annoys my mother (and likely others, though I try to avoid it when I'm working with a patient). All of us have bad habits, some clearly more self-destructive than others. We generally know what our behavioral blemishes are, yet we often fail to rid ourselves of them. And like with so many New Year's resolutions, why is it so hard to bring about and sustain change? I'll give you one guess as to the word I'm thinking right now? (Hint: it rhymes with "gout" but unlike it is not prevented by iodized salt alone.)

Cracking my knuckles may not lead to arthritis, but other seemingly simple daily actions may lead to things that are much worse. Every day, we place ourselves at risk for disease and disruption of our health, and often, we know exactly what we're doing. Let's face it. Many of us will die from conditions that are largely preventable. Our inability to put our desires and appetites to the side effectively shortens our lives. We can even be fully aware of this and go right ahead with that extra helping at dinner, that cigarette, and yes, just one more drink will do us fine.

Perusal of the Centers for Disease Control website[32] reveals some notable statistics:

- Obesity is related to about 112,000 deaths each year in the United States.
- Obesity remains an important cause of death in the United States, with 75 percent of excess deaths from obesity occurring in people younger than 70 years.
- The adverse health effects from cigarette smoking account for an estimated 438,000 deaths, or nearly 1 of every 5 deaths, each year in the United States
- On an annual basis, the average number of alcohol-induced deaths, excluding accidents and homicides, is 20,687.

Reasonable minds might disagree over the specific figures, methods of data collection, or the interpretations and implications of these statistics, but few would argue against the weight of evidence suggesting that smoking, drinking alcohol to excess, and obesity lead to significant negative health effects. All of these outcomes are not the result of viral or bacterial infections, some sudden and invisible intrusion into one's body. And even if there might be genetic tendencies making the effects more likely, all of these negative results require people to *behave* in certain ways—by picking up a cigarette, lighting it, and inhaling; placing unnecessary calories and saturated fats into one's mouth; or tipping back multiple glasses of alcoholic beverages.

I am from a family of smokers. And during my own tenure as a puffer, I often pointed the finger at my family's genetic heritage. It seems that everyone on my father's side of the family has lit up at some point. I thought it was not my fault I got hooked on nicotine. My brain was wired to like it, and therefore I was a helpless pawn of my addiction. At a family reunion picnic some years ago, we had no fear of mosquitoes and bugs out in the backyard because with all the smoke from everyone's cigarettes, no bug would dare approach. The only ones not smoking were myself (recently quit), my brother (quit a few years back), and my ninety-one-year-old grandmother (who had started when she was fourteen and only quit the year before due to severe breathing difficulties and threats from her doctor). Of course I knew that smoking was ridiculous and that it would likely kill me if I kept it up. Of course I wanted to quit. The kicker is that, when it comes to lasting behavior change, talk is really very cheap. *Action* is where the action is.

In therapy, there's change that the client *needs* to make (from the therapist's viewpoint), and then there's change that the client *wants* to make at that particular point in time. Problems occur in therapy when clinicians focus too much on what clients need and neglect what they currently want. It's a problem with timing and understanding a particular individual's pace of change. It's very tempting as a therapist to get frustrated with a client who incessantly talks about improving things but who, time and time again, fails to live up to his or her own talk of change.

Whether it be in psychotherapy or for any of us hovering over cheesecake in a yet again open refrigerator or for someone with a finger poised at the bar motioning for another, doubt is the double-edged sword of behavior change. Questioning doubt (i.e., "Hmm, I'm not sure my eating out five nights a week is wise") can help us see junctures for making changes and give us a nudge to do so. Intense skeptical doubt ("Oh, I'm impossibly fat and will never get anywhere with my diet—I'm done trying") can stall us out completely.

AN OPEN INVITATION—TRY THIS

The Doubt Detective

Detectives are paid for their skills of careful observation of details, for noticing the cause-and-effect chain of details leading to inevitable conclusions of criminal wrongdoing. So unless you're about to be featured on *America's Most Wanted* for something far worse than a doubting mind, then let's promote you to "detective" and put you to work.

1. Take your "un-inspiring" list and the doubts you've experienced related to them. On a blank sheet of paper, *sort* them into two categories/columns: those that are mere questioning doubts (the healthy ones) and the more intense skeptical ones. Which are merely looking to create clarity for your decision making, and which are aiming to cloud your mind until you call it quits? Look over your two lists, and notice the different feeling tone you have for each.

2. Focus on the skeptical list. What patterns, what consistent factors, tend to crop up for you just prior to these doubts setting in? What's happening around you (and inside you)? Look for details you may have missed before. And also consider what tends to be happening when the doubts dissipate? What are you doing, thinking, and who or what is around you? How about when doubt doesn't show up at all (particularly in situations where it has in the past)? Go Sherlock Holmes on what's happening when doubt is present, absent, and ending, and see what you can learn.

3. Rank order your skeptical doubts from most serious/hindering to least. For those on the more minor end of the list, how might you double down with a resolute plan to address them? What is something you can do now and in coming days to put this doubt to rest?

4. For the minor doubts, consider using these steps to STOP its effects: (1) **S**top and notice the effects of the doubt in your mind and body. (2) **T**ake a moment to pause and breathe slowly and deeply. (3) **O**ptions might be available to address it. What are they? (4) **P**roceed with an option and evaluate its result.

When the doubts run deeper than mere disciplined problem solving might address, we need to take a different tack. As Gil Fronsdal points out, "major doubts may need to be dealt with directly such as by questioning deeply held beliefs, attending to unresolved feelings or challenging ingrained convictions about self-identity."[33] This can be addressed from many different angles and in different venues. Some good candidates include creation of supportive, authentic feedback loops with trusted friends or colleagues, mentors, or meditation teachers, or even seeking out psychotherapy.

Deep doubt requires support to buoy you through. It reminds me of summer camp swimming and the requirement that we have a buddy to swim with. I hope you fare better than the kid I was paired with one year who was fond of suddenly "claiming" swimming trunks with his underwater stealth operations, leading to games of "keep away" and unplanned skinny-dipping for yours truly. Let's buddy up and go out a bit from shore to work with these deep-water doubts.

AN OPEN INVITATION—TRY THIS

Allowing for Change in the Doubting Mind

Look back at your "un-inspiring" list toward the beginning of this chapter. Turn a few those items into specific self-related thoughts (i.e., rephrase them with "I/ me/mine/my" language).

Take any of these thoughts and imagine they are *not yours*. They are comments made by a loved one or close friend about herself. What would you say to her about these thoughts, and how much she should be buying into them? Notice any emotions or thoughts that show up for you in terms of feeling concerned that this person is being too harsh and rigid with herself. Notice any inclinations you might experience to want to convince her not to think this way.

But now, consider the following questions: What leads you to be so doubting of yourself? Where is the caring and perspective for yourself? Why aren't you dismissive of these thoughts when they arise? Must you be so attached to them?

Take any of the thoughts above, particularly one that suggests you are lacking in some capacity, skill, or quality—ones riddled with self-doubt. It might begin with "I can't" or "I'm not." Imagine placing yourself on a number line that measures the degree of this particular skill or quality. Press yourself to imagine someone who *completely* lacks this skill or characteristic. This person cannot do this or be this way *at all*.

If you had to talk with this person who completely lacks this skill or ability, how would you describe how you fall short in this area? Can you imagine looking squarely at the person, both of you knowing where the other is with this skill, and being able to still speak so doubtfully about yourself to him or her? What happens to your doubting mind?

As you perhaps experienced in the above exercise, doubt becomes less "solid" when you hover over its thought aspects and give them a good poking probe with mindfulness. Gil Fronsdal aptly wrote, "Mindfulness can be strengthened by recognizing how doubt distances us from the present moment and from seeing clearly."[34] But when we allow the mind to make doubting thoughts "beyond" mindfulness, they are so stiff and immovable that it's somehow silly to think they are an appropriate target for meditative practices. Somehow, doubting thoughts are experienced by many of us as separate and distinct. Somehow, our self-related doubting thoughts feel very close—like the very essence of "us." We lose sight of the unarguable fact that these are merely more thoughts—no bigger, better, or more real than any others.

Think of it this way. If you were out for a walk and happened upon someone kneeling down on the ground with an ear plastered to a large rock, you might pause out of either a sudden shudder of curiosity or perhaps out of a graver concern for the person's mental health. And yet, if you knew this person to be a geologist, you would think little of it; your mind would say, "Oh sure, makes sense for them, but it's not my cup of tea."

I'm here to tell you the doubting mind is just as much a worthy subject of your (and my) mindful geological investigation as any other. In fact, it may be one of the more important rocks to dig down to and inspect closely. The illusion of absolute hardness beckons to the mindful scientist to uncover the less-than-solid truth. Let's grab up our tools and go spelunking into the doubting mind a bit more.

AN OPEN INVITATION—TRY THIS

Marching Orders for Sergeant Mind

We all have an inner critic—a "Sgt. Mind"—that labels, criticizes, and gets on our (and others') case. Sgt. Mind is trying to keep you from taking risks or getting overwhelmed (therefore he's not "evil"—just shortsighted), but he often keeps your world small and gets in your way.

What sorts of things does he (or she) say about:

- You?
- Others?
- The world?
- The future?

The trick is to learn to relate to this critic, these thoughts, without getting sucked in. Try the following to get *behind* your thinking and assume the point of view of a witness. You can sidestep the negative pull of doubt by building the habit of making doubting thoughts less "sticky" in the mind.

- Think: *Thanks, mind, for coming up with* [insert the thought here]!
- Take a breath and mentally "place" the thought over in the corner of the room. Visualize its shape, color, size, movement, and sounds. Just watch it there in the corner for a few breaths.
- Regard the thought as if it's a car (a Dodge Doubtster, passing you, as you, the witness, are merely driving along!).

The goal here is to practice any or all of these techniques for shifting from a rigid, absolute frame for the thought about others, yourself, or the tough situation and fostering a new, more flexible relationship with your mental experience in order to reduce your experience of stress.

So you've given some of the bigger doubts a good working over, yet they are likely to reappear at some point soon. This is more likely if we're not stabilizing and sustaining mindfulness in daily life. The Buddha taught that when we are less mindful, our conditioned storylines of thought, memory, emotion, and action (i.e., our karmic patterning) seep right back in.[35] Doubt basically pops up in true Whack-a-Mole fashion (to conjure my least favorite arcade attraction). It's me when I'm standing in line at the pharmacy and my internal Sgt. Mind is reminding me of a faux pas with my editor and—just by the mere fact of mere thoughts arising—I end up deflated and in a foul mood. "Maybe I'm wasting my time writing this book," I tell myself. "They're going to come looking for the advance money back."

When we've allowed ourselves to slip into mindlessness, and particularly if our thoughts or conversations steer into certain less-than-healthy (and conducive to mindlessness) topics, then doubt will certainly spring, and if we keep fostering toxic inputs to our mind-body system, then it may spring eternal indeed. Clarity as to what's wholesome and supportive of mindful, open awareness versus what tends to spark the onset of mindless reactive patterning (e.g., skeptical doubt)—is key. Here's a partial and far from complete list of toxic, doubt-sparking possibilities:

- Poor sleep hygiene when alertness is going to be required of you
- Procrastinating and not preparing adequately for a performance situation
- Eating, drinking, or downright drugging to stave off the jitters and bodily discomfort before or after social gatherings

Personally, I've finally accepted my wife's feedback as to my borderline hoarding issues. I can't see the surface of my desk in the basement (and therefore write and distribute my books and writing paraphernalia throughout the house). She's a genetic declutterer who has convinced me of the benefits of decluttering not only our home, but also my work spaces. "Doesn't it feel better?" she asks on the rare occasions that I make a beachhead assault into my various stacks and piles. And indeed it does, as reluctant as I am to admit. Without the clutter, I'm more "clear" as to what I need to do and where stuff is that I need to get it done. Doubt is less likely because it has less to hide behind on my desk. There is indeed a feeling of clarity that arises when the physical spaces in which we live and work are open and unhindered of mindlessly amassed things.

Applying impermanence to doubt means that we're carefully watching the transitions—the edges of the people, places, things, experiences, and internal states that come and go. Doubt can only live in the unchanging, fixed illusion created by the mind. When we make a practice of sustaining mindfulness of these comings and goings—the beginnings, stayings, and endings of the factors supporting our experience of doubt—it can't stay alive long inside us. Mindfulness helps us see that these factors are temporary, and therefore the "always" and "never" lies of doubt evaporate.

To really put the nail in the coffin of doubt, we have to learn to make a practice of noticing that the coffin itself is empty. It's to that spooky, but nonetheless true, aspect we turn next.

Opening Up Doubt: Clarity Regarding Our "Nonselfness"

It's often incorrectly assumed that the Buddha argued there was no "self." Particularly for the Western mind, this causes more than a pinch of incredulous smirking. To be clear, the Buddha instead emphasized that it's not that there's no sense of a self (which is why we smirk based on our daily experience); it's just that this self-sense and the conclusion drawn of it are mistaken. To the Buddha, all things are nonself[36]—there is no "stuff" that is you and other stuff that is not-you. It's all not-you— including the you you cling to!

One day a rabbi, in a frenzy of religious passion, rushed in before the ark, fell to his knees, and started beating his breast, crying, "I'm nobody! I'm nobody!" The cantor of the synagogue, impressed by this example of spiritual humility, joined the rabbi on his knees. "I'm nobody! I'm nobody!" The shamus, or custodian, watching from the corner, couldn't restrain himself either. He joined the other two on his knees, calling out, "I'm nobody! I'm nobody!" At this point the rabbi, nudging the cantor with his elbow, pointed at the custodian and said, "Look who thinks he's nobody!"[37]

This nonself stuff is much more than Buddhist Friday night party banter. (Don't you wish you'd gotten an invite? But wait—only nonselves would be invited anyway.) It has real, even clinical, implications. In my preferred psychotherapy method (Acceptance and Commitment Therapy, ACT for short),[38] clients are taught to see themselves as less the *content* of the things and personal attributes they suffer with, but instead as part of an ever-changing *context* of relationships (with others, the world, and other aspects of their experience). Many clients (and the hundreds of random controlled experimental trials that have supported the method) have benefitted from learning to say, "I am a person currently interacting with the world around me just as it is at this moment, and I'm experiencing the thoughts, emotional states, and bodily sensations that can be labelled as 'depression.'" Notice the difference between this contextual and accurate (albeit a mouthful) description and the following: "I am depressed."

Really pause and notice how this statement feels. Though it's brief, it's also quite solid and confining. How much does such a self-statement open up possibilities in our daily living? Seeing ourselves as an ever-changing context, versus a permanent "thing," helps inoculate us against the downer of doubting. It can help us shift from avoidance, shame, and passivity to engagement, healthy regret, and corrective action.

In their book, the former Navy SEAL officers (now business consultants) Jocko Willink and Leif Babin present the concept of "extreme ownership."[39] By this, they refer to the SEALs' operating assumption of full commitment to meeting the demands and dangers in front of them, without hesitation, and without focus on oneself. SEAL teams are world renowned for their successes on the battlefield because of this commitment—to owning the changing conditions they face and doing so with unflinching efficiency for their entire team. Their success is evidenced by the success rate of their missions and the very low loss of life for operators in their ranks.

SEALs can't afford doubt. Friends and teammates would die (and perhaps many others would as well). "Doubt is a kind of frivolousness—an indulgence of the mind."[40] A SEAL team member, if wounded during a mission, cannot afford to pause to ponder why he was shot, what error on his part might have contributed to it, and what it means about his future prospects in the military. Obviously, he'd be too dead to linger much longer with such doubting. What SEALs know from their training and field experience is that you must stay aware and tethered to your teammates. You can't separate into yourself, go rogue, and John Wayne your way to victory. You are part of a context that leads to ideal outcomes.

We need "extreme ownership" without buying into the illusion that we really claim experiences, relationships, achievements, or tangible stuff as our "property." The paradox is that we can be most masterful in our work and personal lives when we let go of ourselves as the masters. According to Goldstein and Salzberg, "when doubt is governing your experience, it provides distance, and this gives you a sense of mastery . . . But when you feel how limited this mind state truly is, you can gently let go of it, reconnect, and settle the mind. Then you can bring the attention back to what's actually happening, with a willingness to learn."[41] Ajahn Thiradhammo said the following about his time with his teacher, the revered Ajahn Chah:

> When I was listening to him he would answer the same question differently each time; there was no pattern to it, no consistency. I began to have my doubts about him. And then one day as I listened to him, I suddenly realized there was no fixed entity who was Ajahn Chah. He was not somebody who had a fixed teaching he held on to. There was just a totally present being, responding mindfully and wisely to the situations that arose.[42]

If Ajahn Chah had ever the chance to spend time in the West, he'd likely have noted (as has the Dalai Lama) how strangely self-doubting Westerners are versus folks in Eastern cultures. Every day, we struggle against an epidemic of self-deprecation and self-deflation. Some statistics place lifetime prevalence of anxiety disorders at over 15 percent and depressive disorders at between 6 percent (men) and 12 percent (women).[43] There is indeed a bias toward negativity in the view of self in the West that would (and likely have) make a grown Dalai Lama cry.

We need to bring mindfulness to our experience of doubt in order to give ourselves a much needed confidence boost—a proverbial shot in the arm so that we're again willing to reach out and risk in the direction of what matters to us.

The Venerable Ananda, the monk who was the attendant and closest disciple to the Buddha, was passing through a rural village one day. As he was thirsty he neared the village well, and seeing there a young girl, he requested of her a cup of water to drink. The girl said to him, "Oh, great monk, I'm unworthy to give water to you. Please do not ask this of me for I would only cause you impurity. I am a child of the lowest caste in this village." The great monk Ananda looked at her with eyes of compassion and said, "I did not ask you for your caste, but for a drink of water."[44]

If you've come this far in the book, you've likely spent a fair amount of time practicing sitting meditation with the breath as your object of focus. Perhaps you feel like you're a "better" meditator than that now—that breathing is for beginners. Well, if doubt is poking and perhaps pushing you around, it might behoove you to return to the basics and spend some time building your confidence. You can do this in any number of ways: Focus concentration on the sensations of just one breath, then two in sequence, then three, and then upward to ten or more. You might focus on exhalations alone or the gaps at the top or bottom of each breath. Or you can have some fun and climb up "Concentration Mountain"!

AN OPEN INVITATION—TRY THIS

Concentration Mountain

See if you're willing to stay on the trail as you climb Concentration Mountain. The primary goal is to put your focus on your breathing and climb the mountain if you can keep up your concentration. Obviously, this is not meant to be a daily practice, but it's a fun way for you to begin again with the breath as your anchor, particularly if doubt has scuttled your confidence in meditation practice. A bit of "funfulness" in your practice might also shift the internal balance back toward confident ease.

1. Take a slow, deep breath into your belly. Notice what it feels like in your body as the air comes in, expanding your belly out, and as the air leaves your body on the exhale.
2. Place your pencil on the #1 dot at the base of the slope. Inhale slowly and deeply, bringing the breath down into your belly once again.
3. Keeping your focus on the feel of your breathing, draw a line connecting up the slope of the mountain to the #2 dot. Exhale slowly once you reach that dot. Pause there and inhale again.

4. Move to the #3 dot on the exhale and proceed in this way, all the way up and down the mountain until you've drawn both sides.

5. If you get distracted and lose focus on your breath at any point, no worries! But you'll need to back up to the previous dot (placing your pencil there) and regain your focus. Mountain climbers need to make sure they have good, solid footing before proceeding. Only after you've returned your focus to an inhale of your breath should you again proceed forward on the mountain with your pencil with the next exhale.

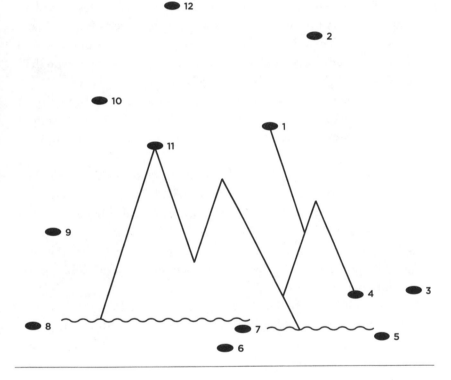

However you do it, the point is to go "back to one" and begin again with shaping your concentration skill with meditation. Do so and remember what led you down this path in the first place—the certainty of the clarity that comes with deeper and stabler concentration. Remember how far you've come, and yet don't rely too much on memory! Doubt likes to ride in on the back of it.

There was once a man by the name of Hua Zi who had lost his memory.[45] It was said that if he was told a thing in the morning, he would forget it by night. He would forget where he was going and at times would even forget how to walk.

His family was quite concerned and burdened by his inability to remember. Though Hua did not seem particularly unhappy or stressed by his condition, his family took matters into their own hands. "We cannot bear to have him live like this," they said. "What life is it to not be able to remember?"

So the family went across the land in search of priests, sages, and all manner of healers who might be able to help the poor Hua Zi. Many tried, and all failed to restore the man's memory. Then one day, the family met a poor beggar—a self-proclaimed philosopher—who had heard of Hua's plight and confidently declared he could heal him.

The family led the philosopher into Hua's bedchamber whereupon he inspected Hua from head to toe. "He will require a special method in order to be restored," the man said. "I will require a fee of half of all your family's wealth."

The family, desperate to have Hua restored, gladly paid the fee. The philosopher bade them all leave him alone with Hua. With the family members gone, the philosopher set about his methods for healing Hua Zi. He first stripped Hua of all his clothing and locked the poor man out of the house and in the garden for the day. Cold and tired, once the philosopher finally opened the door, Hua entered and began looking for and found his clothing.

Next, the philosopher deprived Hua of all food for two days. Extremely hungry and on the verge of starving, the philosopher found Hua in the empty pantry, clawing at the corners for crumbs he found there. The philosopher was overjoyed at this.

For the next few days, the philosopher conducted additional experiments in deprivation with Hua, each time resulting in Hua scrambling about on his own in search of whatever it was that would restore him and provide relief.

After a week had passed, the family returned, and upon entering the house, they were immediately met by a waiting Hua Zi. He recognized them all and called them each by name. But his tone was less than grateful or welcoming. He became enraged and began chasing them and the philosopher around the house and the surrounding gardens with a drawn sword.

A town magistrate was just then passing by and heard the philosopher's and family members' screams. He burst into the house just in time to block a thrust from Hua Zi's sword into the philosopher's chest. The magistrate disarmed Hua and carted him off to jail.

Upon questioning, Hua Zi said the following: "Without memory I was happy and woke up to each day anew. I felt no burden of my wrongs and those of my family—I was free and lived each moment fully. And now that I remember once again, it is all the worse. Now, not only do I doubt myself, but I doubt I will ever return to such a timeless joy again. Now I'm full of the bitterness and rage that comes from the prison of memory."

We doubt ourselves because we (selectively and often negatively) remember. We're especially likely to do so when our history—our conditioned patterning—drives us in that direction like it has for many clients I've worked with in psychotherapy.

I imagined how one of my clients, a boy I'll call Sam, likely got up on cold mornings and walked into the kitchen of the cramped, subsidized apartment he shared with his mom and younger siblings. As he poured out a bowl of cereal, he was reminded by his mother that he'd forgotten to let the cat back in the house "again" and that he must be "stupid" because he'd been told to do so enough times that "any moron" could remember.

After one such morning with his mother, Sam sat across from me during a therapy session and, after a long pause, looked up. "Did you know that the rings of Saturn are full of rocks and boulders?" he asked. Sam was a storehouse of knowledge, though his lack of participation in class and his apparent allergy to any homework papers suggested otherwise. Science in particular fascinated him.

"No, Sam," I said, "I didn't know that. Pretty cool that you do though. You're pretty good at holding on to facts like that."

As if he'd just bit into the juiciest of lemons, Sam smirked away my compliment. It just didn't fit with how he'd learned to think of himself—a round peg in a misshapen hole. "It looks so beautiful and perfect from all these millions of miles away, but it actually is a worthless, orbiting trash heap that gets reflected by the sun." Sam poked at a wad of Silly

Putty I kept on my desk. He stabbed it, voodoo doll style, with a pencil. His story about the cold-shoulder treatment he'd received from his mother that morning, the sudden recital of a lesson about the brutal deception of the "worthless trash" orbiting around Saturn, and his Silly Putty gouging were obviously bound together, like a plastic tie around my kitchen garbage.

Sam, and many clients like him I've worked with, unfortunately learn from an early age that the adults in their lives think less than ideal things about them—sometimes directly telling them so. With enough repetition, these children begin to believe these misdelivered messages, and doubt is primed and prominent in their minds. These messages become shame-ridden scripts these kids continue to act out in their relationships with others, effectively blocking them from attaining the quality of connection and overall life satisfaction they deserve.

I told Sam he was smart and kind on many occasions, but when you've heard "stupid" and "ungrateful [insert demeaning expletive here]" from your most important caregivers—the people charged with watering the seeds of your positive development—hundreds, if not thousands, of times, you're going to grow into something stunted and less than flowering.

There is a very important distinction between guilt and shame that is crucial in understanding this problem of child development. Guilt is correctly viewed as a negative self-related emotion relative to a *specific* behavior one has exhibited. It's appropriate for all of us while we're growing up to experience guilt when we've stepped over the line, when we've transgressed against others in our family, school, or communities. Guilt is a universal emotion that prompts us to redress wrongs and get ourselves back on track. Kids need guilt in order to keep themselves connected. What they don't ever need is shame—a more *pervasive* self-punishment, an *identity* that congeals around "badness" in some way.

There's a fundamental lack for the child (or adult for that matter) in allowing what is (the raw, basic emotional pain) to exist and be fully felt in the present moment. When things go awry—when a child forgets to let in the cat—he or she should feel a pang of regret, concern, or guilt. The feeling should be allowed to rise and fall within like a wave on the ocean's surface. That's natural, and it's what leads us to respond appropriately to the warning signal function that emotions are meant to serve. When we let guilt, sadness, fear, anger—the core, basic negative emotions—rise and fall within our children, they learn that these feelings are survivable and, most importantly, don't have anything to say about who they are as people. They are mere energy within that is meant to motivate us to do something to right ourselves.

Recent research suggests the downside of shame. One study suggested a link between peoples' experience of shame and symptoms of major depression, and a stronger link for shame than for guilt.[46] Pervasive negative emotions like shame have also been associated with inflammatory conditions, such as coronary artery disease. Shame not only hurts; it damages.

We as parents, aunts and uncles, teachers, coaches, and therapists must work to not let kids link their mistakes and failures to their core identities. It is crucial that we not let transgressions fester and that we not rub salt into their wounds with reactive anger and frustration. We should teach children that while there is bad behavior, there are truly no bad kids.

When we encounter a child whipping themselves with shame, we should immediately intervene to point out the difference between behavior to be corrected and beliefs about themselves that should never be called into question. Sam, my young client, unfortunately had been taught from an early age that he was damaged goods—that who he was as a person was fundamentally flawed. This is not the fault of any child. It is the responsibility of any adult charged with the child's care to teach the child otherwise. There is too much left to unfold in any child for any final judgments of character and worth to make sense.

Sam is now on a different, less-shame-filled path. It took positive, corrective input from many caring adults to get things moving in a better direction for him. Unfortunately, I've met far too many Sams who never learn to "surf" their pain—far too many who've been caught in the undertow of shame.

If you've ever been to the Art Institute of Chicago, you've likely seen Georges Seurat's famous 1884 painting, *A Sunday on La Grande Jatte*. If you missed it, it's in Gallery 205. It's simply miraculous in composition and effect. And before you think me an art aficionado, don't, because I have never been to the Art Institute, nor have I seen this painting in person. I was introduced to it years ago while spending an idle weekend afternoon watching the 1980s film *Ferris Bueller's Day Off*. Why do I mention this painting, and why do I seem masochistic in my zeal to disclose, not only my relative lack of sophistication, but my penchant for campy teen angst movies? I do so because both the painting and the movie in which it was embedded are examples of the systemic conceptualization of human behavior I, as a psychotherapist, have come to value. I do so because learning to think in terms of the *context* in which behavior occurs seems important for all of us, important enough for a little author self-ridicule.

As anyone with knowledge of art greater than my own can attest, Seurat's painting lacks any noticeable brushstrokes. Instead, Seurat crafted his work as a pattern of thousands of small dots of paint. You too can approach the painting as did teenaged Cameron, Ferris's woefully depressed and hypochondriac and self-doubting sidekick in the movie, and once sufficiently close to narrow your field of vision, you can see the individual dots of color. Then you will realize that with such a tight zooming in, you've lost the view of the painting as a whole. The "meaning" of scene disappears and back and forth you go, dot to scene, part to whole. And as any undergraduate psychology student can attest (because their exam grades depend on it), the "whole is greater than the sum of the parts." What this means is that, particularly regarding people placed together (as they are in the painting, as they were in the film, and as they are in your daily life), the behavioral "output" of a group is "greater" (or at least very different) than what the individual members could produce in isolation.

In case you haven't seen the movie, it depicts a devious young high school student who decides to take a day off from school. He devises an ingenious plan to convince his parents and school officials of his "illness" and, in the process, gathers up his best friend and his girlfriend to accompany him on his truant gallivanting about the greater Chicago area.

At first glance, the movie would suggest that the sheer force of Ferris's personality made all the outlandish events of the movie possible. And yet, he would've had no hotrod car to drive without his friend Cameron. He would've had no kiss in front of the school building without his girlfriend. The trio came together and made a much more interesting story than if we'd simply watched a movie about a solitary kid skipping school. The *system* created by the interactions of these three friends led to behaviors that none of the individuals would have likely exhibited on their own.

We are all nudged and shaped by our context and the groups to which we belong in our daily lives. When we go beyond the appropriateness of questioning doubt and veer into the void of skeptical doubt, we have lost touch with the truth—we are not separate, solid, and the shame-worthy ne'er-do-wells our minds tell us we are.

Just like with this movie, with Seurat's painting, and with our daily social behavior, a scene, or dynamic, emerges out of component parts. This emergent aspect comes as a result of our brain's normal housekeeping. Our brains evolved to make sense of the millions of bits of information surging into them every moment of every day. As cognitive scientists have indicated, our brains create "shortcut" methods of accounting for our daily experiences.[47] Our brains automatically seek out patterns in order to sort out the meaningful "diamonds" amid all the sensory rough. We would simply be overwhelmed by information if we had to attend to all that our senses receive from the environment. We need our brains to sort information into that which is important enough for our attention. The human brain evolved to see patterns. Consider the figures below:

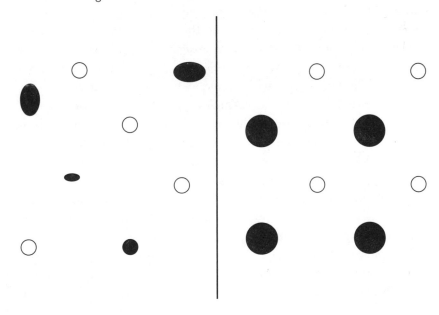

What do you make of this first figure? Glancing it over, most likely, nothing meaningful or notable jumps out. It looks like a relatively random assortment of large and small circles and ovals. But consider the second figure. If you look closely, the second figure contains the same number and positions of the circles as the first, yet it clearly creates the perception or experience of a classic Necker cube. The enlarged, blackened circles automatically create the perception of depth, whereas the first figure, because a random selection are oversized and distorted, creates a sense of meaninglessness and disorder.

The first figure is an example of a "failure" to think systemically, of perceiving the pattern of connectivity between the various elements and creating a meaningful whole. We all live inside situational structures such as this on a regular basis. We enlarge or exaggerate some aspects of a situation and neglect others that may be very important. We distort the facts of our daily lives and thereby fail to find the patterns with the potential to create meaning for ourselves. We end up feeling "superior," "chaotic," "depressed," "anxious," "enraged," "hateful," or any of a whole host of intense, negative, or potentially damaging states of being. We doubt others, the world, and ourselves as a result, and do so in ways that diminish our capacity for joy and effective action.

So, while our brains evolved to see patterns and make sense of chaotic sensory input, sometimes they make errors based, in part, on the enormous demand on our system and the need for shortcuts, and also due, in part, to our own personal learning histories. Unfortunately, we often learn over time to distort and doubt our perceptions of ourselves and others, and this blocks us from seeing the bigger picture.

We often fail to see the system that captures the whole of someone's behavior. We look for the dot of paint to explain everything when we should be stepping back to consider what the full pattern is really all about. *Then* we can do something meaningful. Then we can properly shape which way things can go for ourselves and others in the groups to which we belong.

The seventeenth-century poet John Donne wrote that "no man is an island."[48] As a therapist, I try to remember this and find a route to a fuller understanding of the complete context of a patient's actions.

Let's assume that you're trying to prove the venerable Mr. Donne wrong, that you indeed can be an island unto yourself. Go ahead and mentally maroon yourself. (Go ahead and make it tropical, with a white sand beach and a hammock with a fruity, umbrella-poked concoction of your choosing.) How long would you have to be there alone before many of the things that matter to you (your "treasures") no longer seem to have the same allure? What value will your nice watch have if there can never be anyone to appreciate it? If there's no real need to track the passage of time? And if you ran out of, not only umbrella drink concoctions, but food and fresh water, how long would your contentment continue? Now, hold your breath. How long is this agreeable? The point is that we are all inevitably tethered to the physical and social world around us. We are parts of many larger systems, and we are a piece of what, if we allow ourselves to see it, makes for a meaningful whole.

I should really take my own "day off" and go to the Art Institute of Chicago. I should see Seurat's painting for myself. My bet is that I am there amid the dots on the canvas, and so are all of you. We're all in the same mix (or quicksand) together. Let's do some work now to flesh that out a bit and learn to let go of the doubter within and embrace the contextual, interconnected "being" we all already and always are.

AN OPEN INVITATION—TRY THIS

Fleshing Out Your Stick Figure: Part 1

In a quiet moment (try now!), close your eyes, settle into your holding environment with a few relaxing breaths. And now, conjure the image of something, someone that inspires you to move toward awareness and openness.

Sit for a few minutes, and simply allow the experience of this person/thing to permeate your awareness. Breathe naturally and gently, and allow the experience to flow and amplify, deepening the visualization as much as possible.

Notice what arises in body and mind as you rest into an experience of this inspiring image.

This inspiring person or image likely fosters feelings of openness and expansiveness in you. Take a moment and notice if this is indeed the case. If not, return to the exercise and give it another go. Look deeply as we've done throughout this book, and listen for the echoes of empowerment in body and mind.

And before getting up to attend to your next to-do item, cut your toenails, or do some other mundane activity that will allow doubt to seep back in with you unaware, move to part 2 below.

AN OPEN INVITATION—TRY THIS

Fleshing Out Your Stick Figure: Part 2

1. Take a blank piece of paper and a pencil, and write "me" in the center, and put a circle around the word.
2. Set a timer for five minutes, and begin brainstorming and brain mapping your strengths, capabilities, skills, positive attributes, and valuable qualities—all of them, whether small or large. Use words and phrases, circle them, and then connect with lines ones that seem to feed or link to one another. Don't hesitate—have at it and flesh out your best self!
3. Notice any "But . . ." thoughts (doubt), and mentally wink at them, and return to the exercise.

AN OPEN INVITATION—TRY THIS

Fleshing Out Your Stick Figure: Part 3

Now let's kick it up a notch. Let's push into the doubt as it becomes "you."

1. Position yourself in front of a mirror. Close your eyes, and breathe deeply and slowly for a few cycles.
2. Open your eyes, and silently pose this inquiry to yourself: how am I doing in my life right now?
3. Notice what arises, bodily sensations and thoughts/images.
4. Breathe evenly and gently, and ask yourself: what value am I bringing to the world?
5. Again, notice what arises. Notice the "but" or "can't" or "won't" thoughts of doubt that arise. Notice the sticky sensations in the body arising alongside them.
6. Close your eyes briefly and breathe. Drop the sense of I/me/mine/my. Breathe and realize the *truth* that these patterns of value (and doubt-filled devaluing) are not yours. They are patterns that emerge.

7. Open your eyes, and note aloud to yourself the patterns of value, skill, contribution, positivity that you bring forward in daily life, and name them aloud without saying "I" or "me." Just name them as the patterns they are (e.g., "writing book-length discourse on the importance of opening to uncomfortable patterns and grateful for all that has come together for this to arise").

The point here is not to see the patterns of value and strength and build on them, but to see them *and* the less than desirable ones as impersonal—not about you at all. If you see them all accurately, the value will be less prone to the dampening effects of doubt (which require a strong, solid "I").

Japanese martial arts (such as aikido) refer to the concept of *mushin*, loosely translated as "no mind"—that state of clarity and decisive action that flows forth when the self gets out of the way and valuable patterns (such as aikido training) are allowed to meet the demands of a given challenging situation (such as an enraged assailant). There can be no doubt when there is mushin—no mind.

The nonduality meditation teacher Rupert Spira[49] uses a wonderful metaphor to describe the fiction of the self, which, in the case of doubt, is a particularly tricky story we bind ourselves up in (and thereby use to conjure much of our suffering as a result). I've personally found Spira's metaphor extremely useful in my own personal and professional practice. In it, he suggests that our daily experience is like a movie projected on the big screen. Whether it be an enthralling action flick, a heart-warming love story, or the most harrowing horror show, these films compel and draw us in—in fact, we suspend reality and for two hours or so assume the movie *is* our reality.

Where we get stuck though is in this assumption of the film as who we are—that the thoughts, emotions, memories, detailed story lines, sensory experiences, and mental images (the "self") *are* the core, essential truth of being. And yet, if you've ever sat down in the front row and turned and looked sideways at the screen and the theater and the audience, the illusion betrays itself. You see the light passing through the air and over folks' heads and onto the screen. From that sharp and close-up viewing angle, the film's characters and story are more clearly seen for what they truly are—light and color dancing about on the screen. Hour by hour, day by day, various movies play on this particular screen, yet the screen never changes. It is never dented by action movies, ripped to shreds by the horror film, or pulled off balance by a strong tug on heart strings in that Valentine's Day runaway hit. No, the screen is not only unaffected; it *contains* all of the films. The films show up on *it*.

As Spira so beautifully points out, you're not the movie; *you* are the screen. All the thoughts, feelings, sensations, stories show up *in* you—they aren't you any more than you leave the theater, drive home, and begin introducing yourself as *Star Wars* or *How the West Was Fun* (a particularly forgettable family film with a certain young pair of identical twins "cowgirls").

With doubt, it's particularly important that we learn to see the movie of the mind as these thoughts and associated feelings are playing on our essential big screen. So a big two thumbs up to opening mindfully to the truth of the doubting self!

Compass Check: Opening to Doubt

Once upon a time in ancient China, there were two brothers.[50] Both worked hard and accumulated much wealth. One day, they were traveling on the road when it started to rain. They were still far from the next village, so they looked around for shelter. They found an abandoned temple at a nearby cemetery.

They went into the temple and saw that an old man was already inside. They noticed he held a small gong in one hand. Curious, they asked him about it.

The old man said, "I am a messenger. My job is to go to the door of people who are about to die and strike this gong three times. It is the signal for them to pass away."

The brothers were taken aback, but then they thought the old man was most likely crazy. Seeing their expressions, the old man said: "I know what you're thinking. You don't believe me. Well, it so happens that the two of you will die next week. You can see for yourself when your time comes." Then he vanished right in front of them.

The brothers were shocked. They resumed their journey after the rain stopped, but both were disturbed by this most unusual experience.

The old man's words weighed heavily on the older brother's mind. He kept thinking, "I worked hard to accumulate this wealth, but what's it all for? I have only a few days left, and then I will be gone." He lost his appetite and couldn't sleep. Soon he was sick. When the day came, he was too ill to get out of bed. He heard the sound of the gong being struck three times and died, exactly as the old man said.

The old man's words also weighed heavily on the younger brother. He kept thinking: "I worked hard to accumulate all this wealth, but what's it all for? I have only a few days left, and then I'll be gone." Then he thought: "There is no time to waste. I must do something with this wealth and quickly!" He jumped into the task of divesting his possessions. He went around his village to give money to worthy causes as well as public works. The villagers were surprised by his generosity and also very grateful. They got together and decided to hold a celebration in his honor. They all showed up in front of his house and had a big party. Musicians played music; people danced and toasted his kindness. Everyone was having a great time.

The old man showed up with his gong. He saw that is was very crowded and noisy. He had a job to do, so he got as close to the house as possible and struck the gong three times.

No one heard him. People assumed he was one of the musicians. The younger brother was so busy talking to people, accepting their thanks, and clasping their hands that he didn't even know the old man was there. The old man tried again—and again. He was having no luck at all. Finally, he got frustrated and left.

A week later, the younger brother was busier than ever. People saw him as a community leader, and many wanted him to work with them on various projects or get his opinions on issues of common concern. Between appointments, the younger brother found himself wondering: "Wasn't that old man supposed to show up at my doorstep? Oh well, no time to worry about that. There are still many people I need to help."

In this chapter, we've turned over the stone of doubt and given it a (not-so) solid inspection. With deep investigation, mindful awareness helps us see the nuances of sensation, thought, and our well-rehearsed and memorized histories of "evidence" for doubt's conclusions.

We've pried doubt apart by watching it fall away due to its inevitable impermanence, as well as its sneaky self-affirming sleight of hand. With tools at the ready, you can (if willing) slosh around a bit more in the quicksand, eventually find your way forward, and grow in awareness and peace as a result.

An Open Invitation: Additional Contemplations for Personal Practice

Below are contemplations for cultivating opening amid the confusion and disorientation of doubt. Add these to your tool kit for loosening the bonds that doubt places on your mind and heart. See if these help you stay the course with your overall efforts to overcome the hurdles of your hindering patterning.

Acceptance in the Face of Doubt

Curiosity is said to have killed the cat, yet doubt is what kills our willingness to get curious about our lives. So unless you want to live in a world overrun by cats, are you willing to cultivate your curiosity muscle and go looking in micro- and macroscopic wonder at all the ways doubt manifests itself in your body and mind? Are you game for making a game of peekaboo when doubt tries to get you to keep your eyes closed to the truth inside and around you?

Working with Time/Impermanence

In the Bible, the doubting disciple Thomas needed to see and touch the piercing wounds on Jesus's hands to resolve his disbelief that Christ had actually transcended death. In essence, Thomas needed proof that Jesus had sidestepped the permanency of death before his doubt would resolve. For your own daily doubts (about your meditation practice, your work, relationships, and even yourself) to lift, are you willing to step outside of permanency as well? You do not need wound holes or resurrections—you only need a willingness to closely watch your own experience (bodily sensations, thoughts, and mental images) as doubt unfolds in you to see that it (in its own time) reveals its impermanent, wispy, inaccurate nature. Basically, are you willing to keep watch and doubt the certainty of your doubting?

Clarifying the True Nature of Self

In his wonderful short book *First You Have to Row a Little Boat*,[51] Richard Bode says the following about his life of sailing:

> I sailed around Angel Island, past Tiburon and Sausalito, and headed toward Berkeley with the wind astern. To port, the fortress of Alcatraz; to starboard, under my sail, Coit Tower and the gleaming city herself draped across a hill. I gazed about, thinking how different this bay was from the one I had sailed in my blue sloop so long before. I had moved across a continent, migrated to another place and another time, but I had not left the essence of myself behind. I had sailed as a boy, I had sailed as a man, and I was sailing still.

Who is this reader concluding this chapter on doubt? You've traveled far in this book and this reader is, inevitably, different—changed. And yet what has not changed a bit? What, like Bode's sailing, has continued unabated throughout? Can doubt touch this?

Your karmic conditioning is as thick and intertwined as any knot. Consider it a Gordian knot.[52] In the fable, Alexander the Great, upon marching his conquering Macedonian army in the Phrygian capital of Gordium in modern-day Turkey, came upon an ancient wagon. This was tied with tightly entangled, "impossible" knots that, according to tradition, could only be untied by one who was destined to rule all Asia. Ever looking for opportunities to conquer, Alexander struggled against the knot until, out of frustration, he paused and then drew his sword. In one swing he cut the knot to pieces, thereby freeing the wagon from its yoke.

Would that we each could channel an inner Alexander to cut us free of our knotted conditioning of desire, hostility, restlessness, sloth/torpor, and guilt with a single swing of our conscious mind! To my admittedly limited understanding, such a sword does not exist. Instead, we must do the hard work of opening the knot strand by strand, applying the gentle, compassionate, and consistently expansive pressure of mindfulness as we move along the limited timeline of our lives.

In our closing chapter, I'll lay out my best recommendations for untying knots. I offer ideas and practices for beginning an integrated, ongoing plucking at the hindering strands that have noosed your happiness thus far.

CLOSING INQUIRY

At the end of any attempt to work with your experience of doubt, are you willing to simply notice whether you are opening as you bring the practice to an end, or are you closing? Don't judge yourself for either; just notice and label your experience. Can you allow yourself to keep returning to the work of not knowing?

8 Karma Chameleon
The Path of Opening Up One's Patterning

OPENING INQUIRY

Leaning into and opening to one's patterning is inevitably uncomfortable. How much do you want to live honestly in the truth of your experience (be it painful or pleasant) or close down in search of comfort and live from conditioned patterning and self-delusion?

Grandpa Abblett was fond of gritty, pithy sayings—some that he picked up in the navy during World War II, some he crafted himself as he watched coal barges pass by on the Ohio River, sitting having a beer on the porch of the log cabin he'd built. As we bring our journey into the hindrances to a close, it seems that one of Grandpa's sayings is apropos. I can still hear his booming voice and see the mirth and naughtiness shining out from his wry smile.

When facing a situation that seems like it has a lot of momentum and you're trying to push back on it—trying to get it to change—Grandpa would say, "Stopping that is like trying to stop a lava flow by spitting on it." Such is the feeling one gets when working to overcome the momentum of one's own conditioning in the form of the hindrances.

And yet, with enough "spitting," you might just turn your karmic lava flow into a Hawaiian Island paradise. It will help you do so if you remember that the hindrances are not inherently "bad." Badness is a judgment of the mind and is itself an aspect of conditioning. As Todd Kashdan and Robert Biswas-Diener observe in their book *The Power of Negative Emotion*, "sadness, frustration, doubt, confusion and even guilt all serve a similar purpose: they signal you to apply the brakes, to retreat within yourself in order to reflect, and to conserve energy and resources."[1] Our current antiseptic, comfort-craving society would have us believe that the true healthy state is free of all hindering emotional and behavioral patterns—that we are the yellow, smiley faces like the one that was my childhood cookie jar. And yet, the hindrances—our conditioned tendencies to close—are there for a valuable reason. Closing is a natural, self-protective function without which we'd likely get run over by buses, taken advantage of by every conniving scoundrel, or be simply unable to develop the resolve and compassion that come from painful experience. No, closing is not bad—it just *is*.

The path laid out in this book is to develop the flexibility to open up without staying stuck after closing down. It's me when I slip and close down by making another impulsive, dopamine-facilitating book purchase on Amazon (as I just did this morning), and instead of devolving into a cascade of hindrances (desire/wanting leading to doubt/wavering leading to restlessness/worrying leading to either more desire/wanting or fatigue/wilting), I can practice SNAPPing awake and come back to opening once again, get back up on my unhindered horse, and keep moving. As suggested by the figure here (initially presented in chapter I), there is an ebb and flow between opening and closing, input and output, inner and outer—not unlike the rhythms of every cell in our bodies. The trick is to bring mindfulness to bear in harnessing this rhythm—maximizing the *timing* of opening and closing so that it serves the expansion of awareness and full-contact living.

It's also very helpful in working with the hindrances to realize there is no self-improvement "hack" when it comes to lifelong karmic conditioning. There is only the melting (at times glacial feeling) from the consistently applied heat of mindful awareness to these seemingly frozen patterns. Ajahn Thiradhammo has noted about peoples' intentions for mindfulness practice: "Someone may take up meditation to reduce their stress level. However, after some practice they may notice that their stress level has increased and give up meditation with the view that it has

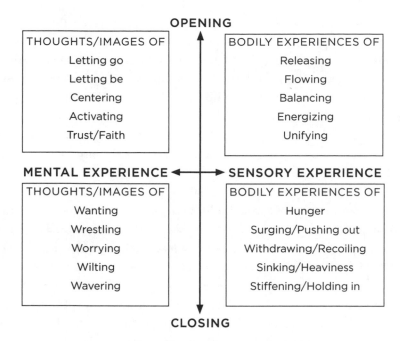

OPENING

THOUGHTS/IMAGES OF	BODILY EXPERIENCES OF
Letting go	Releasing
Letting be	Flowing
Centering	Balancing
Activating	Energizing
Trust/Faith	Unifying

MENTAL EXPERIENCE ◄──► SENSORY EXPERIENCE

THOUGHTS/IMAGES OF	BODILY EXPERIENCES OF
Wanting	Hunger
Wrestling	Surging/Pushing out
Worrying	Withdrawing/Recoiling
Wilting	Sinking/Heaviness
Wavering	Stiffening/Holding in

CLOSING

no benefit."[2] Hindrance work is not about silver bullets and quick fixes. It's about increasingly opening to experience, whatever its feeling tone.

We need a growing foundation of moment-to-moment mindfulness in order to notice the rising up, playing out, and falling away of hindrance patterns and the conditions in our inner and outer environments that support and dissolve them. We have to clearly see the changes as they occur in order to move free of the hindrances. It requires considerable willingness and a wish to embrace a new relationship to emotional discomfort to do this work. In the West in particular, we tend to expect to feel motivated before making necessary changes in our behavior. Truth be told, we must *do* before we're going to *feel* like doing more.

Amma Syncletica, a fourth-century Christian saint, said: "In the beginning, there is struggle and a lot of work for those who come near to God. But after that, there is indescribable joy. It is just like building a fire: at first it's smoky and your eyes sting and water, but later you get the desired result. Thus we ought to light the divine fire in ourselves with tears and effort."[3]

I once had a patient who said she was chronically frustrated by her husband's inability or unwillingness to put her needs first, even to the point of putting on blinders whenever she had evidence that her husband might be having an affair. She would talk openly about wanting to confront him about his behavior and his overall callous treatment of her, but she never acted. I found myself frequently struggling against the urge to tell her what to do, to prompt her to do what was so clearly obvious that she needed to do. "He's cheating on you, for God's sakes, even though you're struggling with cancer. Leave the bum, and take back what little life you have left!"

I had to let go of the normal, socially appropriate desire to expect people to keep their word. "She's told me that she wants to confront him, that she was going to do it before today's session. I'll be damned if I let her slide on this." But let her slide I did, at least in terms of confronting her with her "failure." The point is, people change, and the change is most likely to sustain when it emanates from within them as opposed to from outside pressures. My client already knew she wasn't keeping her word. The last thing she'd want to hear was me pointing it out and making her feel like the failure she already believed herself to be.

In an effort to develop a model of human change, one that cuts across the various schools of psychotherapy, researchers developed a "transtheoretical" model of the change process.[4] In this model, people are believed to progress through a series of "stages of change," beginning with:

- precontemplation (where people in effect say that they are not the source of the problem—others or the situation itself are the root cause) and progressing toward
- contemplation ("Maybe I could consider changing this, but I'm not certain how") to
- preparation ("I'm really thinking of changing, and here's what I might do") to
- action (where actual change efforts are being undertaken) to
- maintenance (where efforts are made to maintain the changes already made).

We all struggle to commit to the change process, sometimes getting stuck in precontemplation, where we deny what we need, focusing instead on what we think we want. What's helped me as a clinician is to realize that even if a client blocks themselves from changing in the direction of what he or she needs, such a person is still doing their best with the tools for change presently available. Believe it or not, alcoholics drink not because they love the taste of bourbon, or because they want to destroy their lives, they do it because the bottle is the one consistent tool they have for managing their experience of stress and upset (i.e., conditioned closing in the service of self-protection). My job, as their therapist, is to help them create new tools that will work more efficiently. I can't, however, simply beat them over the head with the tools I think they should use; they have to fashion them on their own (with supportive assistance).

And as clients and I move forward into the change process, I have to also remember that change is *not* a linear A-B-C process. Change tends to occur in fits and starts, often looking like a slowly ascending spiral, where there appear to be brief periods of setbacks and loss of progress, but overall, there is an upswing over time.

We smoke, drink alcohol, and stuff our mouths with an excess of calories because we want to feel better, even if it's the last thing we need. It's even a partial explanation for why we remain in destructive relationships. We want satisfaction, even if it means denying ourselves what we ultimately need to develop toward our potentials.

It bears repeating that there are no quick fixes when it comes to changing our most entrenched and difficult patterns. When we change too drastically or suddenly, we are moving too far away from our baseline level of functioning, and such massive change is very difficult to maintain. Old habits return when we haven't taken the time and made the effort to build up support for our new patterns of behavior.

A smoker who quits cold turkey has to publicly commit to the change. He or she has to avoid the coworker smoking buddies of days gone by. A drinker might need to forgo bars and clubs indefinitely. An obese person might need to limit outings to restaurants and throw away all takeout menus.

As I've sat here writing this, I've paused more than once to glance at my smartphone, and I've noticed the faint whisper of "Amazon . . ." emanating from it. Clearly, this final chapter is a challenge to write, with lots of positive and not-so-positive experiences rising up, along with accompanying itches to close down with a dose of compulsive comfort: precontemplation stage for sure.

Beyond the individual practices in this book, how does one work with hindrance patterns in a systematic, integrated way? Here I offer suggestions for creating an inner compass of sorts—a rubric for returning to the practice of opening again and again in the service of wider, more sustained awareness. First, we begin with an understanding that the hindrance patterns are not neat, distinctly separate chapters as presented in this text. As I've alluded to throughout, they tend to interact and feed one another, as shown in the figures below:

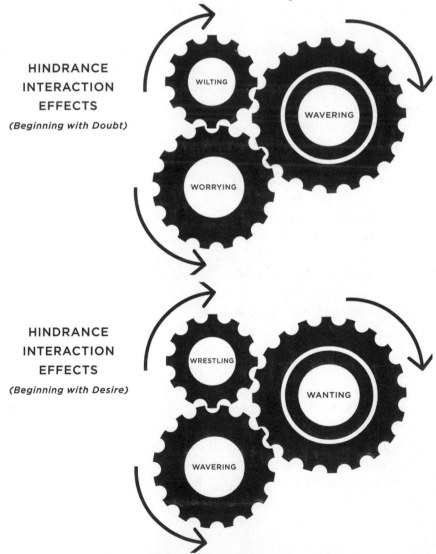

**HINDRANCE
INTERACTION
EFFECTS**
(Beginning with Doubt)

WILTING

WAVERING

WORRYING

**HINDRANCE
INTERACTION
EFFECTS**
(Beginning with Desire)

WRESTLING

WANTING

WAVERING

The possible combinations are endless, with the hindrances sometimes manifesting not singly or even in linear sequence, but as a jumbled mass of mental/emotional/behavioral unfun. Part of what Ben Franklin likely found in his own personal experiments with his virtues is that trying to track and build one in isolation from the others is impossible. Virtues and vices like to commingle and hang out together in the human body-mind.

In daily life you won't have the luxury of taking a "one hindrance at a time" approach. You'll ideally have the tools in place for working with whichever hindrance arises in a given moment—seeing it and relating to it (and its family of hindrance friends) clearly and flexibly. Below is an organizing rubric for bringing together your practices with the hindrances in any given situation.

THE SYNERGISTICS OF
OVERCOMING THE FIVE HINDRANCES

3rd Order Opening: "Leap"	• Action from Awareness
2nd Order Opening: "Look"	• "Seeing Behind and Beyond" Hindrance Patterns
1st Order Opening: "Listen"	• Mindfulness of the Here/Now of Hindrance Patterns

In a given moment of hindrance reactivity, these three steps would apply, with all the practices in this book embedded within them. Prior to listening, you must first realize that you're caught in reactivity. The hindrances figure above is helpful in terms of suggesting thought/

mental and body/sensation components of hindrance reactivity as it's manifesting. It is here that daily journaling can be extremely useful so that you become increasingly cognizant of your own unique fingerprint of how each hindrance shows up in the body-mind. Ideally, you also are soliciting feedback from others as to what they observe of your reactions, which, by the way, helps to magnify your commitment to continuing this work of awareness.

Once you have a basic recognition of having been caught up in a hindrance, you can then apply the "Listen, Look, Leap" rubric:

- Listen. Bring mindful awareness to the contents of thought and bodily sensation.
- Look from that awareness at the context you're in and what most needs to be addressed.
- Leap. Take a meaningful action in the direction of what is important, even if it is uncomfortable.

Listening involves the basic shining of mindful awareness on the manifestations of the hindrance and its supportive conditions in the here and now. Take any of the practices from this book aiming to enhance present-moment contact with thoughts, sensations, and mental images and insert them here. The universal SNAPPing awake practice is ideal here, but whatever practices help you listen to the here and now of hindrance discomfort are fine.

Looking means that with this foundation of awareness, you can now see behind your reactions to the self-protective function they are serving. You now can see the self-soothing your addictive using provides, the voicing of unspoken, decades-old hurt that your hostility communicates. Looking also means that you see beyond this self-protective function to how you might act in ways to serve the expansion of awareness, compassion, and connection to the truth of experience. You know—deeply—that allowing the hindrance's emotional/felt manifestation to burn its way to completion in the light of awareness (and without mindless repetition of the reactive/behavioral aspect) creates the openness necessary for the dissolving of this conditioning, this cycle of suffering you've been caught in.

The third step of the three-*L* rubric is *Leaping*. Here you are taking action (or embracing inaction) that flows naturally and with the quality of wisdom to address the requirements of the situation you're in. This is the elusive sense of timing I love to talk about with audiences of clinicians. Clinicians universally agree that knowing *when* to intervene with a client (and when not to) is crucial to successful psychotherapy. And yet, by show of hands, almost no one ever says they've been systematically or intensively trained in the timing of their interventions. They, like me in my own training, were left to the winds of hindrance conditioning in forming their sense of timing. Whether as clinicians or parents, colleagues or spouses, we can do better. We can leap toward actions (even if it means staying silent) that will be clearly necessary when we've fully listened and looked deeply into ourselves and the situation we're in. Timing for doing flows inexorably from presence of being.

Leaping is evidenced by staying quiet when a family member pokes an old emotional button for you over a holiday meal. It's a soft touch of your spouse's hand in the midst of an argument, perhaps coupled with saying, "I know what I just said was unfair and only makes things worse." Leaping is asking for a raise at work, less because a self-help book tells you it's your right to do so, and more because your own listening and looking underscored the relevance and truth of it as you sit with your boss. Leaping is the small and large doing that makes all the difference in the quality of your relationships with yourself, others, and the world. It's you at the zenith of your potential to create, connect, and have a worthwhile impact.

AN OPEN INVITATION–TRY THIS

Breaking Hindrance Habit Loops by Asking W Questions

By asking the following *W* questions out of a basic foundation of mindfulness, you are increasingly likely to see behind and beyond the limiting borders of hindrance patterns. In any given hindrance-reactive situation ask:

- **W**ho is impacted by this hindrance pattern, both directly and indirectly, and are the needs behind their own behavior being considered? Am I seeing the truth in others, or am I seeing my own agenda for gaining positives and avoiding negatives?

- **W**hat are all the factors influencing this pattern? What else am I missing? What needs do I have that I'm not speaking truthfully? What is my intention, and is it in alignment with opening to awareness?
- **W**here am I right now, and how might this situation be cuing my conditioned patterning? Might I move in closer or farther away from these cues, and with what purpose?
- **W**hen is it wise for me to open to awareness of my experience of this pattern, and when is it wise to temporarily close into my conditioning?
- **W**hy am I walking into and opening to my experience of my hindering patterns in the first place? Why not just carry on with my conditioned closing? Why does it matter?

As you practice with your hindering patterns from day to day, consider these three aspects of opening. Embed your practices, and assess your daily living within them. Get support and feedback from others (yet be careful to make a practice of listening and looking as you take in what others offer about your own behavior). Consider this traditional Syrian tale:

A man had two wives and both loved him, though one was young and the other old. Whenever the man lay down to sleep with his head on the young wife's knees, she would pluck the white hairs from his head so that he would appear youthful. And whenever he rested his head in the other wife's lap and slept, she would pluck out the black hairs from his head so that he should be white-haired like herself. And it was not long before the man was bald. Such is the origin of the saying "Between Hannah and Bannah, vanished are our beards."[5]

Others may have their own agendas for the feedback they offer us.

As we close, a final recommendation: this hindrance, or hurdle, work is not about *you*. We do our best self-work when we drop the self-story. "Thus as unenlightened beings, our basic assumptions are based on permanence, happiness, self and attraction, whereas the truth of reality is exactly the opposite."[6] We must commit to telling the truth without believing that it's about us at all. The philosopher and neuroscientist Sam Harris writes, "A commitment to telling the truth requires that one pay attention to what the truth is in every moment . . . Honesty can force any dysfunction in your life to the surface."[7] Such is the case with the hindrances. If you stay out of the way (which means keeping the self-story of mind from taking hold and solidifying your experience into hindrance half-truths), then you will experience life directly.

This is why the book has proceeded with the structure of both science and Buddhist psychology, clinical observations and the Buddhist three marks of existence (unsatisfacoriness/suffering, *dukkha* in Pali; impermanence, *anicca*; and nonself, *anatta*). From these vantage points, the shining truth of the various facets of hindrance conditioning becomes more visible—and workable. The book has aimed to reorient you toward the truth of reality versus the stronghold of karmic hindrance conditioning.

In assessing our penchant for self-serving dishonesty, Sam Harris writes, "By lying, we deny our friends access to reality—and their resulting ignorance often harms them in ways we did not anticipate."[8] And it's here that I want to drive home a final point: our hindrance work goes far beyond *us*. It ripples out and hinders or helps others. We can either serve as cues to the solidification of others' unhelpful conditioning, or we can open and conspire to co-inspire one another to higher-order living—to a pattern breaking that can leap from one generation to the next.

When we speak our mindful, unarguable truth to one another, we may cause others (and ourselves) transitory discomfort, but we pave the way for compassion, connection, and creative possibility. As a therapist, I've watched couples and families spark moments of intimacy through such truth talking, and I've experienced it in my own life. It is magnetic and contagious. One example of it is what I've come to call "prizing" of others' behavior.

It was that moment when my assistant scoutmaster gave up a Saturday afternoon to sit and watch blue jays and finches flit about the branches in the woods behind my house when I was eleven years old, and with enthusiasm and presence helped me earn my coveted "bird study" merit badge. His setting aside agendas and egoic concerns to underscore what looked to be valuable in me rippled forward such that I wrote him many years later to tell him about the impact his simple act of prizing had on me.

"I am now a clinical psychologist working with at-risk youth," I wrote to him. "And you taught me how to prize a kid and make him hang in with something difficult."

Prizing goes beyond praising. It lets others know not only that they're doing well at something. It also communicates that their actions *matter* to us. It's looking at someone and saying, "Hey, I noticed your effort back there, and that was really cool and very meaningful to me [really made me feel good / helped me to see things differently / etc.]." Basically, we prize someone who's listened, looked, and made a leap, and we're letting the person know we saw it and that it inspired us. This is a pattern-breaking turbo boost of sorts.

Prizing is what a good mentor or supportive colleague does. A great teacher does this as well. The best parenting comes out of this kind of attunement, as do the healthiest marriages. You don't have to be trained as a psychologist like me in order to learn how to prize. In fact, psychologists (due to our very high suicide rate) need a heaping helping of prizing ourselves.

When Mr. Mullet let go of his own agenda for that Saturday—the errands, the lawn in need of mowing, his own children's concerns—he handed me far more than a merit badge. He gave me an opportunity to see possibility in myself. This is the power of understanding karma and choosing to open: the light holding of one's one conditioned patterning as we turn out toward others in compassionate openness stamps our responses with what the Buddha, in the *Anana Sutta*, called the "bliss of blamelessness." We're not adding to the momentum of the patterning, and we can truly give to others, which brings its own joy.

CLOSING INQUIRY

This book's title is a bit deceptive—the hindrances as "hurdles" you learn to "overcome" (i.e., "leap" over). By now (if you've done the foregoing practices), you've realized that's not quite the case. The truth is that the only way out of the pain of your hindering patterning is through it. So here, for the last time in the book, and hopefully not the last of your life, I'll ask: are you willing?

Notes

FOREWORD

1. Paul Gilbert and Choden, *Mindful Compassion* (Oakland, CA: New Harbinger Publications, 2014), xv.
2. Jack Kornfield, "Freedom of the Heart," *Heart Wisdom*, episode 11, retrieved on June 29, 2017 from https://jackkornfield.com/freedom-heart-heart-wisdom -episode-11.

INTRODUCTION

1. Bhikku Bodhi, ed., *In the Buddha's Words: An Anthology of the Teachings of the Buddha* (New York: Simon and Schuster, 2005), 166.
2. Nyanaponika Thera, *The Five Mental Hindrances and Their Conquest: Texts from the Pali Canon and the Commentaries* (Kandy: Buddhist Publication Society, 2013), 1961.
3. Dalai Lama, *The Universe in a Single Atom: The Convergence of Science and Spirituality* (New York: Harmony, 2005).
4. Jon Kabat-Zinn, *Full Catastrophe Living*, rev. ed. (New York: Bantam, 2013).
5. Jiddu Krishnamurti, *This Light in Oneself* (Boston: Shambhala Publications, 1999), 33.
6. Ajahn Thiradhammo, *Working with the Five Hindrances* (Northumberland, England: Aruno Publications, 2014), 145.
7. Rupert Spira, *The Transparency of Things: Contemplating the Nature of Experience* (Oakland: New Harbinger Publications, 2016).

CHAPTER 1: THE KARMA OF CLOSING

1. Ken McLeod, *Wake Up to Your Life: Discovering the Buddhist Path of Attention* (San Francisco: HarperCollins, 2001), 42.
2. Alan Watts, *Do You Do It, or Does it Do You?* (Boulder: Sounds True, 2005).

3. Joan Marques, Satinder Dhiman, and Richard King, "What Really Matters at Work in Turbulent Times," *Business Renaissance Quarterly* 4, no. 1: 13.

4. John M. Gottman, Lynn Fainsilber Katz, and Carole Hooven, "Parental Meta-emotion Philosophy and the Emotional Life of Families: Theoretical Models and Preliminary Data," *Journal of Family Psychology* 10, no. 3: 243.

5. Deborah M. Capaldi et al., "Intergenerational and Partner Influences on Fathers' Negative Discipline," *Journal of Abnormal Child Psychology* 36, no. 3: 347–58; Ming Cui et al., "Intergenerational Transmission of Relationship Aggression: A Prospective Longitudinal Study," *Journal of Family Psychology* 24, no. 6: 688.

6. Adam M. Grant and Sharon K. Parker, "7 Redesigning Work Design Theories: The Rise of Relational and Proactive Perspectives," *Academy of Management Annals* 3, no. 1: 317–75.

7. Henry David Thoreau, *Walden* (New Haven, CT: Yale University Press, 2006), 7.

8. McLeod.

CHAPTER 2: MEDITATION AND HOW THE HINDRANCES HAVE US OVER THE BARREL OF OUR MONKEY MINDS

1. Kate Pickert, "The Mindful Revolution," *Time* (February 3, 2014), 34–48.

2. William Davies, *The Happiness Industry: How the Government and Big Business Sold Us Well-Being* (London: Verso Books, 2015).

3. Rupert Gethin, "On Some Definitions of Mindfulness" *Contemporary Buddhism* 12, no. 1: 263–79.

4. Ibid.

5. Bill Morgan, *The Meditator's Dilemma: An Innovative Approach to Overcoming Obstacles and Revitalizing Your Practice* (Boulder, CO: Sounds True, 2016).

6. Morgan, 23.

7. Miles Neale, "McMindfulness and Frozen Yoga: Rediscovering the Essential Teachings of Ethics and Wisdom," Dr. Miles Neale website (2011), www.miles neale.com/wp-content/uploads/2011/11/McMindfulness.pdf.

8. Ibid., 1.

9. Ibid., 6.

10. Eugen Herrigel, *Zen in the Art of Archery* (New York: Pantheon, 1953), 32–44.

11. Ibid., 35.

12. Ibid., 70.

13. Satya J. Gabriel, "Oliver Stone's *Wall Street* and the Market for Corporate Control," *Economics in Popular Film* (November 21, 2001), www.mtholyoke.edu/courses/sgabriel /filmcourse/oliver_stone.html.

14. Krishnamurti, 35, 50, 131.

15. Krishnamurti, 23.

16. Jon Kabat-Zinn, *Wherever You Go, There You Are: Mindfulness Meditation in Everyday Life* (London: Hachette UK, 1994).

17. Morgan.

18. Thich Nhat Hanh, *Peace Is Every Step* (New York: Bantam Books, 1991), 97.

19. Bhikku Bodhi and Nyanaponika Thera, *Numerical Discourses of the Buddha: An Anthology of Suttas from the Anguttara Nikaya* (Thousand Oaks, CA: Altamira Press, 2000) 344.

20. Edward O. Wilson, *The Social Conquest of Earth* (New York: W. W. Norton, 2012), 193.

21. Paul W. Andrews, "The Psychology of Social Chess and the Evolution of Attribution Mechanisms: Explaining the Fundamental Attribution Error," *Evolution and Human Behavior* 22, no. 1: 11–29.

22. Julie Y. Huang et al., "Immunizing against Prejudice: Effects of Disease Protection on Attitudes toward Out-Groups," *Psychological Science* 22, no. 12: 1550–6.

23. Ibid.

24. Eric D. Green and Charles R. Nesson, *Federal Rules of Evidence* (Boston, MA: Little, Brown, 1998).

25. Martin Larkin and Susan E. McClain, "Cynical Hostility and the Accuracy of Decoding Facial Expressions of Emotions," *Journal of Behavioral Medicine* 25, no. 3: 285–92.

26. Joseph Goldstein, *Mindfulness: A Practical Guide to Awakening* (Boulder, CO: Sounds True, 2013).

27. Dalai Lama, *In the Buddha's Words: An Anthology of Discourses from the Pali Canon* (New York: Simon and Schuster, 2005).

28. Bodhi, 343.

29. Sylvia Boorstein, *It's Easier Than You Think: The Buddhist Way to Happiness* (San Francisco: Harper, 1995).

CHAPTER 3: SIDESTEPPING COOKIE MONSTER

1. Mark Epstein, *Open to Desire: The Truth About What the Buddha Taught* (New York: Gotham Books), 77.

2. www.timessquarenyc.org.

3. World Health Organization, *World Health Statistics 2015* (Geneva: World Health Organization, 2015).

4. Janine Satioquia-Tan, *Americans East How Much Chocolate?* CNBC.com (July 23, 2015), www.cnbc.com/2015/07/23/americans-eat-how-much-chocolate.html.

5. Joseph J. Palamar et al., "Self-Reported Use of Novel Psychoactive Substances in a US Nationally Representative Survey: Prevalence, Correlates, and a Call for New Survey Methods to Prevent Underreporting," *Drug and Alcohol Dependence* 156:112–9.

6. Jessica Marple, "Examining the Strengths and Weaknesses of Netflix's Business Model in the Context of the Post-Legacy Television Market," *Journal of Promotional Communications* 5, no. 2.

7. Sherry Turkle, *Reclaiming Conversation: The Power of Talk in a Digital Age* (New York: Penguin Books, 2016).

8. Ibid.

9. Ibid.

10. Epstein, 21.

11. Jennifer Jolly, "Five Ways Your Smartphone Can Help Your Health," *The New York Times* (November 16, 2015), http://well.blogs.nytimes.com/2015/11/16/five-ways-your-smartphone-can-help-your-health/?_r=0.

12. William Irvine, *On Desire* (New York: Oxford, 2006).

13. Ibid., 279.

14. Goldstein.

15. Irvine, 280.

16. Goldstein, 303.

17. Judson A. Brewer, Hani M. Elwafi, and Jake H. Davis, "Craving to Quit: Psychological Models and Neurobiological Mechanisms of Mindfulness Training as Treatment for Addictions," *Psychology of Addictive Behaviors* 31, no. 6: 1–14.

18. Ibid., 4.

19. Ibid.

20. Amy Fleming, "The Science of Craving," *The Economist: The Intelligent Life* (May/June

2015), www.intelligentlifemagazine.com/content/features/wanting-versus
-liking?https%3A%2F%2Fwww.socialflow.com%2Fpublish#?fsrc=scn/fb/te
/bl/ed/100socialflow=science+of+craving.

21. Kent C. Berridge and Terry E. Robinson, "Parsing Reward," *Trends in Neurosciences* 26, no. 9: 507–13.

22. Britta K. Hölzel et al., "Mindfulness Practice Leads to Increases in Regional Brain Gray Matter Density," *Psychiatry Research: Neuroimaging* 191, no. 1: 36–43.

23. Bhikku Nanamoli and Bhikku Bodhi, *Māgandiya Sutta*, in *The Middle Length Discourses of the Buddha* (Boston: Wisdom Publications, 2009).

24. Solala Towler, *Tales from the Tao: The Wisdom of the Taoist Masters* (London: Duncan Baird Publishers, 2007).

25. Sarah Bowen and Alan Marlatt, "Surfing the Urge: Brief Mindfulness-Based Intervention for College Student Smokers," *Psychology of Addictive Behaviors* 23:666–71.

26. Ibid.

27. Laura Campbell-Sills et al., "Effects of Suppression and Acceptance on Emotional Responses of Individuals with Anxiety and Mood Disorders," *Behaviour Research and Therapy* 44:1251–63.

28. Christina Feldman and Jack Kornfield, eds., *Stories of the Spirit, Stories of the Heart: Parables of the Spiritual Path from Around the World* (New York: HarperCollins, 1991).

29. Epstein.

30. Emily Balcetis and David Dunning, "See What You Want to See: Motivational Influences on Visual Perception," *Journal of Personality and Social Psychology* 91, no. 4: 612.

31. Towler.

32. Roy F. Baumeister and Jon Tierney, *Willpower: Rediscovering the Greatest Human Strength* (New York: Penguin, 2012).

33. Ibid., 30.

34. Ibid.

35. Bowen and Marlatt, 666.

36. Carol A. Steinberg and Donald A. Eisner, "Mindfulness-Based Interventions for Veterans with Posttraumatic Stress Disorder," *The International Journal of Behavioral Consultation and Therapy* 9, no. 4: 11–18.

37. Judy Lief, "Train Your Mind: Change Your Attitude, but Remain Natural," *Tricycle* website, https://tricycle.org/trikedaily/train-your-mind-change-your -attitude-but-remain-natural/.

38. Epstein, 90.

39. Idries Shah, *The Exploits of the Incomparable Mulla Nasrudin* (London: Octagon Press Ltd., 1983).

40. Henry T. Francis and Edward J. Thomas, eds., *Jataka Tales* (Cambridge: Cambridge University Press, 2014).

41. Towler.

42. Epstein, 133.

43. Ibid., 92.

CHAPTER 4: THE BOILING POINT

1. Kennan A Lattal, *Performance Improvement*, vol. 53, no. 10. Review of Aubrey Daniels and John Bailey's *Performance Management: Changing Behavior That Drives Organizational Effectiveness* (Performance Management Publications, 2014).

2. Padmasiri de Silva, "Anger Management: A Buddhist Perspective," *Journal of the International Association of Buddhist Universities* 2, no. 1.

3. Patricia M. Herbert, *The Life of the Buddha* (Petaluma, CA: Pomegranate, 2005).

4. Francis and Thomas.

5. Tenzin Gyatso, *The Path to Freedom: Freedom in Exile: The Autobiography of the Dalai Lama* (London: Abacus, 2002).

6. The Dalai Lama, *Tibet, China, and the World: A Compilation of Interviews* (Dharamsala, India: Narthang Publications, 1989).

7. Ajahn Brahm, *The Art of Disappearing: The Buddha's Path to Lasting Joy* (Boston: Wisdom Publications, 2011).

8. Tenzin Gyatso, *Ancient Wisdom, Modern World: Ethics for a New Millennium* (London: Little, Brown and Company, 1999).

9. Steven C. Hayes et al., "Acceptance and Commitment Therapy: Model, Processes and Outcomes," *Behavior Research and Therapy* 44:1–25.

10. Michael Inzlicht and Lisa Legault, "No Pain, No Gain: How Distress Underlies Effective Self-Control (and Unites Diverse Social Psychological Phenomena)," in Joseph P. Forgas and Eddie Harmon-Jones, eds., *Motivation and Its Regulation: The Control Within* (New York: Psychology Press), 115–32.

11. Edo Shonin and William Van Gordon, "Mindfulness of Death," *Mindfulness* 5, no. 4: 464–6.

12. Steven C. Hayes, Kirk D. Strosahl, and Kelly G. Wilson, *Acceptance and Commitment Therapy: the Process and Practice of Mindful Change* (New York: Guilford Press, 2016).

13. Marco Iacoboni, *Mirroring People: The New Science of How We Connect with Others.* (New York: Farrar, Straus and Giroux, 2008), 119.

14. Tania Singer et al., "Empathy for Pain Involves the Affective but not Sensory Components of Pain," *Science* 303:1157–62.

15. Daniel T. Gilbert and Patrick S. Malone, "The Correspondence Bias," *Psychological Bulletin* 117, no. 1: 21.

16. Osho, *Transformation Tarot* (New York: St. Martin's Press, 1999).

17. Michael Shaara, *The Killer Angels* (New York: Ballantine Books, 1987).

CHAPTER 5: WAKING THE WILTING MIND

1. Goldstein.

2. Ibid.

3. Gil Fronsdal, *Unhindered: A Mindful Path through the Five Hindrances* (Redwood City, CA: Tranquil Books, 2013).

4. Shah.

5. Bhadantacariya Buddhaghosa, *The Path of Purification* (Onalsaska, WA: Pariyatti Publishing, 1991), 530.

6. Thiradhammo, 117.

7. Thera.

8. Goldstein, 150; Thiradhammo, 128.

9. Thomas A. Dingus et al., *The 100-Car Naturalistic Driving Study: Phase II: Results of the 100-Car Field Experiment*, US Department of Transportation, DOT HS 810 593.

10. NHS.uk, "10 Medical Reasons for Feeling Tired," www.nhs.uk/Livewell/tiredness-and-fatigue/Pages/medical-causes-of-tiredness.aspx.

11. Judson A. Brewer et al., "Meditation Experience Is Associated with Differences in Default Mode Network Activity and Connectivity," *Proceedings of the National Academy of Sciences* 108:20254–9.

12. Ibid.
13. Jessica R. Andrews-Hanna et al., "Functional-Anatomic Fractionation of the Brain's Default Mode Network," *Neuron* 65:550–62.
14. Brewer et al., 20254–9.
15. Ibid.
16. Joon Hwan Jang et al., "Increased Default Mode Network Connectivity Associated with Meditation," *Neuroscience Letters* 487, no. 3: 358–62.
17. Goldstein, 144.
18. Thiradhammo, 131.
19. Kenneth S. Pope and Barbara G. Tabachnick, "Therapists as Patients: A National Survey of Psychologists' Experiences, Problems, and Beliefs," *Professional Psychology: Research and Practice* 25, no. 3: 247.
20. Ibid.
21. Ibid.
22. Ibid.
23. Sharon Salzberg and Joseph Goldstein, *Insight Meditation* (Boulder: Sounds True, 2001), 83.
24. Fronsdal, 59.
25. Carl G. Jung, *The Collected Works of C. G. Jung, Volume 6: Psychological Types* (Princeton, NJ: Princeton UP, 1971), 964.
26. Thiradhammo, 118.
27. Fronsdal, 57.
28. Morgan.
29. Salzberg and Goldstein, 87.
30. Goldstein, 150.
31. Ibid., 147.
32. Ibid., 150.
33. Fronsdal, 57.
34. Mitch Abblett, *The Heat of the Moment in Treatment: Mindful Management of Difficult Clients* (New York: W. W. Norton, 2013).
35. Turkle.
36. Thiradhammo, 147.
37. Benjamin Franklin, *Franklin's Virtues Journal: A Companion to Benjamin Franklin's Book of Virtues* (Carlisle, MA: Applewood Books, 2016).
38. Salzberg and Goldstein, 89.
39. Goldstein, 146.
40. Pedram Shojai, *The Urban Monk* (New York: Rodale, 2016).
41. The publication of this book with this sentence's final word fulfills a childhood aspiration—to find an appropriate context for this most difficult-to-place-in-print word.
42. Thiradhammo, 140.
43. Bodhi and Thera, 344.
44. Thera.
45. Towler.
46. William Hoffman, "What Is a Moment?" Radiolab (2009), www.radiolab.org.
47. Spira.
48. Michael J. Mahoney, *Human Change Process: The Scientific Foundations of Psychotherapy* (New York: Basic Books, 1991).

49. Thiradhammo, 132.
50. Fronsdal, 90.

CHAPTER 6: WORRYWARTS

1. Fronsdal, 69.
2. Buddhaghosa, *The Path of Purification* (Berkeley, CA: Shambhala, 1976).
3. Fronsdal, 72.
4. Goldstein, 156.
5. Aaron Smith, "U.S. Smartphone Use in 2015," *Pew Research Center*, April 1, 2015, www.pewinternet.org/2015/04/01/us-smartphone-use-in-2015/.
6. Jack Kornfield, *The Wise Heart: A Guide to the Universal Teachings of Buddhist Psychology* (New York: Bantam Books, 2009).
7. "Attention-Deficit / Hyperactivity Disorder (ADHD)," Centers for Disease Control and Prevention www.cdc.gov/ncbddd/adhd/data.html.
8. Bhadantacariya Buddhaghosa.
9. Thera, 153.
10. Susan Nolen-Hocksema, "The Role of Rumination in Depressive Disorders and Mixed Anxiety/Depressive Symptoms," *Journal of Abnormal Psychology* 109:504–11.
11. Paul O. Wilkinson, Tim J. Croudace, and Ian M. Goodyer, "Rumination, Anxiety, Depressive Symptoms and Subsequent Depression in Adolescents at Risk for Psychopathology: A Longitudinal Cohort Study," *BioMed Central Psychiatry* 13:250.
12. Filip Raes, "Rumination and Worry as Mediators of the Relationship between Self-Compassion and Depression and Anxiety," *Personality and Individual Differences* 48:757–61.
13. Thera, 31.
14. Fronsdal, 73.
15. Towler.
16. Eric Berne, *Transactional Analysis in Psychotherapy* (Castle Books, 1961).
17. Jane Compson, "Meditation, Trauma and Suffering in Silence: Raising Questions about How Meditation Is Taught and Practiced in Western Contexts in the Light of a Contemporary Trauma Resiliency Model," *Contemporary Buddhism* 15, no. 2: 274–97, https://doi.org/10.1080/14639947.2014.935264.
18. Goldstein, 156.
19. Morgan, 13.
20. Osho.
21. Fronsdal, 72.
22. Feldman and Kornfield.
23. Goldstein, 159.
24. Goldstein, 158.
25. Towler.
26. Thich Nhat Hanh.
27. Thiradhammo.
28. Feldman and Kornfield.
29. Glen Schneider, *Ten Breaths to Happiness* (Berkeley, CA: Parallax Press, 2013).
30. Derek Lin, *The Tao of Daily Life* (New York: Penguin Books, 2007).
31. Gerald Edelman, *The Remembered Present: A Biological Theory of Consciousness* (New York: Basic Books, 2000).
32. Ibid.

33. Ibid.
34. Goldstein, 158.
35. Paul Gilbert, *The Compassionate Mind: A New Approach to Life's Challenges* (Oakland, CA: New Harbinger, 2009), 77.
36. Lin.
37. Culadasa (John Yates), *The Mind Illuminated: A Complete Meditation Guide Integrating Buddhist Wisdom and Brain Science* (Pearce, AZ: Dharma Treasures Press, 2015), 88.
38. Lin.
39. Morgan, 21.
40. Carol Dweck, *Mindset: The New Psychology of Success* (New York: Ballantine Books, 2006).

CHAPTER 7: BECOMING A KNOW-(*NOTHING*)-IT-ALL

1. *The Dictionary of Humorous Quotations*, edited by Evan Esar. Bertrand Russell quote (Garden City, NY: Doubleday, 1949), 174.
2. Goldstein, 164.
3. Fronsdal, 84.
4. Maurice O'Connell Walshe, trans., "*Sangaravo Sutta: Sangarava*" (SN 46.55), Access to Insight (Legacy Edition), November 30, 2013, www.accesstoinsight.org/tipitaka /sn/sn46/sn46.055.wlsh.html.
5. Thiradhammo, 169.
6. Bodhi.
7. Fronsdal, 85.
8. William Cullen Bryant, ed., *The Complete Works of Shakespeare: Tragedies and Poems* (Philadelphia: Carson and Simpson, 1891), 919.
9. Osho.
10. Salzberg and Goldstein, 92.
11. Goldstein, 166.
12. Erik Asp et al., "A Neuropsychological Test of Belief and Doubt: Damage to the Ventromedial Prefrontal Cortex Increases Credulity for Misleading Advertising," *Frontiers in Neuroscience* 6:1–9.
13. Niamh Connolly, "The Benefits of a Doubt," Issues and Perspectives, Science website (July 12, 2013), https://doi.org/10.1126/science.careedit.a1300143.
14. E. Bruce Goldstein and James R. Brockmole, *Sensation and Perception* (Boston: Cengage Learning, 2017).
15. Daniel J. Simons and Christopher F. Chabris, "Gorillas in our Midst: Sustained Inattentional Blindness for Dynamic Events," *Perception* 28:1059–74.
16. Nicholas A. Christakis and James H. Fowler, "Social Contagion Theory: Examining Dynamic Social Networks and Human Behavior," *Statistical Medicine* 32:1–29.
17. Liad Uziel, "Individual Differences in the Social Facilitation Effect: A Review and Meta-analysis," *Journal of Research in Personality* 41, no. 3: 579–601, https://doi.org/10 .1016/j.jrp.2006.06.008.
18. David L. Runyan, "The Group Risky-Shift Effect as a Function of Emotional Bonds, Actual Consequences, and Extent of Responsibility," *Journal of Personality and Social Psychology* 29, no. 5: 670–76.
19. Robert S. Baron, Thomas C. Monson, and Penny H. Baron, "Conformity Pressure as a Determinant of Risk Taking: Replication and Extension," *Journal of Personality and Social Psychology* 28, no. 3: 406–13.

20. Irving L. Janis, *Groupthink: Psychological Studies of Policy Decisions and Fiascoes* (Boston: Wadsworth, 2013).
21. Tom Postmes et al., "Social Influence in Computer-Mediated Communication: The Effects of Anonymity on Group Behavior," *Personality and Social Psychology Bulletin* 27, no. 10: 1243–54.
22. Stanley Milgram, "Behavioral Study of Obedience," *The Journal of Abnormal and Social Psychology* 67, no. 4: 371–8, https://doi.org/10.1037/h0040525.
23. Salzberg and Goldstein, 90.
24. Alan Watts, *The Book on the Taboo of Knowing Who You Are* (New York: Vintage Books, 1989).
25. Salzberg and Goldstein, 101.
26. Feldman and Kornfield, 142.
27. Fronsdal, 87.
28. Thiradhammo, 175.
29. Feldman and Kornfield.
30. Morgan.
31. Salzberg and Goldstein, 100.
32. Centers for Disease Control and Prevention website, www.cdc.gov.
33. Fronsdal, 87.
34. Ibid., 86.
35. Goldstein, 167.
36. Thiradhammo, 195.
37. Feldman and Kornfield, 251.
38. Hayes, Strosahl, and Wilson, *Acceptance.*
39. Jocko Willink and Lief Babin, *Extreme Ownership: How US Navy SEALs Lead and Win* (New York: St. Martin's Press, 2015).
40. Salzberg and Goldstein, 92.
41. Ibid., 93.
42. Thiradhammo, 176.
43. www.cdc.gov.
44. Feldman and Kornfield.
45. Towler.
46. Sangmoon Kim, Ryan Thibodeau, and Randall S. Jorgensen, "Shame, Guilt, and Depressive Symptoms: A Meta-analytic Review," *Psychological Bulletin* 137, no. 1: 68–96, https://doi.org/10.1037/a0021466.
47. Daniel Kahneman, *Thinking, Fast and Slow* (New York: Macmillan, 2011).
48. John Donne. *No Man is an Island* (Taurus Press of Willow Dene, 1976).
49. Spira, *Transparency.*
50. Lin, *The Tao.*
51. Richard Bode, *First You Have to Row a Little Boat: Reflections on Life and Living* (New York: Warner Books, 1993), 202.
52. Evan Andrews, "What Was the Gordian Knot?," History, February 3, 2016, www.history.com/news/ask-history/what-was-the-gordian-knot.

CHAPTER 8: KARMA CHAMELEON

1. Todd B. Kashdan and Robert Biswas-Diener, *The Power of Negative Emotion* (Oneworld Publications, 2014), 16–17.
2. Thiradhammo, 180.
3. Feldman and Kornfield, *Stories of the Spirit.*

4. James O. Prochaska and Carlo C. Diclemente, "The Transtheoretical Approach," in John C. Norcross and Marvin R. Goldfried, eds., *Handbook of Psychotherapy Integration* (Oxford: Oxford UP), 147–71.

5. Jane Yolen, ed., *Favorite Folktales from around the World* (New York: Pantheon Books, 1986).

6. Thiradhammo, 179.

7. Sam Harris, *Lying* (Four Elephants Press, 2013), 9.

8. Ibid., 15.

Index